MW01274061

Gabby and I started our
years ago at CFNI in Da
and helped one another through some crazy times! My sweet friend,
this is your time to "soar" wherever Jesus leads you {perhaps even to
Africa}. No more lies, shame, or insecurities...freedom and healing
are yours! Readers, Gabby's testimony, *In His Footsteps*, will equip
you with tools to defeat the enemy as well as lead you to victory!
Gabby will encourage you to pursue freedom, hope & healing in
Jesus Christ. My friend, you have always been a willing vessel, a
humble servant, a seeker of the truth, and a beautiful daughter of
the Almighty...*In His Footsteps* is your reflection!

—Pastor Kristie Julian
Assemblies of God, Michigan District, Women's Director
LifeHouse Church Women's Pastor, Youth Pastor,
Conference Speaker

In HIS FOOTSTEPS

Blessings,

Gabby Hcetter

In HIS FOOTSTEPS

GABBY HEUSSER

CREATION
HOUSE

In His Footsteps by Gabby Heusser
Published by Creation House
A Charisma Media Company
600 Rinehart Road
Lake Mary, Florida 32746
www.charismamedia.com

Unless otherwise noted, all Scripture quotations are from the New King James Version of the Bible. Copyright © 1979, 1980, 1982 by Thomas Nelson, Inc., publishers. Used by permission.

Scripture quotations marked NIV are from the Holy Bible, New International Version of the Bible. Copyright © 1973, 1978, 1984, International Bible Society. Used by permission.

Design Director: Bill Johnson
Cover design by Lisa Cox

Visit the author's Web site: www.gabbyheusser.com.

Library of Congress Cataloging-in-Publication Data: 2013957299
International Standard Book Number: 978-1-62136-729-1
E-book International Standard Book Number: 978-1-62136-730-7

While the author has made every effort to provide accurate telephone numbers and Internet addresses at the time of publication, neither the publisher nor the author assumes any responsibility for errors or for changes that occur after publication.

First edition

14 15 16 17 18 — 9 8 7 6 5 4 3 2 1
Printed in Canada

CONTENTS

FOREWORD

YOU ARE GOING to like this book. It is truly inspired by God. How can I be so confident? It is a true story about a person being healed by God. Healed both inside and out.

Many question whether God really heals or not. Many want documentation germane to God doing miracles and healings. Well, here it is. The best part is that Gabby weaves God's love throughout all these pages. As far as the truth: I can personally attest to the fact that Gabby is a completely different person than when we first met. My prayer for each and every reader is that you take the substance of what Gabby has to offer and be healed, loved, and freed yourselves. Then turn with a grateful heart to love God back and love your neighbors with the power of God Himself.

—ANDREW HEUSSER

ACKNOWLEDGMENTS

FIRST OF ALL I would like to acknowledge my precious Jesus. You are the One that has loved me and has chased me all my life. I am so very grateful that you have never given up on me and have pursued me with your relentless love and grace. Your belief in me has given me the ability to love myself and see myself as you do. I am forever grateful for who you are and what you have done in my life! I count it my highest honor to serve you and share your love with others. Thank you for giving me the courage to write this book. I have loved the memories we have made together!

To my husband and best friend, Andy: What can I say about you? You are a precious gift from my heavenly Father. He knew I would need someone as patient and loving as you! You have taught me more about who God is and His love than anyone else I know. I count it a privilege to be your wife and to live out this life with you. Thank you for letting me be me and loving me through it all!

To my beautiful princesses, Sarah and Emily: You both have walked with Mom and Dad through some difficult times and have become more beautiful because of it all! Sarah, your grace and love shine brighter than the sun to me! Emily, your carefree attitude and kindness are so refreshing and a daily reminder how to let my Daddy in heaven take care of me! I love you both so very much and am so proud of how much you love Jesus!

To my closest friend, Carrie Hammons: What a wild ride we have been on! I still remember the first time you came to church and I called to follow up with you. I never imagined that that day would lead to such an amazing and life-giving friendship! Your unwavering faith in God and His promises over my life have helped me heal and walk out all He has for me. I do not have enough words to thank you! We made it to the other side!

Petra Alvarez, thank you for allowing God to use you to help open my eyes to His amazing love for me. I still remember the day that you asked me if I knew how much My heavenly Father loved me. That question haunted me and caused me to be desperate enough to find the answer. Thank you for helping me find the One that had been waiting for me all along!

Ron and Denise Perkins, thank you for your prayers for not only me but for what God was wanting to do in our family. Denise, thank you for coming over to my house and helping with the girls when I was in too much pain to do so. I do not know if you will ever know in this life how much it blessed me to have you lift my Emily into her high chair and feed my baby. God knows and has caught every one of your prayers and kindness for me!

To my mother-in-law, Nadine Heusser, thank you for coming and helping out with the girls. Just folding laundry and doing the dishes kept me sane during a time that I could not physically do much. I loved watching you and the girls dance around the living room! It brought much needed joy to my heart!

A huge thank you to Teresa Kephart! Wow, I remember sitting at your dining room table going over some of the chapters in this book. Your insight into the world of writing, which was new to me, helped me tremendously! Thank you for your encouragement to me personally to share all that He has put in my heart.

For the rest of my dear brothers and sisters in Christ that I did not name here, thank you! Thank you for the prayers of faith, tears, listening ears, and the phone calls from someone who desperately wanted to see and understand what was going on in my life during this season. God has been more than faithful!

Thank you to my precious family and friends who have taken care of our girls while I was working on this book and traveling to the publisher. It means so much that you frantically worked through your own crazy schedules so I could follow my dream!

A final thank you to all the staff at Creation House. Wow, what an experience so far! This is a whole new world for me, and everyone has been kind, gracious, and very encouraging. Thank you for those of you who have affirmed that I am ready to tell my story. It means more to me than you know!

INTRODUCTION
MIRROR, MIRROR

OR THOSE OF you who have little girls, the saying, "Mirror, mirror, on the wall, who's the fairest of them all?" is likely a familiar refrain. You probably recall it from the thousands of times you have read the story of Snow White. Like Snow White's stepmother, we also have a mirror we look in to assess our beauty and worth. It is not the mirror we look in every morning as we are doing our hair and makeup. It is the mirror that we look in and see who we think we are. Often, that mirror we use is old. It has cracks and is scratched. Ever try to look in one of those mirrors? You cannot see your reflection clearly; you cannot see what you *really* look like. For many of us, we are looking at ourselves through a broken, cracked mirror. That mirror represents our past, our old identity before Christ. The Father wants to take that mirror out of our hands and give us a new one. The mirror He gives us is crystal clear and reflects our image perfectly and beautifully. Sounds like a good deal, doesn't it?

The mirror the Father hands us shows us who we *really* are. When you pick up this mirror for the first time, you may be shocked by what you see. You see Jesus. Where did you go? Who are you? Where did all the cracks and scratches go? You see, our Father wants us to see ourselves the way He does. When He says, "Mirror, mirror, on the wall, who is the fairest of them all?" the mirror answers back, "Jesus!" It says, "My beautiful bride where Christ dwells! My sons and daughters who are complete in Me!"

You see, our Father not only wants to give us a new mirror but new eyes to see clearly.

For much of my Christian life I was holding the wrong mirror. I insisted that I hold the old, broken one. My fingers had a vice grip on it! Then my Father slowly started prying my fingers off it. Just choosing to let go takes a lot of courage! What if I lose my old identity and do not have a new one? What if I cannot make it following this new path? What if? What if? *What if?*

My heart and mind had so many questions. God started putting new *What ifs* in my curious little head. *What if* all the things I have believed about myself are not true? *What if* the devil has been lying to me all these years? *What if* all the wonderful things God says about me in His Word *are* true? Being inquisitive can have its good side. Ask anyone around me—I am inquisitive and ask lots of questions! If you are like that, let Him use it for good. If you are not, it may take a little more effort and imagination, but asking yourself the hard questions and being open to the Father changing your paradigm is worth it. *You* are worth it! The path that He leads you down to freedom and healing is worth it. What and who is on the other side is worth it.

Many, many people are waiting on the other side of your healing that need hope. Will you go? Will you take the journey for them? Better yet, will you start the journey for Him and yourself? Knowing Him better will be the prize!

As you read this book, my prayer is that you will see Jesus, the Author and Finisher of your faith, in a whole new light. He is the one who started you on this journey and will make sure that you cross that finish line. He will be the first one waiting on the other side for you. He knows you're coming. He knows you can make it. He knows you *will* make it. He believes so much in you.

So do I. Even though I do not know many of you who are reading this work, my heart goes out to you. I have been there. But most importantly, He has been there. He is there! Let Him walk, drag, pull, push, or however else He wants to get you closer to your finish line! We all have a race. We all have a journey. This book is the story of mine thus far. Oh, what a journey it has been! I pray that you would not only hear my story but see your own from His view.

In His Footsteps is so much more than a title. It is the living, breathing reality of where He has had me living for the last seven-plus years. Psalm 85:12 is such a beautiful scripture that rightly displays what He has done: "Yes, the LORD will give what is good; And our land will yield its increase. Righteousness will go before Him, And shall make His footsteps our pathway." He so sweetly interrupts our lives so that we can literally follow in His footsteps. Enjoy the journey and know that your heavenly Father is so proud of you! Go get yourself something yummy to drink, get in your comfy chair, and grab a tissue if you are the crying type! Each chapter is a glimpse of all the beautiful and life-giving truths that He taught me about finding freedom and wholeness. Each one expounds on the things He revealed to me along the path. Oh, I have so much to tell you of His great faithfulness! I cannot wait for us to begin!

Chapter 1

TURNED UPSIDE DOWN

HIS STORY BEGINS on a cool but sunny day in March; March 15, 2006, to be exact. You may wonder why I remember the day so well. It was the day my beautiful little Emily was born into this world. The story actually began thirty-three years earlier (my age at this time), but the chapter of my life that God was writing began on that day. I was in labor with my daughter, and the song "Jesus, Take the Wheel" was very popular, sung by Carrie Underwood. To take my mind off the contractions and pain that I felt like would take my life, I remember singing this song in my head. Be careful what you sing, or pray for that matter! Little did I know that God would use the birth of my sweet baby girl, and the events surrounding it, and that song to radically change my life!

A few weeks after giving birth to my daughter, I began having severe lower leg pain. I knew something was wrong—very wrong. There are some things that we experience physically that seem to pass and are no big deal. I remember buying several pairs of sandals for the upcoming summer, and none of them fit right. They were so uncomfortable, and I had to take them all back. I told my husband Andy that I wondered if something had happened to my feet. They looked different. They felt different. Something in me told me that this was a serious problem. I had already made a few trips back to the doctor within the first month due to some health problems related to giving birth to her, but my knees and lower legs ached so badly. I was scared because I did not know what was going on. I can handle pain. I had both of my children with no pain medication!

One day after laying my girls down for their nap I threw myself across my bed and cried out to God. I said, "God, I need you to heal me. I hurt so bad, and I have a newborn and a two year old to take care of. Help!" I was desperate for a touch from Him. I had the thought to go turn on *The 700 Club*, so I did. Little did I know that the Lord heard me and was answering my prayer.

As I watched, they began praying. Terry Meeuwsen had a word of knowledge: "You are having problems with the arches of your feet, and it is affecting your lower legs; and God is healing that." I stood there as if all the blood had gone out of my body. It was eerie, but a good eerie! I knew that God had spoken to me.

Shortly after, as I got back from taking my daughter to swim lessons, I came home, and the words of Isaiah 55:10–11 were in my spirit. It says, "As the rain and the snow come down from heaven, and do not return to it without watering the earth and making it bud and flourish, so that it yields seed for the sower and bread for the eater, so is my word that goes out from my mouth: It will not return to me empty, but will accomplish what I desire and achieve the purpose for which I sent it" (NIV). I knew He was working but could not yet see the hugeness of what He wanted to do. His Spirit kept encouraging me to keep believing there was a bigger purpose than what I was seeing.

I had lived a lot of my life in the natural realm—believing what I felt and could see and touch. His healing seemed a million miles away at times. But there I was, three and a half months after the birth of my daughter, standing in my living room, and Jesus shows up! Wow! I had no idea what was causing the pain, but God not only promised to heal me; He diagnosed my problem! God loves stepping into the middle of our lives and changing them forever. He used this word to begin a season that would last seven years and counting!

Boy, am I glad I am on this side of that word, if I may be honest. Don't you look back on some of the trials you have been through and wonder how on Earth you made it? I bet there are some circumstances, no matter how much God worked in them, you would not want to step back into! God has almost completely restored my body, but the miles we have traveled together and how much He has done are just absolutely crazy!

So, two days after hearing the word God gave me from *The 700 Club*, I had an appointment with a physical therapist to try and strengthen my muscles that were so sore. Ariel was the name of my therapist, and she said to me, "Take off your shoes." She looked at my feet and said the arches in my feet were almost flat and that one side was worse than the other. Good grief, even my arches could not fall evenly! That would explain what was going on. I stood there, not sure what to say because of the word the Lord gave me two days earlier about my arches being the problem. Two days. God's timing is never off! He was supernaturally orchestrating these events and the timing with which He spoke to me. I remember lying on the bed in the room by myself while receiving some electrode therapy just pondering what God had spoken to me about my feet. I walked around the office in almost a daze about what He was going to do. I left that appointment knowing God was up to something!

Over the next weeks and months I found myself in an emotional, physical, and spiritual whirlwind. The word I heard about God healing my feet really challenged me and my belief system. Certainly, I knew God still healed people because I had seen it happen to others and experienced it myself. At times I would have faith to receive that word and look expectantly for my healing. I drove my husband nuts as I said over and over, "God is going to heal me." Actually much of the time I said it with more doubt than faith. It came out to him as a question, "Is God really going to heal me?" At other times, I found myself doubting that He was really going to do it for *me*. And therein lay my problem—*me!*

God was getting to the root of my problem. I did not believe that I was worthy of His healing and that He would arrange something so miraculous for me. Did He not see how much I doubted His promises at times? Did He not see the fear and torment from fear and shame and unworthiness that I felt? He sure did. And that was what He wanted to heal before He healed my body. God, in all His wisdom, knew what I needed way better than I or any other person.

I waited a few weeks before I shared the word from *The 700 Club* I felt like was for me with my dear friend, Carrie. I realized that a part of me felt like hiding what God had shared with me because it was so personal and because it was exposing the need in me to be healed. (Little did I know that He would use her to continue to bring even another prophetic word to heal me—and that would turn my world upside down!) I also shared the word with our pastor at the time, my husband, and a few other who were close friends. Each time I shared the word, I felt like hiding. My shame, at times, was greater than my faith, but God was getting ready to lay an ax to that root.

I remember being so excited for the next few months that my healing was going to occur any day and at any moment. I remember seeing signs around town about events that were coming up and wondered if I would be healed by then! I knew God was going to heal me any day, and I wanted proof to show the doctors. They had given me arch supports to help support my feet and body, but nothing helped. In fact, they hurt me more at times. For the next few months my focus was on my body and the word that God had given me about healing me physically. I went to the doctors but knew that my healing would ultimately come from the Lord.

I wanted to be wise. I began going to physical therapy two times a week to strengthen my legs and knees, which were hurting so badly from my arches that went flat. They told me that the hormones that loosen up your ligaments to prepare you to give birth to a baby are the same ones responsible for the ones that made my arches go flat. The arch in your foot is a ligament, and it is not only responsible for supporting your foot but your whole body. Trust me when I say that you should really appreciate your little footsies (or your big ones for that matter). Each foot has twenty-six bones in it (the bones in both your feet make up a quarter of all the bones in your body), and there are tons of ligaments, tendons, and muscles that support all those bones. Yes, I do believe that I am now qualified to be a podiatrist (foot doctor)!

Though my focus was on being healed, nothing was happening. My pain was getting worse and not better. Why was God not healing me yet? Oh, I remember bending down to feel if my arches were being raised yet. My feet still looked as flat as a pancake, and I continually looked at them in the mirror. I would look at them from the side to see if they had been raised yet! I knew at any moment they would be healed and life would go back to normal. God didn't want my old normal, though!

Was I crazy? I was beginning to think so when I was not experiencing yet what He had promised. My husband and I were so convinced God's healing was coming that we began to take pictures of my feet from all angles. You do not realize how much your body has gone through until you see it in a picture. My feet looked sick and disabled. The blood was not flowing properly, and they had lost a lot of muscle tone. While I had faith that I would be made whole, grief and sorrow also filled my heart about what was happening to my body. My old body before the birth of my daughter was gone, but there were also thoughts and dreams about what I would do when He healed me.

I am so glad our gracious Father does not condemn us for our attempts at believing Him. I had faith to be healed, but I also had doubt that it would really occur. The more time went by and I was not better, I felt unworthy again and discouraged. Welcome to *my* world. I cycled from faith to doubt to unbelief, then back to faith—just to go to doubt, fear, discouragement, shame for not walking in victory, and back to faith. Talk about exhausting! I have a feeling some of you know exactly what I am talking about. The good new is that Jesus broke me out of that cycle, and He will do the same for you if you let Him!

The caption on the front of this book talks of a journey through fear to freedom. Notice I had to walk through it before I walked out of it! Little did I know then what God was up to. But I am not going to let you jump to the end of the story so quickly. I want you to read the whole book! What I will tell you because I just cannot keep it inside is that He is way more faithful than I ever imagined Him to be. I love Him now more than ever.

CHAPTER 2

THE BIGGER PICTURE

*D*ESPERATION HAS A way of driving us to find answers. Much-needed answers. It causes us to look for something or someone to help us out of the mess we are in. Desperation was my gift during this season. It was the gift that God left in the recesses of my heart and mind that would drive me to find an answer to everything that was happening in my life. From the time that God spoke the word to me about healing me until a few months after that, I was in turmoil. I did not understand what was going on but desperately wanted to. God is so gracious to us when we do not see clearly. He hears the cries of our hearts to be free, and He answers them, only in His own way!

I clearly remember the day I was talking to my good friend Carrie on the phone about not understanding why God had not healed me yet. I was venting and looking for answers to my very real problem. What God was going to say to me next would turn my life upside down! My friend was quiet for a few moments on the other end. Then she said, "Gabby, God put something on my heart to share with you, and I have been praying and waiting for the right time to tell you." When someone says something like that to you, it can unearth all kinds of emotions! I felt fear, excitement, and curiosity. She proceeded to share with me the heart of my Father for me.

> What you have borne in the flesh, in your physical body, is much, much more than most ever bear in a lifetime, and only you and Jesus know exactly what that is. God wants you

to know that He knows what you have gone through, and the weight of what you have had to carry is represented in your feet. It has been so great that in the physical sense your body has collapsed.

Your focus at this time has been on Me healing your feet, but I want to heal your heart. As I restore your heart, mind, emotions simultaneously I too will restore your flesh. I want to bear the weight of what it is you have tried to carry until now. I, God the Father, want to carry it for you and restore the places that have not been tended to deep within you. Body, mind, and spirit, you will be made complete in me.

My soul leaps now, almost seven years later, because it truly was a word from my Father that has come to pass. His faithfulness to His word and plans has been so great! In all honesty, I am glad that it is seven years after the all the pain, but I can certainly tell you that His word that flows from my heart comes from His unrelenting faithfulness to me. His faithfulness. *Period.* I would never in a million years trade all that I went through for what I have gained. My friend who has walked closely with me during this season said I would say that! She knew because she had been there in other difficult seasons in her life. Getting the opportunity to bless and edify His body is one of the greatest privileges I could ever have. Bringing Him all the glory brings me exceeding satisfaction! Knowing that He is using my story to bless others is truly humbling! So, indeed, my Father wanted me to see the bigger picture, one I had not ever seen before with these eyes.

It took a while to process the word He had given to me, but immediately He began using me in the church I was going to at the time. I was asked to speak shortly after this, and I could not help but believe that He wanted to use what He was doing in my life to minister to others going through pain. I never really considered myself a speaker or a teacher, but I guess He did! My husband and I were asked to speak on God's blessings in our life, and boy did I have lots to share! It was not a stale message pulled out of a file cabinet but one being lived out in my life at the very moment. (I think God prefers that anyhow.)

There were many emotions and thoughts going on inside me. He was lifting my eyes up to Him and off of my circumstances. I was literally being transformed from the inside out, and it felt like it. Because I was so desperate for Him I became very sensitive to His Spirit, not only for me but for others. I became aware of their pain and how I could help them from my experience.

For someone who walked in such fear and shame, standing up and telling others what God was doing in me was difficult. Being so honest and real felt vulnerable. But now I realize that God (and I) would have it no other way. People have real problems, and they need real answers. As I cooperated with the work of the Holy Spirit, I could tell that I was becoming more focused on what God wanted to do internally and not only about my feet being healed. Oh, I never let the hope and faith go, but there was a new grace to glean all that my Father wanted me to glean from this season. The Holy Spirit had lifted my eyes up.

During this time, at the beginning of this season, my same friend shared something else that the Lord had showed her about what He wanted to do with my circumstances. She first took this word to our pastor to see what he thought. He believed it was from the Lord but told her to be sensitive to the timing of sharing it with me because I may not have been ready. Their sensitivity to God and to me is something that I am very grateful for. After about six or eight weeks she shared God's heart for me through this word. She said that as she was praying for me she saw Jesus walking through the city on His way to the crucifixion carrying His cross, and after this she heard, "*So too as I, Jesus, have carried the cross bearing the sins of man, I have strengthened her to carry her cross and have brought her to a place to be able to bear the weight of the sins man has committed against her. She is ready to carry her cross, and in doing so she will be moved to compassion and unconditional love and forgiveness for those who have sinned against her. She will be moved to forgiveness, and this will bring total freedom."* My friend, Carrie, heard the words, *"The work is done. The one thing left to do is grieve. I have allowed her circumstances with her feet in order for her to learn to grieve—it is a way of release."*

He showed my friend that just as He bore the sin of men, loved them unconditionally, and pleaded with the Father to forgive them, so would I be moved to that very place of forgiveness in an unconditional way. This would produce total freedom. He said that this was not just about the healing of my feet but of my heart. He said that He would make me complete in Him—body, soul, spirit. What an amazing word! I knew it was from the Lord because it confirmed His nature, character, and what He was already stirring in my spirit.

One thing I know now is that when it seems like Jesus is unraveling your life, it is truly so He can put you back together! It may feel like He is trying to destroy you, but once you learn of His loving nature, you will see your circumstances with a different set of eyes. This is what my Father was doing with me. I had walked so much in the natural according to what I could see, feel, and experience. He was showing me that there was so much more to my life; to life, period. Little did I know that in the coming days, I would literally draw all of my strength—mentally, emotionally, physically, and spiritually—from Him. He would become my life.

I remember being in so much physical pain that it was very difficult and sometimes impossible to do my daily tasks. I am forever grateful for a wonderful woman and friend who we went to church with at the time. She would come over and put my little Emily in her high chair and feed her. Lifting my baby was not possible for me. I had so much pain from my feet that had affected every part of my body. There was no getting down on the floor to lie with my little one like I had with my first daughter, Sarah. Just bending over to change Emily's diapers was a huge task for me. (You mothers know how many diapers a newborn goes through in a day.)

Every day seemed the same to me. I would get up every morning, and I knew that if Jesus did not come through for me in some very real and practical ways that day I would not make it. I vividly remember sitting down to eat my breakfast with my Bible and being more desperate for a word from Him than I was for my physical food. I cried out to Him with everything I had. I was so desperate for Him. Yes, I had some people who helped me out in the physical sense, but I was suddenly coming face to face with other things in my life, and the only one who could help me was God. Not a bad place to be, by the way! Mind you, through all of this, I never became clinically depressed or got stuck in a place of defeat. That does not mean that I never felt overwhelmed or like things were difficult, because they were. Looking back, I feel like God literally had me in the palm of His hand. The storm was raging all around me, but He was holding me!

Writing this now, I can hardly imagine how I made it through all of that. The pain in my feet and my feet actually going flat affected the rest of my body. At first, just my feet and lower legs hurt. Then I began to develop pain in my hips and then my back. By about six months after I had Emily, my body felt like it had been run over! For about the first one and a half to two years I lived lying on the couch. Yes, I got up when I had to, but only when I had to. I did only the chores and activities that I knew needed to be done. If I left the house to go somewhere I had to be sure that wherever I went I would be able to spend most of the time sitting down. The thought of standing for more than five or ten minutes caused panic in me because I knew the pain and discomfort I would experience. If for some reason I was in a situation where I needed to stand for a while

I would go home knowing my pain would be more severe than normal for the next several days.

I knew that I needed some form of exercise but was not really thrilled with doing anything that had to do with standing or walking, so swimming seemed like a good option for me! I hopped in the car and headed to our local indoor pool. It really did feel good to have the weight of my body off of my feet for thirty to forty-five minutes a few times a week. At times I wished I could just live in the water to escape the pain in my feet!

I had a newborn and a two year old when all of this started. When my pain was the worst I was happy when I got one basket of laundry folded all week! Running into one store for a quick errand was a huge feat for me! I remember my husband and daughters running into the store as I waited in the car because my body hurt too badly to go in. Instead of staying home and being miserable I went along for the ride. Oh, those precious times with my Savior in the car with the worship music cranked up. I leaned back my chair and sung my heart out to my Father. All I could do was lift my eyes and life up to Him. The worship songs that were popular during that time are forever engrained in my heart and my spirit. We sang one at church today that just about threw me over the edge—in a good way!

Coming out on the other side of this journey I am experiencing some major faithfulness. My faith has become sight!

We took many drives in the evening as a family because that was one thing that we enjoyed that I could do. We usually had to sneak in a hot chocolate or something yummy! My older daughter, Sarah, thankfully was a very easy girl. We read a lot, because that was something else I was able to do. We played puzzles at the table and sang. There was no taking her to the park, pushing her on the swings, or picking her up for a long time.

I can handle pain pretty well, but nothing prepared me for this, for missing out on so much with my two little ones. All along I knew my Father was going to supernaturally heal me. But I was in so much pain, and He seemed to be taking forever! As I prayed about it, I felt Him gently lead me.

> *I will use the arch supports now to help you, but there will come a time when I will not have to use them anymore, because I will heal your feet.*

That gave me peace. I wanted to use wisdom, so I went to the foot doctor and tried to get some custom arch supports made. I have to say that once I got the arch supports they did take away the worst of the pain in my lower legs and made the pain more bearable. However, they never took it away like the foot doctor said they should, and I still had a great deal of pain. He was perplexed as to why they were not helping me when they had helped and completely taken away pain in almost everyone else. He had me tested for arthritis and other diseases to rule out other underlying conditions. I had my back X-rayed to make sure all the discs were healthy. Of course, like I had imagined, all the tests came back normal, and my back looked very healthy!

I remember one day the foot doctor wanted to send me for some tests to find out why I was still having pain after his treatment. So much of me wanted to tell him that God was going to heal my feet. I could not find the courage. You see, for someone who had lived a life of fear and shame, sharing something like that seemed impossible. I will share more of why I lived with these bondages in the coming chapters, but at that time I was convinced he would think I was a total loon! As I was preparing to get the X-ray of my back later in the day, God gently whispered to me, *"I have never been so proud of a daughter as I am of you."* Did He just miss something? Was He really saying these kind words to me? Yes, He was.

I learned something about my Father that day. He truly loves me.

Like, big time. He not only saw my fear of telling the foot doctor about my feet but that I needed to be healed from the years of being rejected and made fun of for who I was and my inability to express who I was. I was still wearing rejection as a heavy coat, and He was removing it from me one layer at a time with His love. He knew that for me to be that bold was still very difficult. I did not feel like I was ashamed of Him but of me. I was still the problem. That is what this whole season was about for me: Him healing His daughter. When He said these words to me, I began to cry right there in the dressing room where I was preparing to be examined. I knew He was up to something bigger than healing my feet. He was healing my heart. Something changed for me that day. I began to see my God and myself in a different light. I realized how much He loved me, not because of how good I performed but because I was His. All His.

I went along with the treatment that the doctor gave me and wore the arch supports. As I said earlier, they did help, but not fully. The worst of my physical pain was gone, but I still had many limitations. It was during this time as my feet improved a little that I decided to get a recumbent exercise bike just to get my legs moving. Going to the pool and coming out wet in the dead of winter was not so fun for me anymore. I thought that I could handle the bike. It would get me off my feet but still allow me to exercise my muscles. In the beginning, five minutes was all I could ride. Just doing that made me proud! Using my muscles began to make me feel a little better. During this time my chiropractor—which is such a great doctor—gave me helpful tips on not pushing myself too hard and letting my muscles get the rest they needed until my body gained more strength.

I really had to face some things about my body during this time that were difficult. My figure is pretty athletic, and I have always enjoyed physical activities like gardening, hiking, camping, walking, etc. Now, I was grieving over all the things that I could not do with my body. It was hard. God knew how much it affected me even more than I did. He knows us through and through, my friends. He let me cry and get angry over it all. Then, in His gracious ways, He gently lifted my eyes up to see Him. Yes, all of my circumstances were still there, but He was becoming bigger through my pain. He continued to show me what He was doing with it all and all of the wonderful things He wanted to accomplish in this season. His Spirit would continually remind me of the promises of healing in His Word and of the specific words He spoke to me. This brought great comfort and strength to continue on and not lose hope.

My wonderful mother-in-law came over and did laundry, dishes, and helped with the girls. I had to learn how to receive during this time. For some this is easier than others. For me, it was hard. Why is that? Why do we do silly things like reject help from well-meaning people? Pride, fear, feeling unworthy—I could relate to them all.

I remember not only the physical pain but the issues God was bringing to the surface. It seems that when God is dealing with you and uprooting things, they tend to smack you right in the face. He sure was right when He said that He would heal me physically as He healed my heart, mind, and emotions. I was seeing His very words coming to pass right before my eyes! I began to realize the weight of all the fear, shame, guilt, unworthiness, unforgiveness, and hurt was literally destroying my body. It is one thing to see these things, but our Father's heart is to heal them. He does not want us to roll around in the mire and stay there. He has much more for us.

I began to realize that what we go through in this life damages our bodies. I felt ashamed of what happened to my body in a weird sort of way. I felt as if there were something wrong with me, and I had to wrestle with those emotions. The enemy would have loved to destroy me during this time through guilt and condemnation for the years that I walked in darkness, but God's voice singing and rejoicing over me was so much greater and sweeter. It was such a beautiful day when I discovered Zephaniah 3:17, which says, "The LORD your God in your midst, The Mighty One, will save; He will rejoice over you with gladness, He will quiet you with His love, He will rejoice over you with singing." If I had not spent lots of time in His presence, this season could have very easily destroyed me.

I remember lying in bed at night when my pain was the worst. Just to get up and use the restroom was extremely painful to my feet. It would take an hour for the inflammation in my feet to subside enough for me to fall asleep. During the time before I could see the bigger picture, I would lie in bed and be angry. I would say things to my husband like, "Why can so many other ladies have babies and their bodies be fine?" or "I do not understand why God is allowing this." I know now that my Father wept with me and over me in my affliction. I just could not see it then.

If we walk in the natural most of our lives, understanding and cooperating with His purposes just seems foreign. He was teaching me to walk out of fear and death and into the new life in Christ that He provided for me. Getting there was the fun part! I was so used to living in fear that this just threw me over the edge. I could not comprehend it and certainly was not the least bit happy about it in the beginning. I was hurt, confused, and angry at God. How could He let this happen to me when I had a two year old and a newborn, for crying out loud? Had He taken a break from watching over me? Some of you may have tears in your eyes now because you have been there or are there now. The purpose of me writing this book, however, was so that we would not stay in a broken and defeated place.

By His grace, I am now a living, breathing testimony to the resurrection power of Jesus Christ not just to heal our bodies but to restore our lives! I believe He wants to restore you also, for His glory. During these days, His very words were life to me. I ate them and looked for Him all day. He was the one who sustained me when I was lonely and in pain. When I did not have the strength to take care of my girls, He carried me.

I happen to have the world's greatest husband and father to our children, by the way. He worked all day and would come home to his bride, who was in so much pain. The house was a wreck because I only did what I could physically do to take care of our children. Looking back, I am amazed at how well they were taken care of! I put all my energy into loving and caring for them and seeking the Lord during this time. Andy, my husband, would come home and make dinner, do the dishes, and help take care of the kids. By the end of the day, I was so sore I really was not up to going anywhere. That would require walking and standing, which was painful.

All of this really took a toll on him, too, in many ways. He wanted so much for me to be healed and whole, not for him but for me. He wanted me to be able to do everything that I had physically done before. I used to work out, go for walks with him and Sarah, go hiking, camping, garden, bake, etc. Not anymore. The couch and I became pretty good friends! He understood and loved me through it all. Most of all he believed God with me for the promises He had given me and what He wanted to do with our lives.

Our oldest, Sarah, was an angel baby. She rarely cried, mostly when she was hungry. She was born five weeks early and was under five pounds. We were not prepared for the difference in temperament when Emily came along! I could tell from the first few minutes of her life that she was a different child altogether. She cried in the hospital and would not sleep for the first twelve or so hours after being born. All she wanted to do was eat and be awake. Good grief, did she not realize that I just did all the work and was exhausted?

Oh, I did enjoy her those first hours of getting to know her! She was stout, and you really did not seem to have to handle her like a newborn! Oh, her dark hair, skin, and brown eyes just captured me. They still do! She was mine. All mine. I loved our first hours together, but at last she needed to go to the nursery so I could sleep a little. She began crying in the hospital, and I remember asking, "Why is she crying so much? My first daughter did not cry this much." The nurses and doctors said, "All babies are different." And boy, were they.

Emily cried a lot. She had colic. Yes, I can hear the sighs now from all you parents who endured colic. Notice I said *endured*, not *overcame*. Colic wins. Every time. So, on top of my pain, she was a cranky little thing. Surely God really overlooked this. As if I did not have enough to deal with, without a crying, cranky baby all day. She did not cry all day, but she would start at about four o'clock in the afternoon, just as Andy was coming home, and cried until about one or two in the morning. I laugh now as I vividly remember asking Andy why he was not bonding with Emily like he did Sarah. All he had to do was to hold our screaming baby up and laugh and say, "Hmm, I wonder why I am having a hard time bonding with her!" He took the bus to work and could hear her crying when he got off at the bus. He later told me there were days that he wanted to keep on riding the bus past our stop! It was tough even for a guy who works at the state mental institution!

Even during the day she was fussy. You would lay her down for a nap and could never expect her to fall asleep. Her little tummy hurt, and she would let you know about it. Just as I would try and get a nap myself, she would start to scream. We tried to take her out for stroller walks, drives, and the like just to help her and give us some sanity. Nothing worked. My darling Emily did not sleep through the night until she was thirteen months old. As much as I loved her and did not take out my frustrations on her during this time, this only added to what I was going through. Fortunately, my older daughter, Sarah, was such a good girl and a great big sister and helper. She would lie next to Emily when she cried and say, " It's OK. I love you!" What a sweetie!

Gradually, at about six months, Emily started to cry less, and so did the rest of us! She slowly became an easier baby, and we were able to enjoy her more! I felt at this time that between her colic and my pain I was missing out on so many things with her. We were all just trying to survive. Looking back on my Father's mercy, He has restored everything and more to me and us as a family. That is just the kind of God we have! As I recount all of this, it seems like this happened to someone else, like I am reading about someone else's life, because things are so different now!

If you did not grab that tissue I told you to, go grab one now, and hang in there to see how He unfolded this beautiful story of grace and healing! Let your gracious Father lift your eyes above the circumstances you may be in now. Let Him show you His lovely face. His face has a way of giving us strength for the journey and giving us vision beyond what we are going through to see where He wants to take us. Buckle up!

CHAPTER 3

WOVEN IN WONDER

REMEMBER THE DAY I had a breakthrough. I was pregnant with my daughter, Emily, and was laying my older daughter down for a nap so we could both get some much needed rest. Actually, looking back now I can see that God was preparing my heart for the season of difficulty with my feet. He was preparing to radically change my life. Sarah was about two years old at the time. I had her in my lap next to her bed and told her that God made her, and she was so good! As I left her room, it hit me—I did not truly know this for myself. I was telling my daughter something that I did not believe about me.

God has a way of wanting truth in our inward parts (Ps. 51:6) and will do whatever He can to have His truth run all through our lives. My Father began to lead me to read Psalm 139 and the beautiful words He has spoken to me. I am convinced that God in all His wisdom knew there would be broken people who desperately needed to hear the words of this beautiful Psalm. These words are life to me and are now written on my heart forever! God began to speak about the beauty and glory He made me with through Psalm 139:13–15.

> For You formed my inward parts; You covered me in my mother's womb. I will praise You, for I am fearfully and wonderfully made; Marvelous are Your works, And that my soul knows very well. My frame was not hidden from You, When I was made in secret, And skillfully wrought in the lowest parts of the earth.

I have to share about the journey that God and I have been on to get to the place of victory and overcoming my past. Breaking free from fear, shame, and all the other things that God has brought me freedom from will make sense only as I share some of where I have walked in this life. Only when you see the depth of the darkness of where someone has walked can you truly see how awesome God is to bring us into such light and freedom!

The lies that for years would become my truth came to me when I was conceived and continued to be re-enforced in me at a very young age. The lies that I believed for so many years took root when I was conceived and continued to be reinforced in me beginning at a very young age. Reading that He formed me while I was in my mother's womb really spoke to me. They caught my attention. You see, my Father knew there were some very valid reasons for me having trouble believing His words to me. I was born to a poor mother in California. Sacramento, to be exact. The day Gabrielle Nicole LaFaye entered this world was September 5, 1978. My birth certificate bears the name of my mother and the name of a French man whom I would never know. All I know of him is what my birth mother told my adoptive mom—that he was not a good man and she never wanted me to find him. This is how life began for me.

Other than my mother's short-term relationships with friends and a few family friends, my mother and I lived alone for years in a small apartment in Long Beach, California. There was a short time when I was one or one and a half that we lived in Hawaii. Most of my early memories are from living in Southern California, though.

My mother was pretty, loving, caring, and fun. I remember her picking me up from preschool or kindergarten and us walking home together. We lived in the ghetto, and I remember walking with her through the neighborhood and by the neighborhood market owned by Chinese people where we would get those little ice cream sundaes in the plastic cups with the little wooden spoons. Gosh, how I still love those! We would walk home, and I would sit down and eat my peanut butter and jelly sandwich and watch *Sesame Street* and *Mister Rogers' Neighborhood*. I loved playing out in front of our apartment complex on roller skates and flying kites in the southern California breeze. Looking way high up at my kite surrounded by blue skies are some of my earliest and happiest memories. Playing with the neighborhood kids on bikes and with Barbie cars filled my days. Those are a few of the happy memories I have from being a little girl.

I remember looking at my mother and thinking she was beautiful. What child doesn't? As I grow and change as a woman, I am looking more and more like her. I get to see glimpses of her when I look in the mirror. Even though I have not seen her in almost twenty years, I have pictures to remind me what she looks like. I get to see different characteristics of hers in my girls also. One thing I remember about her is that she had the fastest growing nails and hair. My girls and I are the same way. We need a haircut about every two to three weeks or we start looking crazy! My daughter has the fastest growing and most beautiful nails of any seven year old I know! Those things make me think of my mother. They remind me of her.

I have a brother also, who I have never met. I am told he is much older than me. It is kind of weird to have family out there that you never have known. I have tried to find some of my family on the Internet, but without any success.

Unfortunately, I didn't grow up in the most ideal circumstances. One of my earliest memories of my mother is when she came in one day to our apartment and pinning me to the floor and excitedly yelling, "We just won the lottery. We just won the lottery!" It seemed bizarre, even as a young girl.

If we won the lottery, it certainly was not much, because we were poor. We often did not have money for what we needed, including food. There were many times I was at home alone without food in the house. I am not sure what she was doing. I remember her coming back to the house with others at times. She always seemed to come home at night.

Now that I look back, I feel compassion for her. To have a daughter and not to be able to take care of yourself, much less her, would be very sad and frightening. I now wonder if she had anywhere to turn for help or if she even knew there was a way out. This went on for the first six years or my life.

During the time of living with my birth mother, I also was in and out of foster homes. When things were rough, I went to the foster home. During better times, I went back home. None of the foster homes were abusive. I do vividly remember looking out of the window and crying and asking when my mom would be coming back. Oh, I remember wanting to be with my mother, even though the conditions weren't ideal. She was my mother after all. I cannot even imagine my girls longing for their mother like that. The thought makes me want to cry. If you have little ones, go and give them a big ol' hug! I do remember that one foster family fed me peanut butter and jelly a lot! Other than that I do not have many memories of my time in foster care.

There was one family in the apartment complex that my mother and I lived in that I believe was sent by God to help take care of me and look out for me. I never lived with them, but they had a daughter a few years older than me. We were best friends. I would play at her house often. She had more and nicer things to play with than me! We played house and Barbies and had tea parties. We did all the fun things that little princesses should be doing! Her family would feed me food and let me stay for hours. They also let me go places with them. Those were happy times, when I could escape the pain at home and know that someone was taking care of me.

The day eventually arrived that would be the last with my birth mother. I remember it as if it were yesterday. Our apartment had two stories, and the stairs were made of those tiny gray pebbles. The manager had an apartment that was upstairs and overlooked ours. I remember looking up and seeing a police man coming from his apartment. As I looked at him, time seemed to stand still. My life seemed to stand still. It was like I knew what was going on, even though I was only five or six. We had been here before. The police removed me before and put me into foster care. This time was different. That was the last day I lived with her.

I went to live with the family that I had been in foster care most often with. Although I would live out the rest of my growing up years with them, the battle for legal guardianship was fierce. My mother asked my foster family not to adopt me because it sounded too final I guess, so they went through the process of legal guardianship. Any courthouse is not fun to do this in, much less the Los Angeles courthouse. It is huge, it smells, and there are tons of people. The process took longer than normal because of various delays. I remember many lunches in that courthouse cafeteria. Not my favorite, by the way. I remember all the cement of the old buildings and the long hallways. When court was in session they would be empty and quiet. When we were waiting for court they would be bustling with people, very interesting people.

By the time I reached seven or eight years old, the process for legal guardianship was finished. I have not seen my birth mother since. I am thankful that my adopted family never did or said anything against her or was anything but loving toward her. They also gave me the freedom growing up to stay in contact with her through letters, so we have written to each other through the years. She knew that I graduated high school and went on to Bible college. I never felt like I wanted to see her in person. I guess I was too scared of all we had been through and was not sure if experiencing all of that was good for me, and now for my family. We sent her an invitation to our wedding, even though I knew she would not make it, and she even called us in Dallas, Texas, where we were living shortly after.

When I was pregnant with my first daughter, Sarah, I wrote and told her, and I sent her pictures after she was born. I guess writing to her felt safe for me and let me feel connected to the one who brought me into this world. My mother never forgot my birthday. She would always send a card and a gift. One time she sent a dress that was way too small for me. She bought it for the little girl that she remembered all those years ago. I just had my seven year old try it on, and she looked like a little Gabby!

I have a box of things and cards that she has sent me. That is really all I have to remember my childhood, besides what is in my head and heart. She told me all our pictures were destroyed in a shed, so I have no baby pictures of myself. The youngest one I have of me is when I was about one and a half years old and we lived in Hawaii. That's it. At times I get sad that I do not know what I looked like as a baby. I did pull one photo out of me when I was about four. I was dressed up for Halloween, and boy did I look cute. This last year, my little Emily dressed up as Little Red Riding Hood. After printing out the pictures I went and dug for the one of me when I was four. Side by side, we look so much alike! I almost cried! It means so much to see my girls looking more and more like me and their grandma. It is like a piece of my life being preserved in them. I will get a glimpse of them at certain angles and see me as a child. Oh, I love it!

After being taken from my mother, I had to go to the hospital because I was having a breakdown. I could not keep any food or water down because I was so upset by everything. Memories of me as a frail little girl lying in that hospital bed are still vivid in my head. My adoptive family took me to counseling to try and get through everything, but I do not remember it ever being that helpful. Looking back now, I believe that this is where many of the physical symptoms I experienced stemmed from—from the trauma that I went through as a little child, especially in the early developmental years.

All of those things affect us. Our bodies do not get to escape. Much of the time they show the evidence of where we have walked in this life. I now know that when God promised to heal me through this journey, He truly wanted to give me something that I never knew as a girl: true health and rest and wholeness. That is why Jesus came. This is why I love Him so! He came to restore us to the image that He made us with. Perfect. No flaws but perfection.

I always remember suffering from one ailment or another, even as a child. Now, He was restoring all things to me. Even parts of me that He always saw, even when I didn't. Simply amazing! This is nothing short of a miracle. I loved that He looked down on me in that hospital bed and had a plan to deliver me from all that life had thrown at me and would throw at me. I love that He has not left me to suffer in any area, including physically. Little by little, the effects of being healed in the deepest places of my heart and the deepest places of my mind have affected how my body functions. It is like they are all lining up together—simultaneously. Like He said. Just like He said. There are many things that have improved, including my feet. It is funny though, how our feet are the foundation of our physical bodies, and how God was rocking and shifting the very foundation of how my life started.

Beloved, He sees us through and through. Every fiber of our being, including these bodies. Every tendon, ligament, muscle. Nothing escapes His watchful eye. Every part of our frame that has had to endure such stress and trauma in this life. I so believe that

Jesus came to make us whole in every area. I am a living testimony to that! Much of the time we neglect our bodies, thinking they are less holy or less His than other parts of us. Our bodies are where He dwells. The Holy One is coming and doing some housecleaning so that where He dwells is fit for a King. He wants our bodies healed and whole so they can display His glory. So *we* can display His glory. As I mention in other areas of this book, I do not desire to condemn any who are living with sickness or disease. What I long to bring out is the fullness of the gospel message—that He came to heal and restore every part of us. Let us seek Him and press into Jesus for all He has for us!

All that had happened in my life not only affected my body, but it affected all of me. It brings us full circle to the place that God brought me to on the day I laid my little one down and told her how God had made her and how utterly wonderful she was. Oh, He definitely wanted her to know it; He just did not want it to pass me over! As He led me through Psalm 139, I read it like it was the first time I had ever read it, or seen it for that matter. I was getting it! Through tear-filled eyes I came to the revelation that I—yes, I—was His work and creation. This was nothing short of life changing for me. He went back with me to the place where all the lies had begun. He went back to the very place of wounding by the enemy.

Watch out when God goes back for something, because it will change when He gets there! Lies will be destroyed with the truth. For me, my emotions always told me how I should feel about myself, and now God was challenging me to believe something different. Here was the lie that plagued me all of my life: there is something wrong with me, and that is why I was rejected by my parents. If that were not bad or powerful enough to keep me down, Satan kept playing that card with me all through my life. If anything went wrong, I thought, "There must be something wrong with me." If someone did something to hurt me, it must have been because there was something wrong with me. Everything that happened was my fault. That lie stuck because I never knew or experienced anything else. That became my truth, even though it was a lie. But as I read the truth of what God said about me and my life, that message began to make more sense than anything else.

Just reading that He formed me was simply life changing for me. If He made me, then there must not be anything wrong with me. The fog and heaviness began to lift, not overnight; but reading His very words through tears and grief, it began to lift. I began to believe Him over my past experiences and what my emotions were still telling me.

Then, I began to feel a righteous anger well up in me. I was angry that I had given my life to this lie, angry that the enemy had stolen so much from me. Angry at all I had missed out on because of my early life. The Spirit of God inside me was tired of being weighed down, and I was mad at all the enemy stole from God's daughter—me!

I began seeing myself differently. I had to humble myself and repent before my Father that I had dishonored Him by treating myself so badly for my whole life. I knew I had never done anything to bring this on myself, but I sensed that part of my healing meant recognizing that His truth and the lie I had accepted could not coexist; by living in bondage to that lie, I had unknowingly turned away the free gift of grace and lavish love my Father had extended to me through Christ. When the Holy Spirit begins to convict us, it is totally different from the shame and condemnation we are so accustomed to. Shame is the enemy's language, but conviction that leads to life and freedom is God's language. I do not believe that in all of the Word of God there are any more personal, beautiful words than the ones penned here in Psalm 139:13–18 by King David under the inspiration of God.

> For You formed my inward parts;
> You covered me in my mother's womb.
> I will praise You, for I am fearfully and wonderfully made;

Marvelous are Your works,
And that my soul knows very well.
My frame was not hidden from You,
When I was made in secret,
And skillfully wrought in the lowest parts of the earth.
Your eyes saw my substance, being yet unformed.
And in Your book they all were written,
The days fashioned for me,
When as yet there were none of them.
How precious also are Your thoughts to me, O God!
How great is the sum of them!
If I should count them, they would be more in number than
the sand.

I will take a little liberty here and show how God made these verses so very personal and life giving to me. I don't know about you, but I really do not care to hear a sermon on going through hard times if the one delivering it has not really been through any. Nor do I care about hearing about how wonderful and beautiful that He made us from someone who really does not know it for themselves! This is not the case with David. He was a shepherd who I believe spent much time communing with His God. Just look at the other psalms that he wrote. He knew that His God loved Him and knew him so intimately. God made sure that we got a glimpse of the intimacy that He and David shared. He wanted us to know that we could have it too!

As we look at this psalm together, I pray that His words would heal our soul. Each verse is so full of truth that I want to share from most of them what He had shared with me about their meaning. There are some days that I still cannot get past the first verse in Psalm 139. As I have been writing this book, I planned to just touch on some highlights or big events in my life, but it became apparent as I was writing that He had some other plans. He just simply would not let me pass over some very significant things in my life. They were important to Him, and by writing them He is continuing to heal me. He has been so faithful in this work. With all that I experienced growing up, I never really got a chance to know myself. It has not been until this journey, and specifically writing this book, that I have really had a chance to do this. That may sound funny to some of you, but to others, you can understand and relate. Oh, many parts of me have been free for years, but much of this message of freedom is coming from someone has been recently broken free and is being broken free at this very moment!

This may be a good time to open your Word along with this book to get the fullness of what He is trying to say to us in Psalm 139. To think that God has searched us and known us. For some of you, that strikes fear in your heart! Don't let it, beloved. Think about when we search for something—car keys, a lost shoe, a scripture we love; it is because we want to find the thing. We are the thing that He is searching for! He wants us! After living the kind of life I did, that comes as such good news! Somebody wants me, and it happens to be the one who sees and knows all of me, as we go on to read. I love verse 2 where He says, "You understand my thought afar off." He gets us! This truly is one of the many reasons that I love Him so.

Thinking back to all I wrote about living in shame and feeling bad about myself, He truly understands why we think and act the way we do. He gets it but refuses to leave His beloved there! Let's not operate in a spirit of fear about God knowing every detail of us, down to our every thought. It is not His heart to condemn us. He wants us to draw *near* because of these things. If He died to save us while we were a wreck as sinners, surely He will keep on delivering us (Rom. 5:8.) If we really understood this, we would be seriously different! Listen for the voice of your Father all through this psalm. He is there! As I opened this psalm it was almost as if He were there just waiting for me to discover the treasure of His love for me! He is waiting for you there, too!

Look at verse 5 with me. It describes how He closes us in or hems us in all around.

> You have hedged me behind and before, And laid Your hand upon me.

The reality of God being so near in our past, present, and future gave me so much comfort. He had seen all the broken roads that these feet had traveled, He saw the *me* who was desperately trying to find healing in my present, and He is already in my future waiting for me! He goes on to assure us in verse 7 that there is no place that we can go to get away from Him pursuing us. No matter how far I was from Him, how hard I fought against His perfect will in my life, or how many times I would fall, He was all over me! Why? Why would this all-knowing, all-seeing, infinitely wise God go to such great lengths to seek me out? "For God so *loved* the world that He gave His only begotten Son, that whoever believes in Him should not perish but have everlasting life" (John 3:16, emphasis added).

Oh, if you thought God was getting personal in the first half of this chapter, buckle your seat belts and hang on for the ride of your life! Verse 13 lets us in on why He is so passionate for us. It is there that we read that we are His creation. It is that simple. For those of you who are parents, I don't need to say any more! This was the message the Holy Spirit was bringing to life the day I laid my little one down for her nap. It was not enough for her to know it; He wanted me to know it too. You see, for me to know that He created me—the deepest parts that make up *me*—was like pouring water on parched land. I so needed to hear it, and more than once! God formed me. Me. You. Us. That truth may seem so simple, but it is truly life changing. It cancels the lie that there is something wrong or flawed with us.

I remember walking around the house as God was revealing this to me saying to myself and then proclaiming out loud, "If God made me, then there is nothing wrong with me!" It canceled out the lie that I had been rejected because there was something wrong with me. The words of this psalm began to replace the words in my head, the words of the accuser of the brethren.

No matter the circumstances or family you were born into, you are His creation. He goes on to say that He literally knit us together in our mother's womb. He cares so much for each individual that He takes the time to form and fashion every detail of us with the same hands and wisdom and might that He used to create the universe! Talk about being special! Satan just hates this chapter! I bet he fought God's plan of including it in the Word. God rejoices over it and over us as we read and believe it! David cannot help but just turn his face upward and shout out some serious praise here in verses 14 and 15. So will we when we truly understand the beautiful work of art we are.

Just think, your God stands back and looks at you with a sense of awe and wonder. We are His work of art! These words and our Creator's heart are echoed in Ephesians 2:10, which says, "For we are His workmanship, created in Christ Jesus for good works, which God prepared beforehand that we should walk in them." No matter what life has thrown at us, Jesus came to restore us to the image that He made us in. I remember Him whispering to my heart that He was restoring me to the beauty and glory that He made me with. Wow! I had no clue what He meant then, but I received His healing words into my heart and made them mine. Because I believed my Daddy, He began to bring it to pass. Then I got to see glimpses of the beauty and glory that He made me with. Others began to see it as I walked it out.

One of the gracious ways that God let me live this out was to use my gifting in the church. Before His work of grace, I was too scared and broken to walk in the freedom to minister. I was always the one being ministered to! God began turning that around. I found a new passion for teaching and preaching that I had not known. People actually told me I was really good and should continue doing it. God was able to express Himself through me because I could finally see my beauty and value to Him and myself and to others. He so wants to open up our lives and let all that He has done be poured out. That does not come by accident; it comes by knowing we are His.

As He was restoring my mind and how I thought about myself, it gradually affected my actions more and more. I began to believe that I was beautiful and made decisions based on His truth. As I saw the words of Psalm 139 in black and white on the pages of my Bible, I also saw them in red, written with the precious blood of Christ, who came to make the heart of our Father a living reality in our lives. The Holy Spirit wove these words together with what Christ did on the cross and the faith in my heart. All of these were becoming a beautiful tapestry! I began to see bits of it come together as my spiritual eyesight became keener to what He was doing. That brought loads of encouragement to keep on in the journey of finding healing.

As I experienced more of His healing to this broken and tattered life, I was continuing to experience more and more healing and release from pain in my body too. It was so cool to see that every time He uncovered another layer that needed to be mended, He also mended my broken body. His work in my soul literally released my body from the pain and stress it was under. Because of this, I began to look forward to what He was going to do next, because I knew my body would be more and more healed as a result! Even on some of the most difficult days of this journey, I now knew He was with me and would sustain me. He would bring me through! To have faith for it is one thing, but to see it in our daily lives in just stinkin' awesome!

I joined with David in praise to God for who He made—me! I never knew the fulfillment of someone rejoicing over me so greatly, much less rejoicing over myself. It was a totally foreign concept to me! God had to remind me often to just chill out and enjoy who He made. As I was getting to know myself, He taught me to enjoy myself. I realized that because of how I viewed myself, I was not able to enjoy Him, me, life, or others. I was carrying lots of weight that I was not designed to carry. When we do that, our mind, emotions, and body break down under the weight of it all. I remember the word He gave me that the weight of all I had tried to carry all my life literally was crushing my feet and body. As He began unpacking the loads off of me, my body began to heal a bit. It was like a chain reaction. I was still full of pain, but I was beginning to see the healing in my body that He said He wanted to bring all along.

God goes to great lengths to describe the beautiful detail of how He made us. David says in verse 14 that his soul knew that truth very well. Gods' truth was woven through the fabric of David's thoughts, feelings, and actions, not just his spirit. God so wants us to get it like that!

The words of verse 16 sent me soaring. To think that before life got really messed up and damaged me, He saw the perfect me He created. He also saw the amazing plans He had for this life. God has dreams, and not just to change nations or see a certain president elected. He has dreams for people—you and me. God gets to live out His dreams through us. If I were Him, I would not put so much stock in us! Fortunately, we are not God. Before He even saw the intricate parts of our being come together to form a human, God dreamed some amazing dreams over our lives. Let's not let His dreams go unfulfilled. Let's love Him as much as much as we can! Stop fighting it and just start believing it!

I had to hear this message way more than once. He also made me with a hard head! So, beloved, we get the honor of having His hands lift up our head above the cloud of shame and unworthiness and walk confidently in the God who made us. My daughter quoted Psalm 18:35 to me as she was memorizing it for school. It says that God stoops down to make us great. What an awesome, humble God we have. He could demand to hold all greatness in His control, but He humbles Himself and lets us share in His greatness. Not His glory, but His greatness. How utterly beautiful. It brings tears to my eyes every time I hear it! He has wonderful plans for His work of art. He gets to choose what He does with His masterpiece.

Even as He was freeing me to minister more and just to be me more, there was still this lie that He was uprooting little by little, the lie that the deepest dreams and hopes in my heart could not be fulfilled, that because of where I had walked in this life I would not be able to fulfill all the things that God had for me. I began to meditate on this His words and reason that if He has my days all written in a book, then it must be possible to walk them out. It would be so unfair to make plans for us that we could not fulfill. God showed me Psalm 139:16, which says, "Your eyes saw my substance, being yet unformed. And in Your book they all were written, The days fashioned for me, When as yet there were none of them." What does this say? God says our days were perfectly fashioned for the people He made us to be. *Perfectly.* He also means here that we are able to live out those plans He has for us. No sin is too big, no stumble too hard.

Oh, I hope this is speaking life over some of you and the dreams that He has for you! God intends for you to be who He has made you and to do what He has given you to do. Period. If you have doubts about that, stop stumbling over your failures and look to Jesus, who makes it possible. Take time to share your deepest fears and insecurities with the One who made you. Trust me, if He can handle all my stuff, He can certainly handle yours too. So what if we have gotten off the perfect path He laid out for us. He makes it possible to get back on, right where we are at. Just turn toward His loving face, and He will lead you. He is so able!

I will end with sharing a few thoughts from verses 17–18. If we really believe these verses, we would never doubt His love. Sometimes they are hard to believe because of the way others have treated us and talked to us—a little less loving than our perfect Creator. OK, maybe a lot less loving. He wants us to see Him for who He is regardless of what others have done or said to us. That is fair, isn't it? I think so. It does take time, though. I will not lie about that.

To know that God is thinking precious and beautiful thoughts toward us can totally revolutionize our own thinking and way of life. That He even thinks about us period probably shocks some of you! To think that He is thinking good thoughts toward you is just about ready to push some of you over the edge. Let it go. Let all the old talk and what people have done to you go. We cannot hear Him clearly and His thoughts toward us until we do. And we cannot let go of the past until we know His thoughts toward us. It really is a wonderfully crafted cycle by God to make us totally dependent on Him and what He says about us. This chapter is just the beginning. You have gotten a little insight on the healing that He began in me. It is a huge beginning, and it happens to be my favorite; but the rest of His Word is so full of what His thoughts are toward us. He holds nothing back. Let's give Him as much of a chance as He has given us. Let's fall in love with Him enough to want to see our Creator's dreams for our lives fulfilled. We were made for so much more than where we have been. And to think that my understanding about how He made me began on an ordinary day laying my little one down for a nap. Maybe today is your day!

Maybe this is the beginning of a beautiful journey between you and your Creator. Wherever we are, I am convinced that He wants to strengthen us all in knowing His heart and His thoughts for us. I'm in. How about you?

CHAPTER 4
HEALING WITH THE FATHER

Therefore submit to God. Resist the devil and he will flee from you. Draw near to God and He will draw near to you. Cleanse your hands, you sinners; and purify your hearts, you double-minded. Lament and mourn and weep! Let your laughter be turned to mourning and your joy to gloom. Humble your-selves in the sight of the Lord, and He will lift you up.
—JAMES 4:7–10

AMES, THE MAN who penned these life-changing verses, is someone that I can relate to. He wrote out of His own struggles with his faith in God. What some of you may be surprised to know is that James did not truly believe in Jesus and His mission when Jesus walked this earth. And he was His brother! You would think that God would at least place Jesus in a family that would believe in Him and support Him and His mission. I will share more about this later in the book, and we will look at it from a different angle. But obviously something changed for James. Seeing Jesus raised from the dead gave James a bit more faith.

While we may never know exactly what occurred between God and James to change his heart, we do get a glimpse here in this passage. By far, humility is the word and theme that stands out here above all else. James certainly had to humble himself before God. He had to admit that he and his ideas of who Jesus really was wrong—and that God's were right. Not a bad place to begin! He had to do something with his brother, who, in fact, did not stay in the tomb and was walking around alive before He was taken up into heaven. If He did not humble himself, he was a fool! How many of us have made fools of ourselves because of our pride? My hand is the first to go up! I am so glad that God does not leave us at a place of mocking us because we are so slow to believe His ways. James says that if we truly humble ourselves before God, He will, in fact, give us a place of honor. He will give us the place that we were meant for all along. He just will not let us get there on our own and in our own pride.

Humility has to precede all the wonderful things that God has for us. As I share my story, you will see the thread of humility that God had to work in me all through my healing journey. If you are honest, you will say that God has taken or is taking you through the same route! None of us get to escape and none of us are done being humbled. However, we never have to fear the way that our Father humbles us. We never have to fear that He will shame and embarrass us. He is not like humans. He is God Almighty. He is the God who desires to draw *near* to us, but many times, we need to take the first step. Let's follow the advice of James, who said to draw near to God so that our God can draw near to us.

All of us are in different places in our journey of faith and our relationship with God. Some may be wondering what believing and following Jesus is all about. Some may be just beginning to follow Jesus. Others may be well on your journey. But all of us could use to draw closer to God. All of us are still being humbled and coming to realize that there is one God, and we are not Him! This very message happens to be the basis for this life and this book!

I joke with my husband that he is the low-maintenance one, and I am the high-maintenance one. At least I can laugh about it now! Before He healed me, that truth would have thrown me into a fit. He also has led me to understand that those who have walked in much hardship and trauma in their lives just have more "stuff" to deal with. I am OK with that now, because my stuff has drawn me closer to Him and has forced me to humble myself and let Him be God. I am so grateful that there is no shame in talking about our broken lives that have been mended and still need a bit of mending from the Father.

Just as the quality of our earthly relationships can be affected by any number of things, our relationship with God can be as well. I am aware that for some of you, just hearing that you can have a relationship with God makes you a bit uneasy. You may have grown up in a religious environment where it was all about going to church, saying prayers in a certain form, and then going back home, where you continued on with a life untouched by the hand of God. Or the heart of God. If you are going to continue to read this book, you may be in for quite a ride. It is a journey into a very real and living relationship with God Almighty, one that was not just meant for me but for every person on the face of this earth. That has always been and will always be God's intention: to have us know Him so closely that He fills our hearts and lives so that we are changed. This is a story about how my relationship with God was affected and weakened as a result of some of the places that this life had taken me. By what this life had thrown at me. Let me take it step further—by what Satan, God's greatest enemy, had thrown at me.

Oh, Satan is not a fictional character that people dress as for Halloween but a fallen angel that was not able to take James' advice. He could not humble himself under God but rather wanted to be God. He found out the hard way that there is only one true God. He was not it. So now, he is His enemy, and when we trust in God, he is our enemy too. He is the one out to destroy us. This story and the glory that comes from it go to the one true God. He has won! My victory did not come easy, quickly, or without a fight, but am I ever so grateful that it came.

Before this season that God allowed with my feet I would have thought that He and I needed no healing in our relationship. After all, I had accepted Christ and had been a Christian for about twelve years! Boy, was I wrong. Through this season in my life He began showing me that I still had many areas that I did not let Him in and that I was keeping Him out of certain areas of my life. You see, God seems to have a bit of a problem with that. When He asks for our lives, He really wants all of us. Oh, we are all gradually growing and changing, but make no mistake, He is after it all. Why? Because of His love for us. If you are married, do you just want part of your spouse's heart and affection, or would you prefer to have it all? I know the answer to that! God is no different.

Following Christ is not just about doing a few good things once a week just to try and appease God. It is about a living, loving, intimate relationship with this God who made everything with no effort at all and wants to love us. And wants us to love Him. He is a jealous God who is angry at anything that gets in the way of that (Exod. 20:5). It did not take God very long to communicate this truth to man. We see it in the second book of the Bible, for crying out loud! It isn't that He is angry at us but rather at the things that get in the way of us loving Him and Him loving us. I found that out quickly.

I also seemed to be smacked right upside the face with how much stuff I let come between God and I. The many things from my past were a huge part of this. Early on in this journey, after He began showing me what He wanted to do with my circumstances and as He lifted my eyes off of them and on to Him, He showed me how much He wanted to heal how I saw Him. The truths that He would reveal to me about this would forever change my heart and my life. That is what this season was about. That and all the wonderful things He taught me as we walked out the truth of who He really is versus who I thought He was. I am grateful for the humbling. I desperately needed it!

What I love more is *how* He does it. For someone who was so accustomed to living and breathing shame-filled messages, His humbling came with a completely different tone and feel to it all together. *How* He humbled me makes me love Him even more. He knew what the years that living in the world and just trying to survive all that I had been through did to me. It made it hard to trust and give my heart to anyone or anything, most of all Him. Some of my worst struggles had to do with trust, pride, obedience to Him, doubt, and unbelief. People may look at the "big" sins of adultery, drunkenness, etc., and think that the things I dealt with are no big deal, but some of the worst things that we can struggle with as people are the issues that stay buried in our hearts and are never healed, the ones that nobody can see.

God began making me aware of these things in my life and how they were affecting my relationship with Him. The season of pain with my feet and all I was going through brought them to the surface. It was like the magnifying glass of heaven was on my heart, which needed to be healed and to learn how to trust Christ deeper than I had ever trusted Him, or anyone else for that matter, including myself. Even anything else. I remember talking to Him about it all as I was taking a hot bath. I bawled my eyes out. It hit me like a ton of bricks. Thankfully, Jesus can do some heavy lifting! As I was made aware of these things, I began to see them for the very first time, and from His perspective. Things really change when we see our lives from where He sits! I told Him how sorry I was for trusting myself over Him and shutting Him out of so many areas of my heart because of fear. I asked Him to begin to heal our relationship. Oh, I had known Him for years, but this was much deeper. I felt so clean that evening, and I knew that I was on a different path—one that was heading *toward* Him and not away from Him.

I had been as close as I knew how to be with Him and had enjoyed a good relationship with Him before. I just did not know how to know Him or trust Him more or like He wanted me to. Now, in His gracious ways, He was teaching me. In the natural we can always become closer with those that we love. We just have to die to more of us. My circumstances made no sense to me, and there was certainly no way that I could figure them out or worry or fear my way out of them. His very words to me about healing my feet brought out my own unbelief that had lodged itself in my heart.

Before this season I would not have thought that I did not have a problem believing Him or His promises, but my reaction to Him proved differently. So much of my Christian walk before consisted of going from trust to fear to doubt to unbelief and back to trust. That is where many Christians live. He has so much more for us. So many beautiful things come from simply knowing Him and trusting Him. I thought my healing would come from some formula or scriptures that I quoted enough times about healing. When those things did not work and only made me more frustrated at my apparent lack of faith, He began to reveal so much to me.

Much of that revelation had to do with the way that I viewed Him. Often the way that we view God has to do with how we were raised and what we have experienced from people. It really is unfair to God, but is the reality for many of us nonetheless. Since people were a source of pain and rejection to me, I pretty much put this on God. Unconditional love was very, very foreign to me. I really thought that I had to earn anything that came my way, and if something was lacking, it was because I was not doing something perfectly. Much of my healing with Him came as a result of learning the truth about who He was. Instead of banging me over the head for living in doubt and unbelief, He began to just love on me. That is what I needed.

As soon as I humbled myself and admitted that these circumstances (and everything else in life) were way over my head, He swooped in to save me. No shame. No "I told you so"; none of that. Just love. Love that would heal my soul. Love that would give me no choice but to believe. Love that would heal our relationship and turn my heart completely and forever to Him and Him alone. He promised to tend to the places in me that had never been tended to. That is what this journey was about: Him healing His daughter. As I took the words to heart from James to draw near to Him during this journey instead of letting my circumstances drive me further from Him, the healing began. And it felt good. My soul was ready for this. My heart was ready for this. My body was definitely ready for this! Jesus was the one I had been waiting for all my life!

I humbled myself and gave Him complete and total control over what was going on in me. I was even crazy enough to ask Him to use these circumstances to show others how amazingly awesome He is and to help others. He, in fact, did make me aware many times that He was going to use this to bring much glory to Him and to help others in what they are going through. So here we are seven and a half later. He got His way! He always wins, so we might as well save ourselves some agony and just give up. He has been waiting for that all along.

One of the things that I am forever grateful for and in awe of about God is that He understands us. For crying out loud, He is the only one that knows us and why we are doing what we are doing. He is the only one that truly gets us. Most of the time, I do not get myself and my crazy emotions and behaviors. My husband has times where he certainly does not get me. My girls think that I am a silly mother much of the time. It is so good and refreshing to be understood totally and completely by God. He knew the very real issues I was facing and the very real causes.

Some may have a hard time with the fact that I needed to repent and ask God to forgive me for my lack of trust and belief in Him after all I had been through. But God does not have a problem with it, and I did not either. If we have a problem with humbling ourselves before Him, we are the one that needs to change, not God. Ouch! If we have a problem with it, we still do not understand His holy and perfect nature. He is not man. He is God. There is one true God.

The most gentle and healing mercy came along with Him showing me these things. The wind of His love blew over my parched soul and began to break up the dry and fallow ground. The rain was coming. A downpour. Over the next several years the rain of His love poured on my heart and my mind and my body, endless amounts of pure, healing love. There was no more performance, no more perfection. Only learning to live in His boundless, limitless love. I had to learn, as I will share through the pages of this book, just how much He loved me and how to receive that love.

I am convinced that as a whole Christians do not know the love of God like He wants us to. His love is the only thing that brought me out of this season alive and well, and it is what will get you through your life as well. I had to learn to know and receive His love to the very core of my being. Each chapter deals with a different aspect of His love and healing. His love is so endless that this small book and all the books of the world put together could not even begin to describe it. That is what our hearts were made for. Humble yourself and open your heart to the only One who can breathe life into your heart.

This was a season where I felt like I had nothing to give but everything to receive. God forced me into a place of receiving. There were so many times that I would sense Him quietly say to my heart, "Just receive my love." I would literally lay on my couch, bed, chair, or wherever and let Him love me. Wave upon wave of endless, bottomless love washed over me. Oh, how I thought my heart would explode! The depth of His love could not do anything but make me whole. Being in the presence of such beauty and perfection *had* to heal me. And He did. Little by little. More love, then more trust. The cycle would continue until He had accomplished His purposes for this season. Oh, I will never be finished, but I have a good start!

During this season He would share His heart with me. More than anything He would affirm me and tell me how proud He was that I am His daughter. Have you heard those words from your Father? If not, He wants to open your ears to the sound of heaven toward you. He began to take me to Psalm 103:8 and teach me more about who He was. It says He is "slow to anger, and abounding in mercy." Boy, did I need to hear those words. It was as if I heard them for the first time. Those words began the long-term surgery and recovery of my soul. His words replaced the angry words and actions of those whose harshness I had experienced growing up. Others' actions had given me the message that He was the same way they were. But God's truth also sunk deep into my heart, which had never heard it. Now, beginning to experience His mercy, I could relax and breathe. For the first time I was free to be me, the real me. I was free to fail. Every facet of His healing has to do with these things. And so much more.

I am so thankful for the words and the admonishment from James to draw near to God. He promises to draw near to us as we let Him be not only the Savior of our lives but the Lord, the one who gets to rule it all. So today, let's go for it. Let's get on with life and what has been holding us back. And more importantly, let's see our relationship with our Father and Creator be healed.

By the way, He never stops doing that. This season has been truly life changing, but there will always be room for me to continue to draw closer to Him and humble myself and let more things go. He is the only one that can heal us, but we are the only ones that can draw near to Him. Let's do like the psalmist David in Psalm 62:5–8:

> My soul, wait silently for God alone, For my expectation is from Him. He only is my rock and my salvation; He is my defense; I shall not be moved. In God is my salvation, and my glory; The rock of my strength, And my refuge, is in God. Trust in Him at all times, you people; Pour out your heart before Him; God is a refuge for us.

Will you go with me? Will you draw near to God and let Him be your *only* refuge and salvation? If we admit it, we have not done so good trying to stay in control of our lives and our plans. We have lost our peace and our joy. We need to be healed. We need to draw near to Him and pour all our hearts to Him, all our fears, doubts, worries, frustrations, and cares. Pour out your hopes and dreams to Him while you're at it.

He is the only one who can heal and restore us to the place we are meant to live with Him. He is waiting to take His rightful place in our lives. He is the only One worthy of all of us. He died to prove it. He is already the Almighty. He is already the Creator. He is already God. We just need to open our hearts to Him more and more so He can be all of those things in *our* lives. This is why we were created. When He breathed life into us and our heart started to beat, His dream was that we would be restored to Him and totally His.

Every time that we turn from our ways and turn to Him we experience healing. I would like to share one of the biggest issues that stood between God and I being closer than we were. The freedom that I share about here will be woven all through the book as I share my story. I feared others more than Him. I had a huge case of fear of man. For those of you who have walked there, it is not pretty and will lead you down paths that you never wanted to go down. I believe one of the reasons that I had such an issue with this is that I received so much wounding from people. I feared them too much. I was afraid of what they would think and of gaining their approval. I learned at an early age to have an unhealthy view of the world around me, including people. When you are broken, so is your thinking about how you relate to others and them to you. People usually end up placed up on a higher pedestal than they ever should be placed. It is almost like we think that people are our God. It certainly was that way with me.

You see, He wanted to start this journey together on the right foot. He would certainly need to be God in order for me to receive all that He had for me. The thing about Him showing me this issue in my life was that there was a great sense of His mercy and hope alongside of what He was showing me. He gave me hope of breaking out of the things I had learned just to survive life. He showed me that I did not need those ways anymore. It sounds so simple, but it took a while for me to learn these new ways!

One of the passages of scripture He used to free me was out of Isaiah 50. This is a beautifully descriptive chapter about Christ and His surrender to the Father. Let's look at it together beginning in verse 4:

> The Sovereign Lord has given me a well-instructed tongue, to know the word that sustains the weary. He wakens me morning by morning, wakens my ear to listen like one being instructed. The Sovereign LORD has opened my ears; I have not been rebellious, I have not turned away. I offered my back to those who beat me, my cheeks to those who pulled out my beard; I did not hide my face from mocking and spitting. Because the Sovereign LORD helps me, I will not be disgraced. Therefore have I set my face like flint, and I know I will not be put to shame. He who vindicates me is near. Who then will bring charges against me? Let us face each other! Who is my accuser? Let him confront me! It is the Sovereign Lord who helps me. Who will condemn me? They will all wear out like a garment; the moths will eat them up.
>
> —ISAIAH 50:4–9, NIV

At first that group of scriptures scared me more than a little bit because my life was so far from this! Then He gave me hope that my life *could* look like this.

This was the first time in my life that I understood the truth about how I was to view people. They are just people, not God! I had gone through counseling trying to get free from what others had done to me. I have since been to some godly counseling, but nothing compares to getting a good dose of truth that sets us free—free to have Him be my God and not be controlled by others and what they think or say about me. He was so patient with me as I learned these things. He truly is a good Father. This is where my healing began, with learning to let Him be God. It was not good enough for it to be printed out in black and white in the Book of Isaiah. He wanted it printed on my heart.

I believe seeing how Jesus surrendered helps us to do the same. I am so glad our God gets us. He gets why we do what we do, and He knows exactly how to restore each of us to Him. He is just so good! I realized that fearing man and placing people above God was hurting others and myself, but most of all it was hurting Him. When we truly understand the beautiful and intimate qualities of God, we understand that His heart can be hurt like ours can. He did not create me to live for the approval and praise of others.

He began to heal my deaf ears and taught me, like Jesus, to be awake to His voice, what He wanted to say to me. I was in such bondage to what others thought of me that hearing His voice brought freedom. He began to speak to me about what He wanted to do with these circumstances in my life. I began to hear Him over the noise of the world and those I let control me all my life. He showed me that just as Jesus was in full surrender to His Father's will I could be too. I had never really believed that about myself. I looked at everyone else walking in intimacy and freedom in their relationship with God, and there was a part of me that thought I could not have that. Before Jesus could do God's will, He had to have His ears open to it. I know, I know. I can hear some of the arguments that He was God, so it was not hard. But He was also fully man. That is where He had the same struggles and temptations as us, temptations to give up, follow the crowd, be second rate. But He didn't.

Many times God's words fall on deaf ears because our hearts are hard and we are stubborn and rebellious. We do not want to obey Him. Not really. It seems like it will cost too much. I can write in great detail about this because I have been there! On the other side of this season I see it cost way more *not* to surrender to Him. The enemy has sold us a pack of lies that says God is holding out on us. He is holding back the best from us. I promise you that if you humble yourself under His mighty hand, He will exalt you in due time. He will exalt you to see His lovely face, His loving wisdom. But most of all, your relationship with Him will be whole and healthy. We are able to walk in this. Jesus came as our example to show us that this is possible. I have experienced it, and so have many others.

What do you have to lose? I can promise you that when you turn from your ways, that when you turn around, you will not come face to face with an angry God just waiting to beat you over the head. He truly gives grace to the humble (James 4:6). As He showed me a new way to live, His grace made it possible to see this huge mountain topple before my very eyes! Humbling and healing with God always lead to a renewed sense of His love in our lives.

Another quality He had to reveal about Himself to bring healing to our relationship is that is He is merciful. This took a lot of faith for me. Not only did I have the issues of lacking many things that I needed early in life, but I had experienced harshness, anger, and lack of mercy growing up. The part about God being slow to anger really got my attention. Hear those words, beloved: slow to anger. Let them sink in deep. Let them go deeper than the hurts that came from those who were angry. As I began to believe that He was merciful and did not fly off the handle easily, I could learn to breathe and relax. God's Word is alive and powerful and sharper than any two edged sword

(Heb. 4:12). Let His Word do the work of cutting out what needs to be cut. Trust Him to replace it with something better.

It is amazing the growth and healing that occurs when we are free to be us. Free to mess up. Free not to be perfect. Let me remind you, because of where I made my home, it took years to get free from the heavy coat of guilt and condemnation I wore. Hours of laying in His presence, hearing His voice, and letting His love and mercy wash over me. I had to believe what His Word said over how I felt. There were times that I would go to make a decision, and I would hear the voice of those who were hard on me telling me what I should do. Then I had to make a decision if I would fall back into those patterns or trust what He was showing me. Being in His Word and presence a lot gave me new perspective. True perspective. I knew what He was saying was true. His mercy and love brought freedom to my soul. I had room to move and was not so hemmed in. His Word says that He puts our feet in a wide place (Ps. 18:19).

God showed me that the healing in our relationship would touch everything else in my life. Everything in my life would flow from that place of love and trust with Him. The healthier and more based our relationship with Him is in truth, the greater our freedom. I wanted to be closer to God, but I had to surrender it all to have what my heart desired. His promise that I started this chapter with is true: if we humble ourselves and draw near to Him, He will draw near to us. I am convinced that we are as close to God as we want to be. I don't know about you, but I want to be so close to Him that I can feel Him breathe and know what His heart is beating for. Let's go!

CHAPTER 5
HE BROUGHT ME OUT

He sent from above, He took me; He drew me out of many
waters. He delivered me from my strong enemy, From
those who hated me, For they were too strong for me.
—PSALM 18:16–17

FEAR WAS MY constant companion as far back as I could remember. Some of my earliest memories were feeling fear. I lived with my birth mother in a very bad and low-income neighborhood in North Long Beach in the late 1970–1980s. Our apartment complex backed up to an alley, and our apartment sat along the alley. For those of you who do not know, lots of weird and bad things happen in alleys, especially at night. Somehow at a very early age I was aware of that. I remember being very afraid to use our bathroom at night because it was on the alley.

Now mind you, all kids have fears—some of the dark, some of other things. I have two children, and both of them experienced fears of different sorts. This was different. Because of not having the security in my own life, tormenting fear became the natural progression for me. Now I understand this, but for years it dominated my life and seemed to define who I was and what my experiences were. I never felt safe. I have many memories of being places and feeling alone and afraid.

Much of my fear came as a result of not having a nurturing environment to thrive in during my early years. It was as if I had to care for myself and make sure I was being cared for. As a child of a few years old, that was impossible. Not only did I feel like I had to care for myself, but subconsciously I knew I needed to care for my mother.

Looking back, I see how the stronghold of fear got its grip on me early. As I grew up, fear continued to be a constant in my life. I did not realize until my Father began to free me that it really was my identity and how I saw myself, even long after becoming a Christian. I never knew it was possible to live without fear. It was all I had ever known. I do not mean to put anybody down here, but many of the people who had a direct influence in my life, including Christians, operated in fear themselves. Sometimes when you see something modeled to you, you just accept that is the ways things are. Sadly, I saw fear modeled more than trust. God sees our living in fear as a result of not living in His perfect love. In 1 John 4:18 we see this. Yes, fear is an issue, but God wants to go so much deeper. It's like the fruit we see on the tree is fear, but the root, or real issue, is love, or lack thereof. I believe some of those close to me cared and loved me the best they could. I am forever grateful for the love they gave me. Though they did the best they knew themselves, God's love was lacking in some areas of their lives. I pray with a heart of humility that one day they will be able to rejoice in His love for them.

God used many things to get my attention about how I was letting fear dominate my life. His Word was on the top of the list. Since His words are alive and powerful (Heb. 4:12), they convicted me that something was not right about being tormented by fear. I love that those words never condemned me to more fear but slowly began to free me. He used people who taught His Word with power, love, and anointing to show me that fear is not how Christians should live. Slowly, I began to believe it but still could not find the way out of this deep, dark pit.

If God is truly seeking to free us from something, He has many, many ways of doing this. Some are less fun than others. Sometimes

He has us go through the very things we fear to set us free from it. It all of it He shows us who is really living on the inside of us. Little did I know that my deliverance from fear (and a whole host of other things) would come as a result of the circumstances God allowed with my feet. We absolutely have to trust that the words of Jesus in Matthew 10:29–30 are true or we will lose our minds:

> Are not two sparrows sold for a copper coin? And not one of them falls to the ground apart from your Father's will. But the very hairs of your head are numbered.

Some of you may be wondering where I am going with the bird analogy! Jesus was talking to His disciples, His people. He was telling them some of the things they would face in this life, but He told them they did not have to fear because of how valuable they were to their heavenly Father. Jesus wanted them to know that their lives were safe with their heavenly Father. Let me say it again. We are safe with our heavenly Father! It may seem like all heck is breaking loose, but we are safe. Whatever God may allow in our lives is ultimately for our good and for His glory.

Jesus was also telling them that nothing could come into their lives apart from their Father's knowledge of it. God not only had knowledge of it—intimate knowledge—but He also had to allow it. I do not believe this was just God knowing about it but really weighing out what He was going to allow to come in their lives. Jesus was teaching the disciples that if God was aware of birds being sold for a certain amount of money and knew every hair on His disciples' heads, then He was certainly aware of what was going on in their lives.

Sometimes we have just been taught wrong. Some of those things include the argument that God will never allow difficult, trying circumstances in His people's lives. I am all for faith and claiming His promises, but I do not want to just believe God for what I want.

Enough of me has died now to say that I want His best and perfect will. If we are going to be like Jesus, we have to live like this. I am not talking about accepting illness, disaster, or trials. What I am saying is that we have to know His Word and heart well enough to discern what He is allowing to enter our lives. If you need help with this, search His Word, spend time in prayer, and seek wise counsel if you need to. He wants us to get past the whys and get around to the what. What do you want to do with this? What is your purpose is all of this? Some things in our lives are just a result of living here on planet Earth, and others are consequences of our own choices. God can redeem them all.

My heart is not to argue about theology here, but to get us (myself included!) to a place of total surrender to what He wants. That was Jesus' heart as well. He was living this out right before their eyes. He knew why He had been sent and what trials He would endure to redeem mankind, and He came anyway. Talk about surrender! Do not be afraid of this. If you are, bring it to your Father, who can speak, "Peace, be still!" Trusting in Him is the safest place in the universe we could be! These are the life lessons I was learning through my trials. He was teaching me that He allows trials in our lives to work His purposes out in us *and* through us to reach others. I felt impressed many times, especially on difficult days, that what He was doing in me would be used to bring Him much glory by helping others walk through similar things. To Him be the glory! He can be trusted!

John 8:32 says we will know the truth, and the truth will set us free. If we are lacking in freedom in our lives, we are lacking in experiencing the truth. This was Jesus' desire for us when He spoke these words. He wants to become our truth! He began to teach me through this passage that there was nothing that could come into my life without Him allowing it to. That set me free! Yikes, that sounds downright scary to us. We get afraid of what

He may allow. If we are afraid, it is because we do not know His love for us the way He wants us to. No condemnation here. Not from me. I have lived there. He is still freeing me from some things I have feared. I bet He is doing the same with you also!

In a weird sort of way, fear was what kept me feeling that everything was alright and that I was in control. So God began using His words from Matthew 10 as I was desperately trying to figure out what on Earth was happening to my body and why on Earth He was allowing these physical problems. I had lived in a dark pit of fear and despair, and now it seemed like those old ways were just not going to cut it. I am sure many of you know just what I am talking about. God allows some trial in your life, and your old ways of surviving just will not work any more. It is as if He is laying the ax to the root. Well, to put it bluntly, He is!

It seemed as if fear was being magnified in my life. When Jesus is trying to uproot something in our lives, it seems to get bigger—but only for a time. Do not be afraid of that, but instead trust Him to become bigger in your life! I had to decide if I was going to let this fear control me or if I will surrender it to the foot of the cross.

I remember wondering and fearing what my life was going to be like with this physical pain. I was terrified. Would it get so bad that I would not be able to walk? What would it mean for my children and husband? Would I ever be able to run and play with them at the park or to push them on the swings? Even after God spoke the word through my friend about what He wanted to do in my life, which included physical healing, at first I still feared it would not happen. Looking back now, I know my Father was watching over every fear-filled tear that rolled down my cheeks. He caught each one and will catch yours too. I knew His many promises in the Bible about healing but feared it was not going to come to pass for me.

At night when the lights were out and the house was quiet, I was scared, scared to get up and have to live in all the pain again tomorrow and to take care of two young children in the middle of all of this. In the midst of that turmoil, I let my desperation drive me into the arms of my Father and not away from Him. So many times we let pain in our lives keep us from drawing closer to God. We let it drive us away from Him. *We let it.* Let's let those words sink in. We do not have to let it! Everything within me is crying these words out now! In my own flesh, I am such a scaredy-cat weakling who does not like to put up with a lot of difficult things. But in Christ, who *He* says I am is who I really am. That makes all the difference.

I was desperate for peace and for answers. I was desperate for Him. This is what He wanted all along! All of me. In all my brokenness. In all my fear. He wanted me. His fierce passion for us constantly amazes me! I remember at times the nearness of His presence overwhelmed me. It was like Jesus walked into the room and spoke peace to my heart. I began to know everything was going to be alright, even though nothing had changed. He did this with His disciples who were so afraid after some life-shaking events in their lives (Luke 24:36–38.) Their lives had been turned upside down also. Please hear the heart of your Savior for you: do not let desperation drive you anywhere but to His feet. Stay there as long as you need to until He, in His gentle mercy, raises you to your feet. Do you notice as we read in the Word that those who threw themselves at His feet are the ones who received the very thing they needed? Really, what other option do we have? Go crazy and lose our minds over some of the things that happen to us? People, we are called to much more than that!

I made a choice. This season and what I was going through were not going to destroy me. I grabbed hold of Him with everything that I had. It did not feel like much then. I began to dive head-first into His Word. In the morning while feeding my babies His Word was open on the table. It became my necessary food. I knew

I needed it more than physical food to survive. Don't get me wrong; I had read the Word regularly before and loved it. Now I desperately needed more of it. Fear, doubt, shame, and my own thought patterns would take me out for good if I did not consume His Word. It was my medicine and deliverance. Without it I would have never been free—or stayed free. Neither will you. You cannot get free and live free without the Word of God. Please do not even try. You will only make a bigger mess out of things! Oh, how I know! I am not being legalistic here. I am aware of how much some of you have been bashed over the head with "you need to read the Bible" messages. That is not His heart. He wants you to live, to be full of life. Christ paid a huge price to give you that life. But we cannot have it if we do not know what it is! God so wants His Word to become real in our lives. He wants to give us a love for His Word. It is yours for the taking! It is yours if you are desperate.

The enemy has lied to us to keep us from the only thing that will set us free, God's Word. Satan plants fear in our hearts using our past hurts and disappointments with people so that we fear Him getting too close and seeing the real us. So we stay out of the Word and far away from anything that gets too close to our heart. We fear that He will understand the deepest parts of us and worry if He even cares. When we open the precious pages of the Word of God, we will see something much different. He wants to give us eyes to see, not eyes filled with fear and anxiety about how much He sees and knows about us but eyes filled with wonder that He is really as good as He is!

God was definitely making the most of this opportunity to show me how much He really loved me. When Jesus walks in to our lives, fear just cannot stay. He is the perfect love that casts out fear (1 John 4:18). I remember being home and feeling His presence so strongly. I really needed that. I had major trust issues, so for Him to come so gently and sweetly was huge for me. He did not come and rebuke me for living in so much fear; He just came and loved on me. He showed me how close He wanted to be with me if I would continue to let Him in. How did I know this? Through reading His Word and letting Him speak His words to my heart. He had spoken to me many times before, but there is something that being desperate brings out. A greater sensitivity. A greater hunger.

After several weeks and months of this, I noticed I had more peace and an assurance that everything was going to be alright. His Word was coming alive more and more. There were so many promises in there—for me. When we are desperate for God, He will never disappoint us. He may not answer when and how you like, but He will not disappoint us. His amazing love and grace will wash away whatever we thought we wanted that was not Him. So the way out of fear is love. It really is that simple. Oh, let Him in. Let Him love you.

If you do not know where to begin, "Help," is a great prayer! Ask Him to show you His love. More than once He reminded me in many ways how much He loves us and how we can receive His love. The first step is to believe all that He did to give us love. His life, death, and resurrection are proof of His love for us (Rom. 5:8). If we cannot believe that, we will have a hard time believing that He keeps on loving us through all of our tumbles in life.

He showed me to simply spend time in His presence. He shows us love in so many different ways: Him speaking something personal to our hearts, a song, a scripture, or something beautiful in nature. Just let Him be Daddy to you! I needed a father's touch in my life because I had lived so many years without one. Find scriptures on love, and read and think on them like crazy! You may have days where you feel like every few minutes you need to be reminded of His love for you. This is totally alright and a part of the process of learning to be dependent on Him. He loves it this way!

As I began to grow in more peace in my relationship with God and the fear began to decrease in my life, the Holy Spirit began to teach me about the role of the deceiver, Satan, in walking free from fear. There were many times in the process of getting free that I felt confused and could not understand why I would still feel fear even though I could tell I was gaining more and more freedom. I also seemed to be more jumpy. It was like my emotions were super sensitive during this time. Before freedom started coming for me, I was pretty much scared of everything. I joke I was scared of my own shadow! Taking my girls to the park frightened me because I thought of the harm that someone might inflict on them or myself. I never got to the point of not leaving my home but still wrestled with fear constantly and can certainly understand those who have struggled in this area. Being at home at night without my husband scared me too.

The Holy Spirit taught me that just because I still felt fear did not mean that I was actually bound by it. This is a lie that Satan would like to keep covered up. To be honest, while God was setting me free there were times I actually felt it more. This may sound weird, and I do not want to confuse anyone but desire to share with you the reality of what breaking free actually looks like. There is intense spiritual warfare over getting free from fear, because once the enemy cannot intimidate us with his lies anymore the battle on his end is lost. Do not get me wrong; Jesus can free anyone from anything in a second. But often because He is building our dependency and relationship with Him He takes us through the process of getting free. I bet you can testify to this in your own life. When you have been in terrible bondage to anything in your life for a long time your mind gets used to thinking a certain way, and your emotions get used to reacting a certain way. It is during this time that the enemy will throw some crazy thoughts and feelings our way to make us think nothing in our lives has changed. He truly is a deceiver. But Jesus wants to come into our everyday lives and set us free. No more waiting until going to church on Sunday to get free. Brothers and sisters, Sunday is here!

Relationships and people scared me, which is what I want to talk a little about. The reason I am going here is because this is where many of us have lived and do live now. My worst fear was definitely the fear of rejection and the fear of not having people's approval. You see, for me, to experience rejection or lack of approval was to validate the lie the enemy wanted me to believe since birth: that the reason people rejected me was because there was something wrong with me. Little did he know that my Redeemer was alive and well and coming to my rescue with His love! I made so many decisions based on the fear of being rejected. Many of my decisions were made to please others. Because of this, I didn't discover who God made me to be until the most recent years of my life. There were people in my life who were wounded themselves and took advantage of fear and insecurity in my life. They were able to manipulate and control me because I was weak. I so feared any hint of rejection that I just became who people wanted me to be. This is not a good place to live. More of how God has healed me in this area is woven in other chapters of the book, since His healing my heart in this area took place as He was healing other areas of my life.

Much of my relationship with God had been based on fear also. I feared that I was not good enough for Him or was not doing enough to please Him. Fear of Him really knowing me and then rejecting me like many others in my life was very real for me. I did so many things to try to make Him love and approve of me. My view of Him and our relationship had to change in that area if He would continue to accomplish all He wanted to in me. Little by little, over the years, He has been setting me free from this, but then, for the first time, the ax was being laid to the root. All of these lies are what His love freed me from! I am not sharing the intimate details of my life to be dark and depressing. My heart is for Him to get all the praise for freeing someone so bound! I also want to give you hope. Many of you have walked in deeper and darker pits than I, but He is able to do what is humanly impossible!

God the Father has given us the precious Holy Spirit as such an amazing teacher. He knows each one of us so personally and makes the words of our Father so real to us. Let these words from the beginning of John 16:13 sink into your heart and mind.

> However, when He the Spirit of truth, has come, He will guide you into all truth.

Oh, we do not have to fear not getting or *staying* free when we stay close to the Father. The same truths that set us free are the same truths that keep us free. The Holy Spirit stands waiting for us to open ourselves up to His guidance. It is what He is there for! He will never lead us astray, and we do not have to fear because He is such a precious gift from our heavenly Father!

Please do understand, while I was not going crazy, the enemy really intimidated me while I was getting free, especially from fear. That is what he is based on. He tries to control us through his lies and intimidation. He really loves to degrade us and make us feel worse about ourselves when he can constantly intimidate us. I could just jump up and down now because Jesus untangled me from the enemy's web! I love Him so much for pulling me out, little by little!

God began to teach me that to be really free and to continue to live free forever would mean that His Word could not only be in my heart but it had to come out of my mouth. Mind you, I went to an amazing Bible college that taught us these things. But something new happens when your very sanity depends on the reality of His Word in your life. One scripture that God really used to teach me about speaking His Word is Mark 11:23–24, which says, "For assuredly, I say to you, whoever says to this mountain, 'Be removed and be cast into the sea,' and does not doubt in his heart, but believes that those things he says will be done, he will have whatever he says. Therefore I say to you, whatever things you ask when you pray, believe that you receive them, and you will have them." He began to teach me about the life-giving, mountain-moving power of speaking His words—*His* words and not my usual "I feel afraid" or "I can't" or anything else I was so used to going around saying. I was not even aware of how much I did that. He began to show me that this was part of the reason I was so defeated all the time. However I felt and whatever thought dropped in to my head was how I lived and what I made choices based on.

The Holy Spirit began to teach me to declare what My Father was declaring over my life. Second Timothy 1:7 was a huge truth that helped set me free. It says, "For God has not given us a spirit of fear, but of power and of love and of a sound mind." Those words, mixed with my faith, began to ignite an explosion of freedom on the inside of me. And the outside. I could actually see the effects of His Word mixing with my faith, and it was so encouraging to me! To realize that life-sucking, victory-stealing fear did not come from God was gigantic for me. I was waking up to the reality of who God said I am in His Word and was learning how to believe what the Holy Spirit was teaching me more every day! Another one of my favorites is Jeremiah 31:3, which says we are loved by God with an everlasting love. If you do not believe me about how much I spoke these verses and many more out, just ask my family. They will tell you. My little ones were learning to talk, and this was part of their vocabulary. I am so happy that it is! These and many more scriptures on God's love for me, and on freedom from fear and trusting God, were and still are on the tip of my tongue for when I need them. There were many days in which all I felt like I did was quote these scriptures out loud.

Little by little, I saw victory. For the first time I started to believe not only what came out of His mouth but what was coming out of mine. And for the first time in my life did I start to believe and act like a victor instead of a victim. How refreshing! It was as if the Holy Spirit was blowing His fresh wind over my dry and broken soul. He will do it for you too. All you have to do is believe His words over your feelings and past experiences. His Word changes everything.

When I first started speaking out His Word around the house, I have to admit I felt foolish. I really did not want my husband and children to think I was some kind of nut. Well, call me crazy, but I am free!

During this time, God began to use me at our church more and more. Because of all He was doing in my life, it naturally opened up opportunities to minister to those who needed Him all around me. I began to teach these live-giving truths from His Word, and I loved the new freedom of being able to use the gifts that seemed to be dormant in me for many years. It was another step in getting free from fear. Standing up in front of people and sharing anything, much less very personal things that God is doing in your life, sure has a way of making you trust God like never before!

I would like to say something else about breaking free from fear. Sometimes we get the idea that when we truly realize that Jesus has set us free from fear all of it will just disappear from our lives. I wish! Even though we are free from its ruling power, we do not always get to escape the feeling of it and having to press past the feeling of fear to do what God is asking us to do. Here again, Satan wants to trap and demean and degrade us if we feel it. Listen, when we really know who we are and who God is, we are just going to have to do some things while yet afraid. This is courage, my friend! Each person is different, and depending on the amount of fear that we have walked in the process of getting free may be longer and more tedious than the next person. All I know is that if we let the feeling of fear stop us, we will not be doing very much! Please understand, I am not trying to paint a picture that we are going to have to walk around afraid all the time. I just want to say that we live in this flesh and experience all kinds of emotions because of it, including fear. I do not want you to be confused when God is breaking you free from it that you are still bound. Lift up your shield of faith (Eph. 6:16) and keep on walking. God has you covered. Let us not put our trust in our emotions but on Jesus, who leads us into victory.

God taught me that in order to be truly free from the ruling power of fear I would simply have to do some things afraid. He set me free to be courageous. Writing this book and knowing that people will read it makes me a little afraid. Will people like it? Will they want to read it? Well, the good news is that I trust the One who asked me to write this book. It is His story, and I will trust Him with the outcome. I am His, and He loves and accepts me. That is really all I need. Oh, OK, I want you to read and enjoy the book, too! So yes, in the natural I have a bit of fear. If I did not, I would worry that I was not human! Him showing me and teaching me those lessons of life makes me forever grateful.

That is how the fear subsides in us, when He comes in as the gentle and amazing Father that He is and teaches us and tends to those deep places in our hearts. Like I said earlier, fear has to go in the presence of love. When we do things afraid that He is asking us to do and come out the other side alright, a new sense of power and victory become a reality for us. Experience with the Father just whoops up on the devil! No longer are we tossed around by our emotions, but instead we are controlled by the power of His Spirit inside of us. Then we will have this scripture to add to the ones we declare out loud: "Yet in all these things we are more than conquerors through Him who loved us" (Rom.

8:37). Let your God rejoice over you as you begin to walk out the victory He has given you!

I can now see that God, in the midst of setting me free, was laying a good foundation of love and trust in my relationship with Him. A person is not able to grow, heal, or change in an atmosphere of fear. Little did I know how much more freedom He was going to bring in the coming years. Sitting here now, telling my story, the pieces are coming together better for me. He has been such a faithful Father who knew how much I needed His touch and love in my life. He knew the journey I would continue to walk with Him would need to be covered in His love and great amounts of grace. Now that I had a better understanding of His love, I would be more capable to receive more of it and to continue to walk into more and more wholeness.

Chapter 6

BREATHE

He also brought me out into a broad place; He
delivered me because He delighted in me.
—Psalm 18:19

LOVE THE WORDS penned by King David as we get a
glimpse into his praise after God delivers him from his
enemies. In Psalm 18:19 we see that David likens being delivered to
having a broad place to put his feet upon. We have the same privilege. We do not have to be closed in or trapped. To be enclosed
or hedged in by God is a beautiful thing, but to be hedged in by
lies and fear are not. The only real way the enemy can defeat us is
by lying to us, by the way. There is no truth in him. When I realized I was free from the enemy's tactic of fear, I felt as if God was
releasing me to run, play, laugh, and jump in a huge, open meadow.
The meadow was full of green, luscious grass and wildflowers—
daisies, to be exact! I literally felt like I could breathe for the first
time in my life! I am not really sure what I was doing the rest of my
life up until that point, but I knew He had given me a wide open
space to live my life. The trap was opened and I was free.

He so much wants to free us and then to bring us out in to a
wide open meadow and let us breathe deeply the fresh wind of
His Spirit. He will blow off any residue from our former bondage.
When He frees us, we are able to make decisions based on what
He wants and on truth instead of reacting to lies. When He frees
you, you will feel like an innocent, carefree child again.

I never had the sense of being either of those. My Daddy was restoring both to me right before my eyes. He says He delivers us because He delights in us! Oh, I felt the delight of my Father. Mind you, I had not felt the delight of a father on many occasions before. Suddenly, however, I would wake up and hear this scripture in my spirit. I began to believe it too! When this truth becomes our reality we are free to run, jump, and dance before Him in jubilant praise! Listen, this is not a time for just quietly praising Him in our heart with hands folded. Sorry, I am not here to mess with anybody's idea of what worship should look like, but it should involve all of us. So this is what I began to be able to do. My body began to be more healed and free to praise Him!

At this point, I was still wearing arch supports that the foot doctor gave me. They helped take the most acute pain away, but I was still experiencing a good deal of foot, leg, hip, and back pain and fatigue. It never went away. I remember that during the process of God freeing me from fear my pain gradually began to get a little better and was easing up a bit. I began to notice that different places on my feet hurt, but in a different sort of way. Usually the bottoms and arches of my feet killed me. Now that was easing up a bit, and the tops of my feet and my ankles were more achy. I began noticing the tops of my feet were getting higher and stronger. This was about a year after I began wearing the arch supports. The foot doctor did not think this should be happening this far into wearing them. God was beginning to do something with my feet that medicine could not and that could not be explained! I was beginning to see God healing my feet, even as I wore the arch supports.

As I mentioned earlier, I began to take pictures of my feet after I received the word about God healing them because I knew they would look different. When my husband and I started taking pictures of them, they looked like flat, mushy pancakes! No muscle tone or health was there. I knew that God was using the arch supports to help strengthen my feet. Now muscles and bones that I had not seen in quite a while were appearing before my very eyes! I remembered back to when He told me that for a time He would use the arch supports, but there would come a time when He would not use them any longer and that the healing would occur supernaturally. I clung to that word daily. Even though I was wearing the supports and my feet were changing, they never did what they were supposed to do. My foot doctor said that people who wear these are fine and should have no pain. Not me! He just could not understand why they were not working for me. I believe it was God's mercy in letting me get some relief from the pain until He restored them the way He wanted to.

Before wearing the arch supports I was on my way to seeing a pain management specialist and was ready to try heavy-duty pain medication just to deal with the pain. My pain was so extreme that even after God began using the arch supports to help me, just walking my daughter from our car into her preschool hurt badly. I would try to avoid the anxiety that just getting out of the car produced in me. My mind and emotions had to find ways to cope with what my body was experiencing. Having these limitations seemed to preoccupy my mind. They made me tired and a bit cranky, too! Gradually through that year, which was about one and a half to two years after having Emily, the pain subsided more. The anxiety of having to deal with all this gradually subsided that year as I saw Him very gradually heal me. I no longer had to spend every waking moment calculating if what I had to do would cause more pain. God had mercy on me and on all those around me, because I am such a lightweight when it comes to medication. I cannot take much more than Tylenol without getting loopy!

Before my very eyes I began to see His Word come to pass about healing me physically as He simultaneously healed my heart and mind. If that did not cause me to jump and shout, nothing would! I literally felt like air and life were being breathed into my very being.

His breath was breathed into my life! I began to experience peace—true and abiding peace—for the first time in my life. All the seeds of His Word and the love He was planting in me were growing. Peace and rest were the result.

At first I did not know what to do with myself. I would sit around the house on the couch and just almost be bored because I did not have anything to worry about or to fear. It was a totally new concept for me! This was a really big breakthrough for me. I never, ever remember experiencing such peace and a sense that I was alright and that everything would be alright. Even though I still had some difficult physical circumstances and things that He was still uprooting in my heart and mind, I knew I was safe. My Father's arms were tightly around my life, but I could breathe.

Oh, when the enemy has a tight grip on your life, the last thing you can do is breathe, my friends. He chokes the very life out of us by his lies. Never once did I have someone so dependable and safe that I could relax with, like I was now finding in God. It was like I had been holding my breath all my life just waiting for the next tragedy to occur. Now, by His grace, I could sit back in His arms and relax. Oh, the life and joy that brings us! The noise and what I call traffic in my head was clearing, and it was happening dramatically. It was almost like I remembered the pain of all I had been through, but His love and tenderness were making it as if it had not happened to me. The deep pain of it was gone. My times with Him and the peace that I had were my new experience now. I could breathe. At times, I would literally just sit back and do just that. I enjoyed the freedom of just *being*. I would sit or lie down and just breathe, breathe in His love, peace, and goodness over my life.

By this point, He and I cleared up some issues on who was going to be holding the reins to my life. He won, by the way, and kept on showing me that He wanted more of me.

Once we had dealt with the issue of fear, He continued to build on the foundation of love and trust. I love what an amazing architect He is. He never stops building! Ephesians 2:20–22 says, "Having been built on the foundation of apostles and prophets, Jesus Christ Himself being the chief cornerstone, in whom the whole building, being fitted together, grows into a holy temple in the Lord, in whom you are also being built together for a dwelling place of God in the Spirit." Jesus wants the foundation of our lives to be built on Him and what He had done for us. This scripture spells it all out. We are being built brick by brick! I do not know about you, but once He knocks down the faulty foundation, it sure feels like He is putting us back together pretty slowly at times! When He is finished doing it we will be the complete building for Him to dwell in. How glorious! How beautiful! No wonder He has to tear down all that is false. It is because He desires to dwell in us and with us (John 14:17).

You will be amazed at how He builds your life and puts you together. You will not be disappointed and will not regret letting go of all the old rubbish, I promise. You will get to breathe—breathe in the deep faithfulness of your Father who has freed you and breathe in the power of His Spirit.

What God was continuing to build in me was the ability to trust and how to keep letting go of the fear of being alone and abandoned. You may say, I thought He freed you from all your fears. Yes and no. He showed me the truth about fear and that I did not have to fear it, bow to it, or to let it be my master anymore. He showed me that by the power of His cross and blood I was free from its ruling power, and that is how I would continue to walk free from it for the rest of my life. God began to show me that I still feared being alone and without anyone in my life.

Once I had learned the reality about what fear is, we could in a healthy way tackle some more fears that He wanted me to let go of. The fear of being alone is why I clung to people and relationships too tightly, because I was afraid they would reject me and leave me like I experienced in the past. He was showing me what health and wholeness looked like. More of my fingers were being pried off of my life!

This part of the journey was so personal and tender that I cannot share it all. I will share some of the highlights and things that I learned so that you can learn more of who God is and how He may want to work in your life. I remember during this season that the fear of being alone and abandoned actually seemed to increase. I was feeling more insecure and sensitive around people, especially those close to me, like my husband, friends, etc. In my own wisdom I seemed to want to try and suppress these feelings, but after trying that and it not working for a while, I began to question God about what was going on. He spoke tenderly to my heart, which was afraid, and whispered, *"The little girl in you that was abandoned and left alone is coming out. Let her come out, and I will heal her."* I am not a counselor, but He is. This is what I needed. I needed to stop trying to be so spiritual and pull it all together when I was dying inside. He wanted me to allow myself to feel the pain of all that had happened to me and the pain of being alone much of my life. Jesus walks into the middle of the pain and begins to apply His love and care to our wounds. He listens, He comforts, and He mends. He teaches truth about Himself and ourselves, which enables us to live out healthy relationships with people. When this happens, we no longer feel like we have to control them because we are afraid they will leave us. We are free to be us because we know how deeply we are loved. We become secure in His love. Let the Holy Spirit lead you to the painful places so your Father can heal you. Stay there as long as He says, but not any longer, because it will stunt our growth.

For me, I never acknowledged the pain of being a little girl and having to take care of myself and how that affected how I saw myself and the world around me. Because God had been establishing a healthy view of who He was, I could now trust Him to go to these deep places with me. I could trust that He would never abandon me and leave me here. This was another huge piece of truth that would free me from fear—He was with me and would never leave nor forsake me (Heb. 13:5.) The truth from Psalm 27:10 came alive to me: "When my father and mother forsake me, Then the LORD will take care of me." He was going to continue to lead me on to wholeness and healing. As He continued to heal me, I felt as if I were in that wide open meadow again breathing in the great love of my Father! Jesus began showing me that I could rely on and trust Him in every place where I learned how to trust and rely on myself. Letting go of my ways was at times a difficult process, but on the other side, it was so worth it! There was a new grace in my life to trust my Daddy. He was waiting in the pool as I jumped off the high dive into His arms. I grew more and more confident that He was not going to let me fall.

One of the things that He taught me during the time I was healing was to be very kind to myself, because this would enable me to continue to heal. For someone who grew up with a lot of self hatred, this was life changing! Since I never learned to love myself, hating myself was just the natural route that I took. When we are against ourselves, we cannot continue to grow, heal, and to change. I could no longer look down on myself either because of all the things in me that needed to be healed. Oh, I just hate our enemy who tries to destroy our lives and then kicks us while we are down, don't you? God wanted me to stop joining in with him. During this part of the healing process I knew I had to continue to agree with God and what He said about me, or I was just not going to make it. It is that simple.

As I drank in more of the Word and the truth about Him healing the brokenhearted, it was like a healing balm that went over my soul. Yes, I could breathe even more of His life in as I let go of my old life! His breath was breathing on my heart and making me whole. Just learning to relax and know that He was the one to heal my body because of His great love for me actually brought that very healing to me. Little by little, as I began to relax in His presence, more healing came. No more formulas. No more striving to be good enough or say enough scriptures to be healed. No, this was something that He wanted to bring about by me believing and receiving. Oh, I spoke His promises over my life that had to do with Him healing my body, but now they were coming from a heart that believed and trusted Him. I knew now that I could trust Him to do what He promised, and that is what He wanted all along—my heart, for my heart to breathe, for my heart to see that, like He spoke in the beginning of this journey, the work was already done. I just needed to let go of the old.

So there I was, letting go and grabbing hold of the One who had already accomplished all things for me. Yes, this is grace! This is what makes us breathe! Beloved, He wants us to get so in His face that we feel His breath breathing on us. It is warm. It is beautiful. It is the most wonderful thing on Earth, and I would never trade any memory in my life for the ones of the days that He was so close I could feel Him breathing on me. Oh, I am still so close to my God, but those days were so precious and tender to me. They made me fall in love with my Daddy more than anything else. That the God of the universe would seemingly stop everything to rescue His daughter made me draw closer and closer to Him.

This was just a little glimpse into His healing during this time in my life. Take a step closer. Let Him breathe on you. His purity will blow off all of your pain. You will be able to rejoice with King David, who knew that His God had stopped heaven and Earth to rescue Him.

CHAPTER 7
BRIDGES

*E*VER FEEL LIKE you're tied to something? To someone? How about to what they have said or done to you? To your past? This chapter is about God breaking you free from all the things that He wants us to be free from. It is about finally living in all the glorious things that He has for us.

We say we are free and act like it on Sunday morning, but our reality is that many are not free. The Word says in John 8:32, "And you shall know the truth, and the truth shall make you free." Funny thing is, Jesus was talking to people who thought they were already free! He does the same with us today. You really can be free. Sometimes it is almost impossible to believe this because where we have lived is so far from being free it is not even funny. We can believe God's Word and His faithfulness to do this for us. I can say this with such certainty because it is exactly what He has done for me, set me free. In the last chapter we just read about God bringing some beautiful truths to me that really were life changing. Both He and I would be doing everyone a great disservice if we did not tell you how to get there! That is what this chapter is about. I actually consider it to be the most important and crucial aspect to any healing and journey of finding freedom.

One word will change your life. You really can be free. I wanted freedom for so long that it became like a mirage in the desert that was always out of reach. I guess the thirst for freedom was so great that I just kept being determined to find it at any cost. I was desperate. Forgiveness was something that He wove early into this season of my life. After He established some much-needed trust, He began to work in this area and has weaved it into every part of this healing journey. Everything was tied to it. All my freedom. Everything had, for me, been waiting on the other side of this.

Much of my life was like driving looking in the rearview mirror! Can you imagine if we drove a car like we do our life? There would be accidents everywhere! And we wonder why our minds, lives, and relationships are such a mess. We are living in the past. How do we get free from the chains and cords that tie us? I could be really spiritual and say the correct answer: Jesus! And He is the right answer, by the way, but how does He do it? I am very practical. If someone tells me to do something, I also want to know how to do it. Good thing God is very practical, too. He wants us to get what He is saying and He wants us to know how to obey Him.

Forgiveness is the way out! OK, so I probably just lost some people. This topic has been preached to death in the church, and still so many people are not free. Jesus wants us to know the truth about forgiveness and how it affects our life.

One of the things that set me on the journey or process of forgiveness was learning and experiencing my Father's great love for me. There is something about receiving His deep, passionate love for us to the depths of our heart and soul that makes our heart softer toward others. Then there is the reality that comes to us that we have sinned and hurt our Father many, many times; this truly humbles us. How can I hold on to what others have done, when He let it go on the cross? We really do not fully understand what He has done for us. Being in His Word and presence makes it real. If you are struggling with forgiving others and beginning that process, the most important thing I could tell you is to let Jesus love you and then in turn learn to love Him passionately. He knows those who have hurt you, how it has affected you, and what it will take to let go. We think we are so smart and know how to get out of the mess we are in, but we do not. It takes His presence and love washing over us and reaching to the deepest crevices of our hard, stony heart. When we see His beautiful face smiling over us, suddenly what they have done begins to lose its affect. We have to choose to start the process of letting go and forgiving.

Many times God wants to show us the end from the beginning to encourage us in this process. He knows our flesh is weak and that some of us need a good shove in the right direction. In the beginning of my forgiving those who hurt me, He began to show me pictures and give me impressions in my heart of what the end would look like—awesome, peaceful, joyful, abundant, fruitful, amazing freedom and love! I did not know then that those things would carry me through a few rough years of learning to forgive. Our soul is so tied to the past, that for some of us He literally breaks one chain at a time. He is so merciful and compassionate to show us the end result. He does not have to. He could just say, "OK, now just forgive and move on!" I remember on one occasion He showed me a picture of myself in a beautiful flower garden with a white fence. It was so peaceful, and I was so peaceful that it almost seemed like it was not real. It was kind of like one of those backgrounds they pull down at the portrait studio! I remember thinking this as He showed me. I was walking, enjoying the garden and myself in perfect peace. Little did I know then that the very picture He gave me would provide strength and encouragement for the hard days and nights of learning to let go, grieving like He said I needed to.

He is so faithful to give us just what we need right when we need it. The Holy Spirit would remind me of that bright, sunny picture on the dark days. Since I am very motivated by what lies ahead and by the destiny He has for me, He gently impressed on my heart that all of the good plans that He had for me would not come to pass if I continued to hold on to the bitterness and anger of all that had happened to me. His words were enough for me to make the choice to let go and forgive. He showed me that by not forgiving those who had hurt me I was actually still connected to them as if they were wounding me today. Since I had such a passion for total freedom I knew I had to continue on the path He was showing me.

Beloved, He wants to be faithful to you also. He may not show you a picture like He did me, but ask Him for what you need. We are all different. We are so unique, and He is so intimately aware of our needs and desires that He will give you what you need. He wants to provide for you! He longs to encourage you to press on. Go to your Father and pour your heart out. If you need encouragement and strength, He will give it. He just wants to hear your voice asking for it. You will be amazed at how He provides. Expect it! Look for it! He will never disappoint you. The words of Psalm 25:3 say, "No one who waits on You [will] be ashamed." Wait on Him. It is in the waiting that we get to know Him and His heart for us.

I remember God explaining forgiveness like this: It is a bridge to get you from where you are now to where you want to be. That made sense to me. And since He knew me so well, He knows that I thrive and do well under pressure when it is taking me somewhere really good! Many of you are probably like this too. Like Paul says in 2 Corinthians 4:17, "Our light affliction...is working for us a far more exceeding and eternal...glory." He knows we need motivation like that. Paul needed it, and God gave him a revelation.

As Christians, so many times we want to be free but do not know how to get there. We want to live in freedom from torment, guilt, fear, shame, and a whole host of other things that come from unforgiveness but need a road to take us there. Or a bridge. Forgiveness is the bridge to freedom. You will be so amazed at the freedom we get when we let go. Forgive. I can hear the chains breaking now, falling on the floor. The dust is flying off them as we walk free!

I cannot give a formula for forgiveness, but there are some steps that make up the process. God may lead us differently through the steps, and for some He may even add some. I think where we fall short of total forgiveness is when we think it is just something we say after someone has done us wrong. Just saying, "I forgive you," is not enough, especially when the wound is deep and the hurt has been lodged in our soul for a long time. That is just the beginning. He has so much more for us.

God explained forgiveness like this to me: Forgiveness is not denying what happened to you; it is looking at it for what it is and choosing to let it go, letting go of the person, situation, words, and the hurt. We really do have a choice. We are not powerless. The power of the living Christ is in us! Satan wants us to believe that we always have to be a victim to what happened to us and the effects of it. Not so! God wants You to know that you *can* be free today. As we spend time with our Father in the safety and security of His love He will show us the situation, people, words of hurt, and rejection from His point of view. Much of the time, our own hurt and pain keep us from seeing what has happened to us truthfully.

Anybody following me? He desires truth in our inward parts (Ps. 51:6) and will show us the truth if we really want freedom! You see, God sees what man cannot. Sometimes all we see is the hurt, pain, and the anger we feel because of all that has been done. If we are really going to be free, then we have to see as He sees. We have to trust that He is telling the truth. I think that it is fair to say that much of our relationship with the Father grows through this process. It is more than a quick prayer to forgive but is instead the process of becoming more like Christ. Remember the words of our Savior on the cross, "Father, forgive them, for they do not know what they do" (Luke 23:34).

Jesus knew the hearts of all men. He created them. His eyes of fire can see past all our sin and guilt to the real reason we do what we do. I so love that about Him! He sees the pain that you have suffered because of others' sin. He cares so deeply that your soul and life have been affected. Neither He nor I am saying that we need to turn our eyes away from justice and wrong that has been done. He is a God of justice. Forgiveness is letting Him have justice and make wrong things right. Only He can do that. When we hold on to the hurt, we are still trying to get justice and make them pay.

So, back to the looking at the situation for what is really is. I believe that is one of the first steps of the process. As you spend time in His presence, ask Him to show you His ways and His perspective. A funny thing happens in His presence: freedom. Loads of it! As we begin to experience Him, all that happened begins to lose its power because He is far greater! His face is lovely and warm, and His arms are open wide. Who would want to continue in death when we begin to experience such life? The things He speaks to us through His Spirit and His Word will flow together and bring freedom.

One day after putting my girls down for a nap I went to spend time with God. I was in the throws of this step of the process. He began to show me like on a movie screen of my mind why people were doing and saying the things that they were and what was really happening. I would never have figured this out in a million years. As He began to unfold the truth, it hurt. Bad. I had no idea so many people were also tied into the same web of hurt and shame that I experienced. I thought that my birth parents were the only ones who really wounded me. That was true, but He began to unfold more as I was ready.

He desires to reveal the secret things to us if we ask. He wants us free more than we want freedom, beloved. First I had to take a step of faith to even believe the things He was showing me were real. By this time I had enough experience with Him to know I could trust Him. He will never give us more than we can handle.

I had to face these truths about people who were very close to me. He had me in this season for a while. I remember being so desperate that I would pray in the Spirit almost continually because I knew if He did not save me, then I would be lost. Step by step, He kept uncovering truth. The cool thing is, not once did I ever sense His condemnation toward these people. I sensed His love and mercy toward them and me. I did sense Him grieving over all I experienced and lost due to these things. His mercy was so near that my heart could rest in His hands. He really does weep and grieve with us. Let the tears flow and let out your grief however you feel like you need to. He is there and waiting to take it from you. Remember, He is showing us so we can be free. Remember that all during this part of the process.

I do not recommend purposefully trying to remember painful things. I do recommend letting the Holy Spirit reveal the things He wants to. There are things we do not need to remember. I have found that He will usually deal with the things that our heart and mind remembers well. It is those things that He will show us truth about. Let Him speak to you about what really happened. Then we get to express our anger, frustration, hurt, or whatever else we need to.

Remember the words of the psalmist David in Psalm 62:8, "Trust in Him at all times you people; Pour out your heart before Him; God is a refuge for us." He wants us to be real with Him. I have found that He is the greatest counselor we could ever have! God is not afraid of our emotions or angry words. In fact, I find if we do not have a safe place to express the pent-up anger in our heart over all that has been lost or done to us, we will become bitter, and our heart will grow cold. Let Him hold your heart and massage it in His warm, loving hands. He made us for so much more than a cold, lifeless heart.

He does not want us to stay angry our whole lives. I think anger gets a bad rap in the Christian world. It is almost like a sin to say we are angry. God says we can be angry and not sin in Ephesians 4:26. Let the anger come out no matter how many Christians tell you that it is sin. Just listen to Jesus and allow Him to show you what to do with it. Let Him turn it into something beautiful. Only He can. He wants to go back to the situation with us. He is our mighty Savior and wants to save us from it if we allow Him. He is so gentle and considerate as we go through this painful process. His Spirit is so close to us during this time. He gives us the ability to see it all and then choose to let it go.

Wherever we may be at in our Christian walk (or for some who may not know Christ yet), many times forgiveness is the way to get to the next place He has for us. From the very second we accept Christ until we leave this planet, we are on a journey. A journey of knowing Him more and letting Him bring maturity and healing to all that life has thrown at us. For many of us, we are waiting on God to bring us a new place in our life, while He may be waiting on us, waiting on us to forgive and let go of the past. We are the only ones who can do it. Even God, who is all-powerful, cannot and will not do this for us. For too long we have been immature and did not own up to what is in our power-to let go. When we do our part, then God will do His part. We cannot free or heal ourselves from the past, but we can let go of what ties us to it so He is free to work.

When God and I began taking this journey of forgiveness I remember going out for drives to our special spot in the country where I liked to stop to pray, read, and spend time with Him. The Holy Spirit began to bring people to mind that I needed to forgive. Those He first brought to mind seemed pretty easy. The things they had done were hurtful but not devastating. I had a sense that He was leading me to forgive people and things that they had done that were devastating to me. I sensed His compassion and mercy as He let me work through the easier things. All the while, His

Word and Spirit were at work in me. As I read the Word, the Spirit brought life to it, and He began to set me free. I would meditate on who I was in Christ and picture myself living in that freedom. For so much of my Christian life, true freedom was just a mirage in the distance, but I was beginning to see glimpses of it.

As God began to heal me more, one night I had a dream. I dreamed that I had met my birth father for the first time. We were at a bowling alley, and we were sitting at a table together talking. We talked as if there were no hurt, rejection, or broken relationship. I had perfect peace in the dream. I woke up and knew that Jesus had healed me from the hurt of never knowing my father. I knew God was showing me that I had truly forgiven him. I had never met him but had only seen his name on my birth certificate. For years I tried to make him and others pay for what I did not get as a child from him. Mostly, I carried the shame, rejection, and hurt inside.

Holding on to the past hurts us more than anyone else. Yes, I was angry with him for leaving me as a child, but somehow the enemy lied to me and told me that everything was my fault. Then came the many years of bondage to shame, guilt, condemnation, and self-torment. By forgiving him and letting go of what I could never get back, I began to experience more peace. I began to see more of who I really was in Christ instead of what my circumstances told me I was. Little by little freedom began to come, and it brought encouragement to my soul that had been so battered. I began believing God more and more that I could walk in freedom. Me! I guess I realized that I always believed that freedom was for everyone but me. But Jesus walked into my life and into my past and showed me what was rightfully mine.

After releasing my dad, then came the time to release my birth mother. I could remember her and had a bond with her, so forgiving her seemed harder than forgiving my father. The more of a bond, relationship, or attachment we have to someone, the deeper the wounds, many times. It is harder for our soul to understand how someone could hurt us so deeply. If we were wounded as a very young child, there is not the maturity in our brain or emotions to process things correctly. We need a reason for what happened to bring us peace and security inside, and many times that reason points back to us; it was our fault. When God began to help me to forgive my birth mother, I did have many emotions about it all. I think that in my earlier years as a Christian I forgave the best I knew how, but I did not know how to continue to walk in healing from all that happened.

I never fully realized until this point in my life what a root shame had in my life. Everything was affected by shame. Shame is not a new problem that we have to deal with. It began in the garden. Sin came; then shame. Shame is always the result of sin, but sometimes the sin is not ours. Sometimes the sin is another person's.

The enemy comes to us and lies and says that what others have done is because there is something wrong with us. This is the essence of shame—something is wrong with us. Couple that with rejection, and we get the lie that others have rejected us because there is something wrong with us. Thankfully, there was *someone* else in that garden ready to give us hope that one day freedom would come! I could shout now! Beloved, you do not have to live in any form of shame, hiding, or condemnation, because Christ has come to see us free from it all (Rom. 8:1!) There is a reason this message is called the good news!

I remember the days of walking around my house and the light of His Word and Spirit penetrating the darkness and heaviness that had always weighed my down. Oh, the freedom! Oh, the joy! It felt like a wet, heavy blanket had always been on me, and now I was beginning to see the light! His written Word and His Word to my heart began to lift my head above the cloud of shame and unworthiness I had always lived under. In the coming months and even over the next few years, God did begin to show me those who had wounded me most deeply in my life. There were some people in my life that I had been so wounded by, and I never really understood that by not forgiving them I was the one suffering, and seriously.

Like I said, I really tried to forgive earlier as a Christian, but sometimes when you are in relationships with people who are wounded themselves and you are part of the system and way of life, you just do not recognize it. I have a feeling that God is touching a similar cord in your heart. Oh, I had gained some freedom, but God wanted more than some. Christ died for more than some. He wanted me to walk in all the freedom He had suffered and purchased for me at the cross.

As I became aware of those around me who were dysfunctional and wounded and who were hurting me, it got harder. How was I supposed to deal with them and all of the hurt being in the middle of it? Somehow when the hurt and the people were long ago and are not in our face daily, it can be a little easier. I really have had to pray, read the Word, and seek wise counsel over this. God led me through the same process of forgiveness as He did with my birth father and mother but taught me a few more steps to the process.

One thing He taught me is to see those who are hurting others as hurting themselves. I am sure glad that He has been able to see the *why* behind the dumb things I do. He began to give me mercy and help me to see these people through His eyes. As I would pray for Him to show me His ways and how to continue to walk in forgiveness, He did. This is truly a prayer that He will answer. The Holy Spirit always answers prayers that have to do with walking in the ways of Jesus!

He was so faithful to teach me so many things. During my quiet times or just driving or cleaning my house, He would begin to tell me things and show me things. I remember one day as I was cleaning the toilet. (Yes, if God is going to talk to us moms, it is often going to be when doing laundry or cleaning the toilet!) He started talking to me more about forgiveness and teaching me how to do it with those who had hurt me so badly. He started to reveal things in their own lives that were painful for them and how they were acting out of their own insecurities and hurt. It made sense to me, and I could receive it because I knew I could trust what God was saying to me. Another time I was cooking spaghetti, and God just touched my heart with compassion for one of the people who hurt me. He started sharing specific things that this person was going through. I sensed His compassion for her, and then I had compassion for her. I longed for her to be free. I prayed for her to be free and to come to know His great love for her. Now that I was experiencing such amazing love from my Father, I wanted the same for her. I did not want her to be insecure anymore. This is such a huge part of forgiveness. When we get to the place of really wanting to be free, and to love like Jesus, we will always come by this way. Letting God flood our hearts with compassion for the very ones who have hurt us softens our hearts. What they did does not seem to matter as much because His love and presence is so much greater and now affects us more than what they did to us. We have to hang in there in the process until we get to this point.

The word God spoke to me in the beginning of this season gave me the encouragement that total freedom was waiting on the other side of this. I promise you, if you persevere, you will get to this place of healing and forgiveness. The real issue, again, is us being conformed to the image of Christ. He is perfect. He loves perfectly and is so kind. He is the image of everything that is so perfect and true in life. That is why God desires us to be like Him. He saw why we rejected Him and did so many dumb things. I am glad God has taken the time and energy to really understand me. People may not understand you, but God does.

Through this process God really began softening my heart.

When I tell you I had a hard heart, I am not lying. Many of you who know me now are shocked, but I am telling the truth! I had several times, like the ones above, where God softened my heart toward others and helped me to understand them. This really helped me and showed me the truth: it really was not about me.

Another powerful tool God put in my hands was not to talk about the hurt and those who hurt me all the time. Yes, there are times when we need to vent and to get our feelings out, but in these instances it is for the purpose of getting healed and getting some healthy counsel and advice on how to go on. I realized that talking to others about all that had happened to me all the time made me feel depressed! I had to be careful during the healing process whom to talk to. I needed to use wisdom. Not everyone is the right person to help you through what you are going through. Ask God for wisdom and for the right person if you feel like you need to talk to someone about your situation. If that is what you need, He will bring them. Even when you do talk about it, be careful not to talk too much. As women, we really like to talk! I know I am not telling you anything new here, but really, sometimes we just need to zip our lips! Talking too much about our hurts and situations keeps it alive in us and stirred up. Forgiveness is truly letting go. We are not able to let go of what happened to us if we are always talking about them. It is kind of like picking at a wound that is trying to heal. The body forms a scab to protect the wound as it is healing. When we continue to talk too much or even think and focus too much on our problems and pain, it is like picking the scab off of the wound, which does not to allow the wound to heal properly or even at all .I had to learn this as God was healing me. Thankfully, there were some godly leaders in the body of Christ that helped shed much light on this through their teachings.

I can almost hear some of you asking a very real and valid question: "Just because I forgive someone, do I need to continue to have a relationship with them?" The answer to this is going to be different for each person. For me, the hardest people to forgive were the ones who I was still in relationship with on a regular basis. They were also the ones who continued to hurt me the way they always had. I came to a point in my healing process that I knew I had to limit exposure to these people in order to continue to become all that He had made me to be and to do. Proverbs 4:23 is a scripture that is truly freeing in this area. It says, "Keep your heart with all diligence, For out of it spring the issues of life." We are given a command by God to value and protect our heart, which is who we are. If we are surrounding ourselves with people who tear us down, instead of help and encourage us to be all God made us to be, we are harming ourselves.

For me, guarding my heart meant coming to a place where I had to limit my time I spent with certain people. Sadly, as of now, I am not in a relationship with them. I have already said this process of forgiveness has been so huge and life giving to me, but some of you may be wondering, If it is so life giving, then why do some relationships have to be limited or even come to an end? I am sorrowful that so many Christians in particular do not understand and live in the truth. I have been accused of not acting Christlike for not having a relationship with some people in my life. For me to continue to let people run over me, put me down, gossip about, and humiliate me is just plain dumb. It is not keeping my heart like Proverbs tells me to. Wow, it took me years to get to this point. It took me going through all the stages in the process of forgiveness to get here. It took me learning how to love myself as He does to get here.

It really does take a lot of healing and maturity as a person and a Christian to be able to set healthy boundaries. For some of you, God may be asking you to put up with certain behaviors (though not abuse) for a season while God is working things out in the other person. God can be trusted. He never wants you to be in harm while He is working. For others of you, God may be confirming to you that you are to distance yourself from destructive people like I had to. Trust me in this; it will not be easy, and those who you set boundaries with will accuse, blame, and ridicule you, even if they are Christians. By the time you get to this point in your life and follow the Spirit, the Word of God, how He leads you to forgive, and by seeking wise counsel, you will be ready for it. Living in freedom to be and do all He has called you to will be so much more important to you than what others think. I would have never in a million years thought I could make the decision to set some very firm but healthy boundaries with those close to me. I was too insecure, too chicken, too afraid of going against the flow—and definitely too fearful of being rejected and not getting the approval I had always looked to from others. That is what forgiveness does; it really sets you free.

Remember the bridge analogy? Without going through the forgiveness process with Jesus, I could not be here today. I remember how I so badly wanted to be free to be my own person and to make decisions on my own without worrying what others would think. It was not until I forgave those very people that I was free from the hurt they caused and free from needing their approval. As I let it go the chains dropped off. I could see the freedom in the peace I was experiencing in my mind. The level of peace in our mind is a good indicator of how we are doing as a whole, especially when it comes to forgiveness. God will not let us walk in peace while we are holding on to offense. It is a law, just like that running a red light will get you a ticket.

Satan has a heyday with our minds when we do not forgive. It is like giving him access just to torment the heck out of us and beat us up until we are flat-out exhausted. The difference was night and day as I began to forgive. I experienced loads of peace and rest within my heart and mind. I found that God has given me His approval, and He loves me and knows exactly who I am. I was free from the rat race of trying to please everyone. He knows that I do not hate those I have had to limit contact with. I so long for their freedom and for them to know the love of their Father so they do not keep hurting themselves and others. I have feelings of love and compassion for those who caused great hurt to me. Oh, the journey Jesus and I have had to take together to get here. What a work of grace!

Often from the time we choose to forgive until the time that it actually gets into our minds and emotions is quite a while. If you are not yet at the place where you feel love and compassion for those who have hurt you, hang in there; it is coming for you too! You too will come to the place where what *they* did does not matter anymore. Who He is, who you are, and what He is doing in our life becomes our new focus. It fills all those empty places where the hurt was lodged.

This is where another huge piece of forgiveness comes in. Jesus says in Matthew 5:44–45:

> But I say to you, love your enemies, bless those who curse you, do good to those who hate you and pray for those who spitefully use and persecute you, that you may be sons of your Father in heaven; for He makes His son rise on the evil and on the good, and sends rain on the just and on the unjust.

Loving our enemies concerns us seeing them through God's eyes like we talked about earlier. Blessing our enemies and those who do not treat us right has to do with out mouths again. *To bless* literally means "to speak well of"! OK, I know I lost some of you again. God had to teach and still is teaching me to control my own mouth and what I say about others. When they come up in a conversation, I usually hear the Holy Spirit whisper, "Just keep your mouth closed if you do not have anything good to say!" When I obey, I have peace, but when I do my own thing and rant and rave about people who have hurt me, I sense the Spirit is grieved. God knows why we are talking about them. If there is a godly purpose and we are not gossiping, He does not mind. He has even challenged me to be kind and use my words to bless those who have brought me great harm. When I do this, it is like giving the devil a black eye! I love to do that by the way, for all the ones he has given to me! I sense God's pleasure and anointing when I just say something nice and loving toward those who have come against me. I will do anything to experience His presence, even if it includes blessing my enemies.

Many problems come when people, and especially Christians, are still living broken. We all are broken to one degree or another; let's face it. But that is no excuse to go around hurting and wounding those around us. Get a grip and get some healing, for crying out loud! Those near to me argued as I shared my hurt and pain that came from their hands that I was too sensitive and that this is just the way they functioned. Basically, they told me to get over it. For me, Satan kept using this as a tool to lie to me and get me to think, again, that something was wrong with me. For years I would try and set healthy boundaries with these people and talk to them openly about how what they were doing was hurting me, to no avail. After every conversation I became more convinced it was my fault and not theirs. This continued for years; not months—years. I know some of you can relate, probably this very moment.

I lived in so much guilt because of the messages that were communicated to me. It came as another form of rejection. Like I shared earlier, it literally paralyzed me. When you are used to living and functioning in a certain way, it is just plain hard to break free. Let me say something here that I am praying will set many, many free. You do not have to receive messages of guilt and shame from anyone. Let me take it one step further. You do not have to receive them from Christians or those who are close to you, or any combination of the two. Satan has sold us a huge pack of lies that goes like this, "You are in sin and wrong to separate from those who are Christians." As he comes as an angel of light, we believe him. Why? Because we have lived in the darkness and with lies so long that we are used to it. However, First John 1:5 says that in God is light and in Him is no darkness at all. The enemy is darkness and uses manipulation, fear, guilt, and shame to keep us in bondage to him. I was all wrapped up in a system of living that was based on fear, not on love. My relationships with those who wounded me were based on fear, not the freedom of love. In fear you are not free to be yourself. In fear you have to do what everyone else says or you are bad or wrong. Sorry, they are not your God, and even He does not communicate truth like that! I am starting to get to know who I really am in God's eyes because I have had to choose to separate myself from the negative people.

The lie of the enemy is that we are bad if we do this. For someone like me who was already extremely insecure and thought I was wrong most of the time, I bought this lie, hook, line, and sinker as my fisherman husband would say. It was not until I began to get healthier and He gave me healthy, loving people to be in relationship that I began to realize the lie of where I was living. I knew I had to make a choice to distance myself from people, but I was literally paralyzed that I was doing something wrong and that God would be mad at me. I lived with a pretty constant and heavy dose of guilt. Religious guilt is the worst kind there is. It results when people use God to justify their behavior and say that you are wrong when you go against the flow. If we are going to choose Jesus, we are going to have to live like Him. Sorry, I just have to live by the principles in the Word. You do too, if you ever want to be free.

Let me interject some truth here. Many of you are probably

totally getting what I am saying because you have known you have needed to make some decisions for your own sanity. Others may be a little confused. I am not talking about leaving relationships and people behind because they irritate or even hurt you. Even those we love most may unintentionally hurt our feelings or leave us frustrated. My husband, friends, and some family have hurt me and will continue to do so until the day we leave this planet. That is the nature of relationships and life. Even love. They irritate me, and I irritate them! We can never escape that and should never try to avoid that because we will miss out on some great connections that He has for us. Please do not run in fear from people because you are afraid they will hurt you. Let me calm your fears: they will hurt you! But if these people really love us, they will give us the freedom and respect that when they do hurt us, they will be truly sorry. They will not blame, shame, or guilt you for being hurt or too sensitive. They will truly care enough to accept responsibility for their humanness. In those situations it is our responsibility to truly forgive. Sometimes we may even need to be the ones asking forgiveness from them for reacting wrongly. We must be able to give ourselves the grace to recognize that though we may also hurt others, God simply wants us to repent and keep moving forward in His plan for us. Thank God He has taught and is continuing to teach me how to walk this out on some wobbly little legs!

When I say to distance yourself from people who are hurting you, I am talking about abuse—mental, emotional, physical, and even spiritual abuse, using you for something that you were not intended for. *Abuse* may sound harsh, but let's just lay it out. Sometimes breaking free from this kind of behavior when it is in group form is even more devastating. Let me explain. When there is extremely unhealthy behavior amongst a family, church, or group of people, it seems like the pain and the problems just escalate. I have experienced this too.

God's heart so beats for reconciliation with those that have hurt us and those we ourselves have hurt. He desires that our hearts be wide open to love and freedom in relationships. This is why He made us. He is also a God who understands reality too. He gets where we live and the roads our feet travel. He knows the difficulty of just simply loving and relating to others. I lived in kind of a limbo state of forgiving those who hurt me and wanting to be reconciled with them so badly, but I was not sure how to do that. Because of the huge amount of guilt and shame and blame that I walked in, I allowed the enemy, for a time, to lie to me that because I was not reconciled with these people, it was my fault. It did not help that they were also sending me these messages. Seems like they and the enemy were in agreement. I really had to pray and seek the Lord for some kind of word or truth that specifically dealt with this issue. You will, too. I really wanted to know His ways and His heart for this. Here is what He told me, and it completely set me free. He said, *"Gabby, I have died for the whole world and done everything for the world to be reconciled to Me, but there are many, many people who are still not reconciled to Me."* What He said made perfect sense. It always does when we are ready for truth, doesn't it?

We, like Him, can do all in our power to see peace in our relationships, but ultimately it comes down to the choices of the other people, doesn't it? Even God Himself gave all of us crazy people down here the choice to choose a relationship with Him. He is the perfect God who has done everything perfectly. Everything. Some have chosen Him, and some have not. How He lives with the tension of that everyday is beyond me. He is God. I guess it is just that simple. Let this truth settle in, not just in your spirit but your soul: if you have done all you can and have searched your heart openly and honestly before God, and man if necessary, then let it go. He has to. So do we.

As you do, watch the chains fall to the ground. Watch as the dust gathers at your feet and you walk free. Watch as the enemy is left kicking and screaming over your choice to keep following God over all else. Over guilt, over shame, and definitely over unforgiveness. Unforgiveness and being offended are just traps that Satan has used to bait us into his dark and horrible way of existence. Oh, we are made for so much more than that! We are made to soar with our Creator! We are made to live in the light and be free!

Make the choice to keep loving people, even if it has to be from a distance at times. Above all, let the Holy Spirit, who knows the heart of the Father and your heart perfectly, lead you into all truth when it comes to forgiveness.

Remember the bridge we talked about it the beginning of this chapter? As we forgive, let's turn around, look over our shoulder, and see it in the distance. We have crossed over to the other side. It wasn't so bad after all, was it? We made it! We are free to walk into the bright future that He has waiting for us. Him living inside of us has made it possible for us to forgive and let go. As we let go, what others have done no longer entangles us. It no longer binds us and connects us to our past but frees us to fully live in the present and for what is ahead. Looking back now, the journey through learning to forgive was way worth it! As our feet step off the wooden planks of the bridge, we realize they are on the steady ground of His faithfulness. We are free from our past. We are free to live in all the beautiful things that He has for us!

CHAPTER 8
OUT OF THE SHADOWS

OY, I THOUGHT God uprooted a huge lie in my life when He freed me from fear, but I had no idea He was getting ready to uproot something that went just as deep in my life, if not deeper. Shame. I am so joyful that some of you cannot relate to shame in your life. What I am more aware of, though, is how many of you dear brothers and sisters know what it is like to live in shame. Some of you may have many negative things that you deal with because of shame. You have been living ashamed of what you have done, or what has been done to you. But the most devastating shame is being ashamed of yourself.

Maybe your issues with shame do not run as deep as mine did, but you know the feeling nonetheless. Maybe you have one or two issues that just seem to gnaw away at your confidence and cause you to feel ashamed. I am aware of some of my dear brothers and sisters who have gone through a divorce wrestle with the shame that you could not keep your marriage together. Maybe someone in your family or close to you is making some choices that could bring shame on you.

Whatever the issue may be, Jesus came to free us from all shame, whether you have loads of it or a little. He does not even want us to live with one ounce of it. If there are things He wants to bring correction to in our lives, by all means, let's let Him do it, but we do not have to be ashamed of them. God wants to teach us His ways. You may not have been able to put your finger on why you struggle with so many things in your life that you do not want to, but today God Himself in shining the glorious light of freedom on you! It is only because of His deep love and compassion that He is pointing out what is really going on in our heart. You can take this next statement to the bank: God will never shame you. Listen again. Never will He shame you. Yes, I just wrote that twice. I wish I could tell you that I only had to hear it twice to believe it, but He had to say it over and over again to me because I was in such bondage to shame. It was right up there with fear. In fact, those two lies were all entangled in a huge web built by Satan himself.

For those who may need more clarity on what shame really is, here it is in a nutshell. It is the belief that something is wrong with you. It is a belief and feeling of being unworthy, an embarrassment, and a disappointment as a person. Try carrying that around all your life and see how it works! It doesn't. When we face the life head-on we begin to see it for what it really is—a lie. For so long it has been what we have believed, so it has become *our* truth. Let me share some more of my life and how Jesus set me free from it. I pray that as you see yourself in this story, you also see the strong hand of your Redeemer coming for you.

Shame, along with fear, was my constant traveling buddy. I realize now that I never grew up feeling good and worthy as a person. As you have read my story, I have talked about how that lie began because I never knew my birth father and because of the environment in which I grew up. In my immature mind, there was something wrong with me that caused these people to leave me. The enemy weaved that lie into every fabric of my being. Because I did not have a good, healthy foundation and view of myself, I was a great target for his lies. We all are, really, if we are not secure in who we are.

Can I just stop and say something here that I have wanted to say for a while? I am so weary of Christians and Christian leaders who only focus on the spiritual part of people. They focus on their gifts, what they can do, how they can "perform," how much they go to church, or whatever it may be. Jesus came to bring back wholeness to every part of us. He did not just come to bring our dead spirit back to life but our mind, body, and emotions. The church needs to stop trying to get everyone to do a bunch of stuff if they are still really broken and hurting. Many, many people in the body of Christ and those who are entering His kingdom desperately need some time to heal and be restored. Yes, many times that comes as we reach out to others, but too many times we just trade one bondage of perfectionism for a more seemingly spiritual one. We must take time to learn about God's unconditional love and acceptance of us. Just get to know Jesus; then let Him do what He wants to do with you. Jesus so wants to tend to all the deepest parts of us as people. He wants to restore the places that never were able to develop because of pain and trauma. I was growing spiritually, but if I did not let my Daddy heal the severely broken parts of me, I could be in serious trouble. So could you. He loves us way to much to let that happen.

As a little girl some of my earliest memories were of me hiding and feeling embarrassed of myself. There was very little concept of my value and worth as Gabby. I did not realize how cherished and beautiful I was as a person. Because of the way I was raised, my growth and development were stunted. My life so revolved around trying to hide and protect myself from further harm and rejection that it became a way of life for me.

When I came to my adoptive family, it was close to Halloween. I dressed up as a cheerleader. I was five and already had the tan and blonde hair to complete the look, thanks to the California sunshine! Now I see how cute I was, but then I felt alone and embarrassed of myself. My new family had a Halloween party to celebrate, and we all dressed up. My new uncle was a jokester. He looked at me and laughed and said, "You need to take your mask off!" He was just joking with me, but for someone who was already really insecure, I felt embarrassed and wanted to hide. I hated it and got really mad at him.

It would be many, many years before I again heard the words, "Take off your mask," but this time it came from my heavenly Father. I was ready to hear them then because I knew how much He loved me and who I was in Him. Until then, however, I wore a mask much of the time to hide the real me. After all, if you could not see who I really was, then you would not be able to hurt and reject me. I reasoned that I had experienced enough of both of those things, and I was not signing up for any more, thank you very much!

Within the next few years after that first Halloween with my new family, some friends of our family who were in the movie and commercial industry asked my mom if I wanted to be in a commercial. They thought I was cute and would be great for cereal commercials. No way was I going to go on camera in front of everyone! I said no, and thankfully my parents did not pressure me too much to do it. Mind you, many kids do not mind in the spotlight, but I had no idea about how to be myself, much less how do it with a bunch of people watching me! Now that I have children it makes me wonder how they would respond to this type of attention from the media. Out of my two daughters, one would probably have no desire to be in a commercial, but the other one would be hamming it up in front of the cameras. (For those of you who know me, you take the guess about which one is which!)

Our family had a video camera growing up. Man, we videotaped everything. I mean everything! Who really cares what we were eating for breakfast on June 3, 1986? Someone apparently did! I get so seasick from watching the video camera spin around. In the videos I notice many shots where I was hiding. No cereal commercials and definitely no videos of me, period!

Another huge thing that contributed to me being ashamed of myself was that while I was living with my birth mother I was sexually abused by some men who lived in our apartment complex. I have vivid memories of my close friend and I being in their apartment and them abusing us. As I look back now I see that I was more vulnerable to abuse because there was really nobody around to protect me from harm. I could not fathom how much these episodes of abuse would affect my mind, emotions, and view of myself for many years to come. Being abused sexually caused me to walk in sexual lust that really came into full swing as I entered my pre-teen and teenage years. I was not able to see my body or my sexuality as God had made them, so I turned to sexual pleasure and lust to fulfill that deep longing to be loved by someone.

My peers at school were not a good influence for me either. I so longed to be noticed, and all of these things were going on inside of me and nobody knew. Again, I felt alone and like there was nobody to talk to about what was happening on the inside of me. I remember that I never felt like a part of the crowd. Even though I was in sports and dated a popular and athletic guy, I still did not feel like I fit in. I remember as a little girl being in school and sitting by myself. I had a sense of loneliness and feeling that something was different and wrong with me. This sense of loneliness continued with me throughout my school years. Although I was able to participate in limited activities such as sports, not being able to involved in more sent me the message that there was something wrong with me. There were many things that I was not allowed to participate in at school, which made me feel different from the other kids. Part of that was due to my hiding, and part of it was that there were not many people for me to turn to for support. Seeing my peers around me participating in and excelling in so many areas continued to pound me into the ground with shame.

My adoptive parents got divorced when I was twelve, and that really changed our family dynamics. My adoptive father made good money, and we had what we needed and a lot that we wanted; however, we never shared a sense of emotional closeness. This caused me to feel like there was something missing and wrong in my life. More than ever, not being able to bond with my adoptive father only strengthened the lie of Satan that I was the problem – that something was wrong with me. I never felt like the little princess that every girl deserves to have a profound sense of. This led to me finding and learning new ways of hiding who I really was. It also led to me feeling like I needed to continue taking care of myself and defining my own identity.

I felt ashamed of the things that were going on inside of my head. I experienced lustful thoughts and could not control how I felt about anything. I felt ashamed because of some of the choices I made, but I did not know how to get free. Shortly after becoming a Christian when I was fifteen, I felt so guilty about some of the thought patterns that were still in my mind. The guilt was so strong that I actually felt nauseous and sick to my stomach. I now know that was not the voice of my heavenly Father but of the accuser, who wanted to keep me down. Looking back I see how much I abused and mistreated myself because I never learned my worth and value as a person. Because music, friends, magazines, and television influenced my decisions, I hated what I saw in the mirror. I determined that I was going to do something about it. Losing weight and looking good at any cost became my obsession.

As a result I developed an eating disorder and several issues of insecurity when it came to my appearance. Deep down inside I really wanted to be beautiful and to feel good about myself. The way I went about that was wrong, but it was all that this very broken young girl knew how to do. I had no concept then that the One who made me and saw everything about me still loved me so deeply. Oh, how what I did to myself hurt Him. It had to have been very hard for Him to see me standing in front of a full-length mirror as a young girl whose body was changing and despise what I saw. I see that now. All I saw then was myself. That is the thing about shame. It really is all wrapped up in us. We become so aware—even hyper aware—of who we are. Every flaw becomes magnified. He came to destroy that way of thinking and living!

I grew to hate my own body. The music that I listened to was gangsta rap, and that certainly did not help me form a healthy view of a woman's body. At about twelve, as my body began to change, people, especially the boys would make fun of me for being chunky. I hated it, and it made me feel more embarrassed about myself. I really did not open up about it to my family, so I just internalized all these feeling and determined that I would fix it. My basic personality can be pretty perfectionist if I am not controlled by the Holy Spirit, so this became my new goal, to be perfect in every way so I would be loved. What a nightmare!

At about thirteen or fourteen I began to only eat five grams of fat a day. I carried a gallon of water around. I watched every bite that went in to my mouth. Self-torment and fear would come if I did not follow this plan perfectly. I was afraid to gain the weight I had lost, so I worked harder and harder. The one thing that saved me from having a worse eating disorder than I did was the fact that I did not want to starve myself completely because I liked food too much, and I hated to throw up. Instead I just balanced my eating almost zero fat with excessive exercise. I would run, play volleyball, and lift weights. I ran before school, then again at track practice. There is nothing wrong with a desire to excel in sports if it is not controlling your self-image. I lifted so many weights because I not only wanted to be thin but to be muscular. Looking back now, doing all of that may of negatively affected my lower back and overworked my body.

I remember riding my exercise bike in the one-hundred-degree heat of my upstairs bedroom while watching the summer Olympics.

Sweating so hard and wanting to look like those athletes was my obsession. I was tan, pretty, and toned. That sure got people's attention—especially the boys at school.

Some of the guys I dated just flat-out treated me terrible. While dating me, they also had other girls that they were sexually active with. This did not do a lot to help my self-esteem! I had been dating a guy in high school, and our plans were to get married when I was sixteen. Boy, I am glad some things just do not work out the way we plan! Let's just say that my family was not very fond of this guy.

At the time, my mom noticed the changes in my body and the amount of time that I worked out and expressed concern. But she left it at that.

So, I continued to build up my own identity little by little. By this time I was well entrenched in how to hide myself. I think to survive I focused on the external things I was involved in. That is really all I knew how to do. I felt like life and taking care of myself were all on my shoulders.

It was during this few years that I came to my worst place mentally and spiritually. I did not even have the smallest clue that Jesus was working behind the scenes to make a dramatic takeover in my life. I love recalling the workings of God to redeem us to Himself, don't you? It is nothing short of miraculous for any of us that we would be willing to follow this Jesus and walk away from a life of sin and shame. My heart aches for the Christians who have begun to follow Jesus but cannot get free from the shame of their past.

Something began to happen in me during my sophomore year of high school. I began looking at my life and realized there must be more. My relationship that I put so much hope in with my long-term boyfriend did not seem to be satisfying anymore. Sin really did not seem to be so appealing, but I really was not sure what the alternative was. After learning of some of the things my boyfriend was doing while dating me, I became depressed.

Something new began to happen in my life. I noticed that I had more of an interest in other things besides partying, dating, and being popular. I just was not sure what the other things were. My mother began going to church after her and her husband divorced, but I never was interested. My boyfriend, friends, and I would make fun of church and "God stuff." She would take me to church, but my heart was not there. I filled a seat, like many people do. I am so thankful that His heart is not for us to just fill a seat but for Him to fill our lives!

Our pastor at the time was praying with my mother for me. I was so ashamed of my behavior and myself as my mother gave him letters to read that were from my boyfriend. I know my mom had others praying for me also. I am forever grateful for that and that my adopted family introduced me to Christ. I remember the pastor sharing a word he had for me. He saw army tanks and a war going on for my life. Boy, was he right, and I happened to be right in the middle of it, without any way of knowing how to get out. I just was not into the whole Jesus thing. It was fine for others, but not for me. I just wanted to keep living my life and for Him to leave me alone.

The next one to two years would turn out to be a life-changing season for me in more ways than one. My mother met and married a Christian man. He is a wonderful man in so many ways. By that time I was attending high school in St. Paul, Oregon, and my family decided to move to Salem, Oregon. During the summer going into my junior year I started a new high school. God really was working in my life, because over the summer I had given my life to Christ. Moving away from my peers, boyfriend, and the pressure to perform at my old school proved to be a great thing for me. I felt like God had given me a new beginning. After things go to an all-time low with my boyfriend and I, we broke it off. Actually, I did. It was a few months before our family moved. For me to do that and to stand up for myself was God. He began to give me new desires even before I actually became a Christian. I look back now and see how He was softening my heart and preparing me for some major life changes.

I still kept in contact somewhat with a few of my close friends from my old town, which was only a half an hour away. My best friend and some others thought that I had become a nun because they all grew up in a Catholic town. They did not understand what being a born-again Christian really meant. I am not sure I understood everything about it either, but there I was—and I was one!

I began to read my Bible. One day my friends from my old high school came over and saw my Bible on my nightstand and asked about it. I remember feeling embarrassed and wanting to hide it from them. I may have been saved, but God still had some major work cut out for Him! I knew it was not right to hide something so important to me, but that is what I was used to doing, hiding. God knew He had to completely take me out of the surrounding of my friends and old influences for me to decide to walk with Him. There was just too strong of a pull on my heart where I was at. I also believe that He knew I would not have the boldness to choose Him in the middle of my friends. He understands the weak and frail and broken parts of us, and He chooses us anyway. I so love Him for that!

After I became a Christian I seemed to have it all together. I prayed, I witnessed, and appeared totally changed on the outside; inside, however, my soul was a wreck from the years of bondage I lived in. Oh, do not get me wrong, I had a new heart and purpose for life, but people still did not know the real me. I remember being so frustrated with the war that was going on inside of me. Before I was a Christian it seemed like there was no war. Now I was learning about the new me and the old me. I would read the

Bible and see all the things I should be but was not and got easily discouraged. I remember I would go to leaders in my church and ask them to pray with me about some of the changes I believed God wanted to make in my life, but they dismissed me as not needing prayer and being perfect. I did have some leaders who helped, encouraged me, and prayed with me after receiving Christ. But what about the others? What the heck? I was beginning to open up and trying to be a real person, and people, including these "God people," totally dismissed it. OK, I am over it now, but for the sake of those Christians and leaders who are still acting crazy like that, stop it! I remember walking away from those times of trying to be humble and honest about what I was struggling with feeling so defeated and hurt. I felt like I needed to be open and honest with my need for freedom, but it seemed elusive in my church.

Many of you may be stuck in the same situation. I pray that God will bring you the freedom you desire. The message that those people gave me in my church was the message so many have been given: just put everything you experienced behind you and be fake. Fake your way to healing. Fake your way to victory. Sorry, Jesus and I just hate religion and false external systems. So should you. Run away from them and those bound by them with every ounce of energy that you have. Use your determination to run into the arms of Jesus. Trust me in this; if you are determined to be a whole human being and get over your past, there is not anything or anyone who can stop you, not even the religious folks. Run right past them into the arms of your Father. He will pick you up. If you need the love of His people, and you do, He is able to pluck you out of your surroundings and put you into a whole new environment. How do I know? That is what He did with me.

God used the wonderful man who helped disciple me to help me find how I was supposed to walk out my calling. Shortly after becoming a Christian, I felt an instant desire to become a missionary and to tell people about Jesus. God gave me a picture of myself in Africa, and I was helping feed people. It was hot and dusty, and the color of their skin was dark. I knew it was Africa, and I knew I would be going there. The picture in my mind's eye is as clear today as when He showed it to me many years ago. I joke that the fact that I wanted to go and do anything for anyone else was proof that Jesus had changed me! I was so self-absorbed and really always had me on my mind. Much of that probably came from having to care for myself so much in my life. I asked this dear friend, Ralph Cruz, if he knew of any Bible colleges or places to go to help prepare me to do what God was putting on my heart. He instantly said, "Christ for the Nations." I looked at the magazine they put out and prayed about it. I knew I was to go.

A few short months later Jesus and I hopped on a plane at midnight with all my possessions in a few bags and went to Dallas, Texas. Little did I know how much He would actually do to prepare me for what He called me to. Aren't you glad He does not tell us everything beforehand? Aren't you glad He keeps some things to Himself? We would just freak out if we knew it all. Oh, my time at the college was so life changing. There He began to uproot things in my life that I did not even know were buried. Layer upon layer began to come off in His wonderful presence.

In many ways Bible college was like a new beginning for me. I could leave behind old friends and even some people who did not really understand who I was and what God had called me to be and do. I am so grateful for my parents and church, who supported me in many ways as I followed Jesus. As I was in such an atmosphere of praise, worship, amazing teaching, and the anointing of the Holy Spirit, I realized that I had been a Christian for two years and had suppressed the old me, the *me* before Christ. All the pain, shame, fear, and guilt of who I was and who I was not came flooding in. I knew then that it was my Father tenderly opening my fragile heart, which had been so damaged. Christ for the Nations did not only focus on what God called us to do but who we were as people. I cannot emphasize how important this is. Those who serve there know that life just beats you up sometimes! They allowed the Holy Spirit to minister healing and deliverance as He wanted to.

The first time I ever really "got" that God loved me was in worship before classes began. I can tell you exactly where I was sitting—in the back section of the Institute Building (the IB). This was where worship was held each morning. Some days the Holy Spirit just took over, and the teachers cancelled classes as we lingered in God's presence. *That* is what changed me. Oh, I remember the awesome teaching, but the Holy Spirit was our greatest Teacher. How I am forever grateful for those times. With hands lifted high and my face toward heaven, I *knew* that He loved me. Little did I know how much deeper that love was for me and how much more I would come to know it.

After becoming a Christian I was not sure what to do with all my baggage. Sometimes hearing that we are new in Christ and old things have passed away is a little vague. What the heck does that look like? Some of those at my previous church seemed to place me on this pedestal. The problem was is that I kept falling off. The stool was lopsided. My foundation needed some work. Yes, I was beginning to learn about the gifts I had as a person, but how to be me was a whole other story. So, God took me across the country to place me in an atmosphere where I could grow. And be healed. And then go out in His name. One thing I remember was being in worship and feeling like the spotlight of heaven was on me. That spotlight shows the flaws, damage, and anything else that needs to be repaired. Sin that needs cleansed. Guilt that needs to be replaced with freedom. I remember sharing these things over the phone with my dear friend who recommended the school. He was rejoicing on the other end of the phone at all God was doing. He was always one person who really believed in me and got me. Don't we all need someone like that in our lives?

Sadly, not everyone was rejoicing with me about all God was doing in my life. There were some in my family who, when I opened up to them about God healing all the years of pain and being without things and people I needed in my life, got upset. I was not sure at the time why they were so angry. I did not understand how they could not rejoice with me. Satan would use that so big time in my life that it would cause me to shut down emotionally and in many other ways for a long time.

You see, I never opened up to people about much of anything. I felt like it would be safe for me to open up to this person about what God was doing. Boy, was I wrong. It was not until years later that God showed me that Satan gained a great foothold in my life that day. Something happened to me. Since I was already wounded and not strong in His love yet, I took it as more rejection. I really do not believe the person meant it as this. I do believe that they did not understand what God was doing and how to react. Some of their life was not open to God moving like this in them, so it was new and strange to them. I do not need to be the judge of them and what happened; God can do that. This person was close to me, and I let what they did and what they said control how I opened up to people in the future. I was already a master at hiding, and from that moment I learned how to get even better.

What I am about to say here is not coming from a place of wounding in me; Christ has dealt with that. I really just want to say that people need help. When they begin to open up about issues or need in their lives, please do not shame them and make them feel worse. If you are not able to deal with the magnitude of what they are sharing, refer them to someone who may be able to. If you are a leader, take some lessons from men and women from places like Christ for the Nations. Be real. Be like Jesus. If you are not like Him when it comes to dealing with people, fall on your face and ask Him to help you love like He does. If you find that you need greater healing yourself, get it; then give out of that which you have. Give people the freedom to open up.

Again, the message that had been so ingrained in me that there was something wrong with me pounded me again. This time it was by Christians and religious leaders, so I thought it must be true. And if it were true, it *must* be the way He thought about me. Thank God He heard my cry, and He hears yours too. I pray He begins to answer your cries through this book.

My time at Christ for the Nations proved to be so fruitful. I am still seeing the fruit of the seeds God planted in my life there. God had more for me there than just ministry. I met my husband, Andy, at Christ for the Nations. Early in our relationship we talked about all the wonderful things God was doing in our life. It felt so good to open up and tell him about how God was changing me. We would sit for hours while we were getting to know each other and just talk about how much I was learning to let God love me. We went out on dates and ate at some of the most amazing restaurants! It felt like a new beginning for me and like I was beginning to get what being a Christian was all about. He loved listening as I talked about how God was like a Father to me. He shared many things about what God was doing in him at college as we both prepared for ministry. Andy and I got married on December 19, 1998. Shortly after being married we moved to Oregon, where my family and I had been living since I was about eight years old.

During that time in my life my mom was afraid that I would meet a missionary and move to Africa with him. I did make it to Africa. I went with a group from our college to Morocco, a beautiful country in North Africa. One week after Andy and I got engaged I boarded a long flight, followed by many train, taxi, and ferry rides, for a three-week trip there. Everything was beautiful—the land, the people, and the food. I would love to go back some day! I still believe God has work for our family to do in Africa, including Morocco.

The love of all nations and people groups was planted in me when I got saved. It was watered while at school. I am amazed at how God does things. I just got back from ministering to my neighbor around the corner, who is from China and is a Buddhist. I have been able to share Christ with her and pray for her healing. God is up to something. His heart is for the unreached people of the world. They are our neighbors, our co-workers, and even our family and friends. He is reaching out to all people and wants to send us to them. Even though I am in the States now, I still get to minister to so many people from all over the world, and it just makes me want to jump and shout!

Coming back home after college and being married was difficult on some levels. At Bible college, most people understand what you are experiencing because God is working in their lives just as much to prepare them for what He was for them. At home I felt different. I was different—not better or more spiritual than anyone; just different. With some, the only time I would gain their approval was when I was doing everything they wanted me to. God had begun an amazing work in me but had not yet finished it. Know the feeling? I believe He allowed me to experience some difficult things with people who were close to me so I could be here at *this* moment writing to you. Sitting here on my porch tonight with the fading blue sky of the evening, it all makes sense. For some time, I wondered why He would allow me to experience such beginnings of victory and healing at school, only to come home and experience some hardships. Now I see it.

Some of you may be stuck in some situations that have you wondering what on Earth the point is. Maybe it is not just for you. Maybe it is for someone else. You're paving the way for their freedom.

I still struggled to find myself and how to express myself. A life of hiding and shame had taken its toll on me and on my relationships. I really got to a place where I was not able to deal with people. What I mean by that is that I had so much anxiety around people and was so tired of being hurt, even by Christians, that I just shut down. This is where my bondage to fear and shame came to a head. At least that is my term for it. It was like I was alive, but not really. Just surviving and functioning. I desperately knew I needed some kind of breakthrough but had no idea where it would come from. All along God had been preparing my deliverance. He had been planning my escape. The battle of my issues was raging too fiercely for me to even think of some kind of escape and what it would even look like. He had been preparing the season of my life in which my foot pain would drive me to Him. With my body and feet and everything else, He seemed to be allowing to come my way.

God knows how to break us out of the prison we are in. It does not matter how long it has been since those cold, rusty bars have been closed. They can swing open in just one moment! Just one word from our Savior, and they come flying open.

Sometimes, however, it takes a little while to realize the door has been opened and that we are free. Walking out of shame was something that I had to learn. It was like my Father took my hand and taught me (and is still teaching me) how to walk in the freedom that He has for me. When you have learned how to walk a certain way and think a certain way, your mind-set has to change before your feelings and actions do. God just happened to place me in circumstances that forced me to come out of hiding. They forced me to live for someone and something bigger than protecting myself.

I remember the first time God made me aware that many of my problems that I experienced were a result of being ashamed of

myself. It was 1999, and we were newly married. I was in our apartment reading Joyce Meyer's book *Beauty for Ashes* about how she
broke free from shame. Before that time, I was never really able to
put a finger on the root of many of the things I suffered with. Now
I knew what was going on with me, and it brought great relief to
know that there was nothing wrong with me. I felt a heaviness
begin to lift off of me and began experience the hope of freedom
from feeling so bad about myself. That was the beginning of the
freedom I experience now, but it would take many years to see it
come to pass in its fullness.

The circumstances God had allowed with my feet were really
what He used to complete my freedom. Everything about it was to
bring Him glory and to see me healed. Here was the catch: what
I was going through could not be hidden. *I* could not be hidden.
When you have physical problems like I did, everyone has to know
about it. I also realized that shame was fueled by pride. Ouch. God
has a way of touching on that one too! For me to need such help
from others and have to learn how to receive was huge for me.
Pride had to fall, then shame.

I kept getting this feeling that life was not about me anymore but
something much bigger. Bigger, like Christ. Unless we have something bigger and more powerful than the pull of our sin, we will
always go back. Every time. Before long my family, friends, church
family, and people I did not want to know I had problems knew.
Just going over the cause of my physical challenges seemed to aggra-
vate the need for me to hide. But I could not. I now know that God's
intent is not to destroy *us* but the false us, the lies and identity we
build up to protect us. They are not really doing that anyhow.

Remember back to the word He gave me about healing my feet
from *The 700 Club*? Just sharing that, at times, would make me
want to run and hide. God heal me? Why would He go to such
trouble for someone who was as unworthy as I felt? And why

would I want to share something so huge with people? But, little by little, I did. Layer by layer the shame began to come off like an old, wet coat that did not fit. It never fit. God began to show me that as I humbled myself before Him I would be more and more free to *be* who He made me to be and to *express* who He had made me to be.

That is where I really got hung up. I had some funky ways of coping with my fear of rejection. We are so funny. I can laugh now. I was not always laughing then while I was in the thick of letting Him break me free, but He is so relentless! One day while spending time with my Father and talking to Him about all of this stuff, He spoke so tenderly to my heart words that opened up my wounded soul like nothing else would. He showed me the truth about why I was acting and reacting the way that I was. There is nothing like getting a huge dose of truth to set us free. He gently reached down into the net I was stuck in and pulled me out, one piece at a time. As He pulled me out I was different than when I went into the net. I thought differently, I acted differently, and I looked different. He was now my Deliverer. In the truest sense of the word. As the layers came off my body was more and more healed. It was nothing short of amazing. I stopped taking all those pictures we took of my feet in the beginning. I did not need them so much anymore, because others and I could see the difference in my physical body.

Oh, here comes some dancing news! During this time I was still wearing my arch supports. They were the same ones my doctor gave me in the beginning. All of a sudden my feet began to have more pain than I had experienced in a while. I still had pain before this, but for some reason now it was worse. What the heck? Then as I started putting it all together, I realized that as my feet were changing and my arches were getting higher again, the arch supports were not fitting my feet properly anymore. Let me tell you, if they do not fit your feet right, it hurts badly. I think I missed my calling as a foot doctor! I took this to the Lord. I talked to Andy and told him what was going on. I shared all of this with my closest friend. I felt a bit like Mary, who pondered some amazing things that God was up to.

I went back to the foot doctor and told him what I was experiencing. He took another mold of my foot and made some new arch supports. I really was not sure what to do at this time. Something had happened during the process of the labs making new supports and me getting them that made the wait six weeks before I got the new supports. That was not a coincidence! God was up to something! To be honest, going without my supports for six minutes caused some major anxiety for me, so the thought of going six weeks nearly threw me into panic. I was not at all interested in going back to the pain I had known before.

During this time I took all of this to the Lord. I knew that the time would come for me to be healed supernaturally, but I was not sure if this was His timing. Sometimes all we can do is take one step of faith, followed by another. If He gives us a promise and we have the faith to walk it out, we will see the reality of it in our lives. That was what was happening.

A few days turned into a few weeks. The first few days of going without the arch supports were filled with anxiety. I was not sure what to think, to be honest. I noticed that my feet were not hurting at all like I expected them to without the supports. My arch supports were not back from the lab, and yet my feet continued to strengthen and heal. The arches, bones, and muscles all got higher on the tops of my feet and ankles. The foot doctor told me before that if I did not have these supports my feet would weaken again, and the pain would become worse. The opposite was happening. This was *His* time to heal me. Oh, He used the medical field for a time, but watch out when you are walking in His timing. He may surprise you! One day can turn your whole life around. One day your healing and freedom can come! For me, that *one* day turned into many. By the time the arch supports came back from the doctor they did not even fit my foot properly anymore because God had restored me so much just in those six weeks of waiting.

I have never had to wear those arch supports again. I have kept them for a memento though! They remind me of His great faithfulness, which made every pain-filled day worth what I was now experiencing. I was experiencing a miracle, one that no man could have arranged or accomplished for me! One that would continue to unfold as He put the rest of my life and heart back together.

Sometimes when we are so used to waiting patiently for Him to come through we are not ready to move when He says move—in an instant. *Now!* God wants us to be on *His* time. The time that beats to the rhythm of His heart. It is not left over from our quiet time last week. We will be ready to move with Him when our time is synchronized with His heart. That is what He wants for us. That is what He wanted for me that day. Heaven touched Earth, the supernatural collided with the natural, and I have never been the same! That very day I realized He was beginning to heal me supernaturally. I really was not sure how He would continue to do what He had always planned. I just knew that He was touching my life and my body. I was simply in awe and amazement at what He was doing. There were times when I just simply wanted to ponder and reflect on what He was doing. All the days and months that had turned into about two years of waiting seemed not to matter as much.

Oh, the work He had to do to get me to the place where I could actually believe that He would do this for me and that I was free enough not to hide it. Let me just interject here something about the graciousness of our Savior. He is such a tender and sensitive Father to us. He knows when we are ready for what He wants to do and when we are not. Before this time, I am not sure if I would have had the courage to tell others about the healing He was bringing me because of my deep shame and insecurity. He knew that and held my heart and my feet in His healing hands until His time came. I could just cry at His faithfulness. I remember telling my pastor at the time about what was going on. He smiled and said, "I always knew God was going to do a miracle with you!" It was so awesome to tell people that God was healing me.

By this time more of me was coming out of hiding, and it felt natural to share what He was doing. There were still times when being so "out there" with what He was doing in my life seemed a little overwhelming to someone who was not used to opening up about her life at all. It was during those times that my Daddy would take my hand and teach me how not to hide. He gave me grace to tell my foot doctor that God was helping my body to get well without the orthotics. This was the same foot doctor that I was too afraid to tell a few years earlier, by the way. He just said that I should keep wearing the orthotics, because if I did not my feet would go back to the way they were before. After telling him I had not worn them for over a year and I was fine, he just dismissed it. Oh well, He missed out on God's glory!

My chiropractor that I have seen for years had a different reaction. I told him that I really believed that my healing was due to God touching my body, and he agreed. He had actually seen me much more than my foot doctor. He still adjusts my back about once a month. He is a wonderful, humble man who was able to receive what God is doing in me. He has seen my children grow up and seen my body get stronger and stronger.

For all the ways I had learned to hide and protect myself, I had to be taught how *not* to hide. He did not want me to go back to my old ways, so He had to place my feet on totally new ground— ground based on His truth about Him and me. If He would not have been holding my hand, I could have never opened up to others about what He was doing in me. He literally had to teach me how to express myself. Some of you can relate. During the time of breaking free came probably some of the worst torment from the enemy. God had to teach me how to use my authority in this area and how to walk out freedom.

Satan truly is the accuser of the brethren. He lives and breathes to accuse God and us. When God breaks shame out of our lives, it closes a huge door to the enemy, and he knows that. That is why he fought so hard against me breaking free. Many, many of you who are reading this can relate to this battle. Good thing the war is already won, and Jesus gives us the weapon of His Word to overcome all the lies of the enemy! It seemed like this time of breaking free from shame caused me to have to draw so intensely close to Him just to survive. I did more than survive; Jesus and I overcame the accuser!

Brothers and sisters, the greater one lives in us (1 John 4:4). You see, shame is the language of the enemy, and when we are agreeing with him we reap the many negative things that come along with that lie. He knows his days are numbered and that all the power he has over us rest in his lies. That is why he works so hard to keep us from hearing and believing truth. When I say that if I overcame shame then anyone on the face of the earth can, I mean it with all my heart. I say that because of how bound I was by that lie of Satan. I love that Jesus does not wait until we are free from our stuff before He just steps right in and starts cleaning us up, one limb at a time. He gets right into the pit of our muddy mess and extends His gracious hand. He gives us a hand up. All we have to do is by faith grab that hand with all our might and let Him wash us off! He is so faithful!

The beautiful way He had me do this was to exchange one way of hiding for another. I know I just lost some of you, so let me explain. He was such a kind and gentle Father in the way He healed and restored me. Oh, He will be and is for you, too! He taught me truth, truth that my warped mind desperately needed to hear. It would be truth that would forever change me. He taught me that it is not wrong to want to be safe. In fact, it is a basic human need. Because of the way I tried to protect myself, I thought it was wrong. He just showed me that the things I turned to for safety—and the people, including myself—were misplaced. He wanted me to hide in Him.

It was almost as if He took me back to the desires I had when I was a little girl. They were all still in me, but they were unmet. He showed me that He wanted to meet the need for me to be safe and secure. Many, many places in the Word show us that He is our safety. For most of my life, that was a totally foreign concept to me. I was always in charge of my safety, not Him, thank you. I fell down on the job. Over and over.

Let's look at some of the beautiful passages He led me to that brought freedom to me. Psalm 32:7 says that He is our hiding place. It also says that He will surround us with songs of deliverance. The difference between hiding in Him and hiding in a lie is freedom. Do you see that? He not only wants us to see it but to live it! He began to teach me how to hide in Him. In the middle of my circumstances and not always wanting to open up to people about what He so clearly wanted me to, I began to learn that His truth and what He said about me were my safety. He did in fact surround me with songs of deliverance.

One big thing He spoke to me that really helped me was to "be Gabby." At first I was a little confused on this one, since this was something I was not very good at. As I pondered what He meant, it caused me to have to view myself outside of my own perspective, which was skewed. It was as if He were saying and having me say to myself, "What would a healed and whole Gabby look like and do in this situation? How would she think and feel, and act?" God is so wise. It worked! Little by little I was able to come out of the shadows of all the messages from people and myself, and the things the enemy had told me that were false.

During this time, another truth that He taught me was to focus on Him instead of how big this whole issue of shame was in my life. He wanted to come and knock down these walls I had built up around myself, and He did not have me do it in my own strength. He began to open up places in my heart that were so closed off, first, to Him and then to others. The truth came flooding into my mind and heart when I was feeling unsafe. So many times before getting together with someone or even going out in public, I would have anxiety. He slowly began to pry my little fingers off of what I held on to, to keep me safe. Hiding. He began to draw on the strings of my heart to hide in Him. He reminded me what His Word said about me and who He was. I was safe with Him. He also was so kind and gracious with me and showed me why I was having anxiety. He can handle it all: our strengths and weaknesses, all of us, all of where we have been and walked in this life.

Oh, I so love Him and want to see people set free. If I can, anybody can be free from the worst type of bondage and shame. If the worst thing that I feared happened—which was people seeing me and rejecting me—I would be able to handle that because of who He said I already was. Most of our fears are really just that, fears of what may happen but usually does not. Either way, if we are bound, we are bound. Let's not compare bondages; let's just get free!

I realized that even going in public at times would produce anxiety in me because I spent so much time hiding who I was. I did not grow up in an open atmosphere where I could be me. Some of that was due to my atmosphere and some was due to my deep-seated fear of others knowing me. My fear was that someone would see me, and I would have to face having to communicate with people. To open up. You have no idea how huge what He has me doing now in ministering and writing is. It is a miracle that I have anything to say and that I am able to do it. I really should not, by all human standards, be able to communicate very well at all. But God echoed the words of the first few verses in Ephesians that said I was already chosen and accepted. Oh, at first how far those words were from making it into my soul. They had to come by faith. This far into my healing I knew I could trust Him, but my soul was protesting.

Freedom and new ways of living do not come easily when that is all you have ever known. My soul had several fits! I just kept clinging to His Word and hiding in Him as He taught me how. How gracious He was, even when I fell down and just freaked out with anxiety around people. His gracious hand picked me back up and taught me how to continue walking in this new way of life. I was learning that freedom to be myself with people came out of my new freedom to be me with Him. Do we get that? Whatever measure of freedom we have before our Father is lived out in our relationships and our everyday life. I never made the connection until He taught me. I can literally say He taught me all I know! If we are struggling in anxiety and hiding from others, we probably have some lack of confidence in who we are before Him. He began to change me as I spent time with Him. Oh, we talked about my "people" issues a lot, but He began to again lift my eyes to something even higher. I am so glad the Holy Spirit comes to help us live out the new life Christ came to give us instead of allowing us to roll around in the mire of our old bondage! When I felt stuck at a certain level of the many layers He was uncovering, He would remind me of this. He is the one that kept these feet pressing on and my eyes lifted ever higher than what I was seeing and feeling at the time. He began to gently break me—the old me, so He could get the new me out. As I spent time in His glorious presence, my desires began to change.

As I beheld Him instead of just my past, I began to desire what He desired. I liken it to a dam breaking. Oh, the many, many times, I would lay broken in His presence in worship, in my prayer time, in my Bible time, or any time for that matter. I began to want what

He was allowing to bring Him glory and not to hide anymore. Let's just say that was a *biggie*! It was no longer about me and protecting myself but about Him being known and seen through me. If we lift our heads above the cloud that many of us walk under, we will see from His perspective too. The Holy Spirit wants to do this for us. In fact, He is the only one who can!

I began to desire for Him to have the glory that He so deserved as God, not just small amounts of glory but massive amounts. During these times of breaking we find ourselves moved in a way that will cause us to pray, say, or sing absolutely crazy things. We find ourselves and our hearts to be completely abandoned to Him and His will. This is what He wanted all along. Silly us and all the games we play before we get here! He does not just break us once but over and over again. When we break, He breaks. Watch out when He breaks something open! The dam that has been blocking the flow of His Spirit that dwells in us opens up. It overtakes us and all things around us. When this happens we are not the only ones that are changed.

I began to share more freely than ever about what He was doing in me at my church, with my family, with my friends, and just out with people. My perspective changed. I saw His face clearer and what He always had for me. I may not have seen it all and still do not, but I began to experience more of His freedom than ever before. I wanted Him to be glorified in my preaching, in my being a wife, a mother, and in how I shared Christ with the lost. I was able to hide myself in Him and find freedom. Loads of it. I was not just free to perform. I was free not to hide who I was from the one who made me. Learning to relax and just be me with Him and myself is one of the greatest gifts He has given me. That is true restoration! My hiding and protecting myself and keeping myself from expressing who He made heaped loads of problems on me. I began to see real change when He began to break the pride of just being concerned with myself more than Him and others.

When the dam breaks it splashes all over, all over the thirsty people all around us. Jesus lived like this every day of His life. Splashing all over thirsty people walking around looking for hope. He gave it to them, and so can we. We can do this when we stop living in the failures of our past. That will keep us pinned down in shame more than anything else. Let the Holy Spirit teach us how to walk in the new creation that we already are.

Another scripture that was so freeing to me is Psalm 34:5. It says, "Those who look to Him are radiant; their faces are never covered with shame" (NIV). I remember the day I saw this. It meant so much to me because I really had problem with people even seeing me, especially my face. It seemed like in my anxiety they were just too close and would surely reject me even if they saw me. I had to get over that one, too. How do we just get over stuff like this? I love that He does not just lead us around our bondage but literally *through it to* the other side. He wants to do such a thorough work in our hearts and minds that we never, ever go back into our old ways. He literally walked me through this verse. He showed me that when we look to others for our identity it will result in shame. People only have so much to give us. When He says those who look to Him will never be ashamed, He is talking about those who trust and literally rely on what He says about them more than their next breath. I had to do that. I was able to entrust all of my hopes, dreams, fears, and the deepest things in my heart to Him. I had to lay it all out before Him, just as David did in the verses before this one. He can handle it.

God is the only one who can handle it, by the way. I was looking to others to tell me who I was, and it resulted in defeat every time. When we truly know who we are, wanting positive affirmation is not always bad. Where we go wrong is when we entrust our identity to mere men. He taught me how to meditate on His Word when I was beginning to feel anxious. Specific words like this verse really helped me. I thought about them when I was in an anxious situation and even when I was not. I needed an overdose of His Word! When we look into His eyes, our eyes see something different. They see and feel His love for us. We come to know we can just sit back and relax in the strong, safe arms of our Daddy.

It may take a while, but like developing any new habit, it will come. Our old ways begin to fade, and we just realize we are making new choices. We are feeling different about ourselves and can just chill out a bit! As I surrendered my whole self to Him, He began to restore and tend to some areas that had never been tended to deep with in me. I saw myself being restored before my very eyes! Pretty amazing and encouraging, isn't it?

Psalm 91 was a beautiful thing for me to read during this time also. It speaks of our hiding place being in the shadow of His wings. See, we can hide—just in the right place. What this whole chapter is really saying is that He wants us to stick so close to Him that we are literally in His shadow. At least that is how I see it. That close to His heart, our ears up to His chest so we can hear all the lovely things He has to say about us. His words begin to cancel out the words of others and even of ourselves that are not true. He so wants us to take time to be this close to Him. Even for those who may have never been through traumatic things in your life, just living on planet Earth takes it out of us at times, does it not? We all need regular, fresh doses of hearing His heart for us.

As He was restoring me, I noticed that traits I saw in my daughters were coming out in me. Let me explain. I have two beautiful little princesses who love nothing more than to twirl and whirl and get everyone's attention—Mom, Dad, Grandma, Grandpa, strangers at the store. You get the point! They do not like it if people are not paying attention to them as they do all their girly things. (Oh, boys are like this, too. It just involves shooting, fighting, and blowing things up! They say, "Hey, dad, look what I just destroyed!" I am not sure I could handle all that! We have the whole drama thing going pretty good here, though. There are days I am not sure I can handle that, either.) I began to notice that for the first time in my life, I wanted to be seen. I wanted to be noticed, not just for what I could accomplish or how well I could perform, but for who I was. For someone who always lived to hide herself from the world, that felt so wrong. Maybe I was being prideful and needed to repent. Before I could head very far down that road at all, God stopped me in my tracks. He gently taught me that He was restoring to me the very thing that my little girls had inside of them. So many times, He has used them and their development to bring freedom and healing to me. He asked me if they were prideful or bad because they wanted people to look at them and to notice them. My response was, "No way!" But somehow, the enemy lied to me and told me I could never have that, the innocence of a child to just be who they are. To enjoy who they are and present that person to the world in confidence, not in pride.

May I just interject here that too many Christians are bound by this legalistic type of thinking. Here is a stronghold that is just waiting to be torn down by the blood of Christ. Somehow we feel so spiritual when we are walking with our heads down, shoulders slumped, feeling terrible about ourselves.

He began to speak some new things to me, very practical things, by the way. One was, *"Lift up your head."* I did a double take on that one, because that was something I had never heard in my life. Nobody had taught me how to physically walk with confidence. Oh, but my Daddy was going back and teaching me things I never learned. How beautiful is He? I know I must have said that a thousand times while writing this book, but I am sorry, He just is! I began lifting my head to Him in worship more and being more confident with Him. I was trusting in Christ in me more than the *me* in me. I did what Paul taught in Romans 6:19. I will paraphrase it for you: "Stop coming before God with all your junk, and come to Him in confidence of your righteousness." I hope that was a good enough paraphrase! I literally began to say, "Here I am, God, your righteous daughter!" What a change. The heavy coat of guilt and shame that I carried was gone and I was free. Little by little. These statements first came by faith and then were followed by how I lived with people. I began to lift my head up when I talked to people. I knew that God had made someone beautiful—someone that He did not make to hide. If I was hiding myself, I was hiding Him. He is that interwoven in us and us in Him. The Word says we are one spirit with Him. Yes, He is that close!

I had the revelation that the more I shared who I was and what He was doing in me through these circumstances, then the more glory He would get. That was my new desire. That was my new norm. To come to know that He actually wanted to use me to bring Him glory just blew my mind. I really had no frame of reference for that besides His Word. So I just went with it!

Writing this book and sharing all that He has done is another huge step in bringing Him glory through all He has done in me. I never imagined writing, actually. Or speaking. Or much of anything that put me "out there." It must be a result of some crazy prayer that I prayed that went something like this, "God, use me for your glory. Whatever you want and need to do in me and through me, do it." Be careful what you pray, or sing, for that matter!

As I began to tell people how He was fulfilling His Word by healing my feet and body, they began to glorify Him, too. That was weird—a good weird! It was, and still is, so humbling that God uses us to expand His kingdom and to cause people to see Him more clearly. He is still healing me and teaching me how to walk in greater levels of victory in this area. I believe the prophet Isaiah revealed the heart of our God when he recorded in Isaiah 43:7, "Everyone who is called by My name, Whom I have created for My glory; I have formed him, yes, I have made him." And again a few verses later in verses 10–13 he writes:

> "You are my witnesses," says the LORD, "And my servant whom I have chosen, That you may know and believe Me, And understand that I am He. Before Me there was no God formed, Nor shall there be after Me. I, even I, am the LORD. And besides Me there is no savior. I have declared and saved, I have proclaimed, And there was no foreign god among you; Therefore you are My witnesses," Says the LORD, "that I am God."

He is saying the same thing to us today that His mouth uttered thousands of years ago to the children of Israel. All of His works in us and around us testify that He is the one and only true God. He made us so we would reveal His glory to the world. So we could reveal who He is, His love, and the fact that He is God. He wants to do such a dramatic work of freedom in all of our lives that those around us are utterly astounded. He wants *us* to be utterly astounded—astounded that He would do something so great with us and our lives, things that will not only change us but our families, friends, neighbors, and even nations. He wants us to drop the false humility that is really shame and pride and lift up our heads long enough to see what He wants to do with us. He made us to carry His glory. Jesus made that possible.

Paul got a glimpse of the redemptive heart of God when He wrote, "Christ in you, the hope of glory" (Col. 1:27). Generations, angels, the saints who have gone before, the prophets who foretold of Christ all desired to see and experience what we have the awesome privilege to experience: Him in us, His glory shining through us. Wow, I have goose bumps just writing this! For any one of us who has been convinced that He has been ashamed of us like *we* have been ashamed of us, these verses just blow the top off of that pack of lies.

You see, the God of the universe made you so He can show off through you. I do not think God would be offended if I said He wants to show us off! Anyone who is a parent can certainly understand that. Let Him use every piece of your life to show Himself through. Jesus comes and makes this such a living reality in our lives. If we have been abused in any way, He causes us to walk in a new grace. We now can throw off the old feelings of unworthiness and walk in a new way. His grace in this area causes us to even walk differently. We hold our heads up, set our shoulders back, and know we are children of the King. If we are women, our femininity is restored, and we can know we are His beautiful daughters who display a part of Him that only we can. Men can walk with their heads high, revealing a strength and grace that a woman cannot. Together, we show the world a picture of who He is. Even the broken and fragmented pieces can be used by Him to make such a beautiful tapestry of grace. When others see you and me, they will see Him. In all His glory.

This is how He has come in and changed my heart and my desires. Let your Savior stoop down and wash your feet. Let Him wash all of you. In His humility, He will wash off all our shame and disgrace, all our need and desire to hide. He will lift off the heavy cloak we have worn for too long. In His beautiful humility He will never look down on you for what you have done or where you have lived. He just wants to lift us up. Let us humble ourselves before His throne of grace and let Him wash us. When we do, our eyes will meet the loving gaze of our Savior, who has been longing to look into the eyes He made. They no longer have to be lowered in shame, not before Him nor anyone else, beloved.

Here is a scripture to back up all I just said. It is such a beautiful nugget placed in 2 Samuel 22:36: "You give me your shield of victory; you stoop down to make me great" (NIV). Oh, wow. He actually wants to make us great. Yes, you. And me. His body.

Jesus humbled Himself and endured such shame and rejection from people so we do not have to live in that defeat. He stooped down out of the perfection of heaven to make us the people we were always meant to be. Can you think of anything greater? Can you think of anyone more humble and beautiful than He who would come and restore us to the beauty and glory He made us with? I cannot. Just knowing how much my Father believed in the person that He had made caused me to learn how to believe in myself. That was a first also! I began to believe that I—yes, I—could walk out who He made me to be and what He had made me to do.

My Father kept encouraging me as I would press on to find total freedom. We had some hard days together in learning how to express all He was doing in me and who I was. His loving gaze made it all worth it. He was the one that would literally keep me going. He taught me that the pain I was feeling during Him healing me was not the same type of pain that I felt from shame and from hiding. God often brings us back through the pain to get to the healing on the other side. When He is healing us there is hope of freedom that comes in mega doses as we let the Holy Spirit encourage and strengthen us. We also get to know Him so much more.

God seems to like to work in the process and not just in the answer. Ever notice that? In all the ways we have come to trust ourselves and our ways of surviving, He wants to teach us His ways, and that takes some time. Do not get discouraged if He seems to be taking more time than you would like as He restores you. Enjoy it. And yourself. If you were involved in a lot of trauma when you were in your developmental years, enjoy Him restoring parts of you that you have never seen. He has seen them all along and is rejoicing in your restoration!

As we close out this very personal chapter on my journey through the bondage to shame, let me leave you (and me) with a few beautiful reminders and promises from His Word on this subject. He knew where we lived and what we would face, so I am convinced He allowed these verses to be placed in the canon of His Word. After failing miserably at being God's chosen people and losing their inheritance (for a time) God gave some very precious promises in Isaiah 61 to the Israelites. Isaiah 61:7 says, "Instead of your shame you shall have double honor, And instead of confusion they shall rejoice in their portion. Therefore in their land they shall possess double; Everlasting joy shall be theirs." Oh, if you are in the middle of a battle with shame of any type for any reason, hold on to these words from *His* heart. They are real. He is faithful. I have seen Him not only restore what was lost to me but restore it even greater than I would have had before. He is just that good! He is so God!

I believe by reading this word, God gives those who have wrestled with shame a special place of honor, a seat at the head of the table, if you will. Oh, we do not have to worry about getting a big head over this one. We can walk humbly to the place of honor He has for us and sit down. When we look at the others seated around the table, we will have such joy and humility at this humble Servant who has placed us there. There will be no time for pride and arrogance, just joy. Our God ends Isaiah 61 chapter with the same thread as verse 7. Look at verse 10: "I will greatly rejoice in the LORD, My soul shall be joyful in my God; For He has clothed me with the garments of salvation, He has covered me with the robe of righteousness." Not only are we seated at the place of honor with Him, but we are covered with the robe dipped in blood that has made us clean. We can lift our heads up and enjoy all the good things He has placed on the plate before us. Our heart can rest and rejoice in all He has done for us!

CHAPTER 9
ALIVE IN CHRIST!

REMEMBER THE FIRST time I felt alive in Christ. He has resided in me since I received Him, and all the power that resurrected Him from the dead was in me; but it seemed buried. Sadly for me, I did not fully get it right when I got saved. I had so much hurt, guilt, and baggage that seemed to still affect me after receiving Christ. It took me a long time to believe that He actually saved me, because I grew up feeling like I had to earn everything and that nothing was just given to us because someone loved us. Oh, it took years for me to learn what grace was!

I vividly remember the first time that I realized that God Himself lived in me and that His power was mine. I was in my apartment at Christ for the Nations, and I felt alive inside. I could actually sense the power of the gospel alive on the inside of me. It was new and amazing to me. Going away to Bible college was truly one of the most life changing and best things that happened to me. God put so many things in my heart that I felt like I could explode! What I did not know then is that He planted many good things in my heart, spirit, and mind, but it would take many years to see it all come to pass.

You just have to understand how broken and hurting I was. The years after Bible college seemed to be great for me if you were looking on the outside, and in many ways they were. I met my husband, Andy, at college; we moved back to Oregon; got good jobs; found a good church; made friends; and even had our first baby. But inside I was still full of the same insecurities and fears

135

that I carried all my life. I do not believe that I was experiencing the life of Christ in me the way He intended.

Because of my past, the enemy was able to use some circumstances to reinforce the lies I believed about myself from childhood—that something was wrong with me and if people knew the real me, they would reject me. He used some people very close to me who I looked to for affirmation to add more rejection and pain in my life. Trust me in this: our biggest pain will come from people. The new life I began to experience at Bible college was being choked out by my past and my current circumstances. I did not know that this experience would cause me to spiral downward into more shame, hiding, fear, and a huge sense of reproach.

Often when we are spiraling down we do not even know how and when we started. We just know that the reality of our lives does not match what kind of life God promised us. Then comes more shame. The enemy loves to kick us when we are down and where we are weak. Remember those words, friends. He could not have defeated me for so long if there had not been a weak place in my life already. He loves to come in and prey on the weak, lonely, hurting, bruised, and vulnerable. We are easily defeated when we are too weak to lift our shield of faith, or do not even know what to have faith in. This is the place that his darts penetrate our soul— our mind, will, and emotions. Our spirit is safe. We are seated in heavenly places. Oh, if we could just realize that. Our enemy wants to keep us from that truth, the truth about who we already are in Christ. I did not know that I would be living in a pit of despair for so long, like, more than ten years. Really, it went back to the day I was born, but it came to a head during these ten years.

When we live that long in one place, we begin to make ourselves at home. We get comfy on the couch and kick our feet up. The problem is that God, our Redeemer, will not let us reside in any place but in His Son, Jesus Christ. God really surprised me by using my physically challenging circumstances and what was going on in my life to bring about the seeds of greatness that He planted in me when I first received Him and at Bible college.

I remember vividly the day at church that I began to feel alive in Christ again! It was a year into the time after my feet had really begun to hurt. In my spirit, I could sense His life. In the reality of my life, it was getting bigger too! I was in worship at church, and I felt like I could explode. It was not just an experience at church, though, because I was seeing Jesus take over my life. He was affecting my thinking and how I saw everything, especially myself. At church our pastor said that the difficult things we are going through are for His glory. I felt something break in me. I needed to break. I went up for prayer with our elder and his wife, who were dear friends of mine. I told them that I felt like I was dying and Christ was coming alive in me, and it felt so good! Oh, how we have been lied to, to think that surrendering to God is going to be terrible. It is the most freeing thing we could ever do! Suffering with fear, anxiety, and pain is hard. Letting go is great!

All of a sudden, it was like I began to understand that all I was going through was not about me and my problems but about God's plan and Him getting the glory. And here we are, and He is getting loads of glory! Trust me, on the other side of your pain it is worth it. He wants to assure you of that today. I would like to share with you a journal entry from a few days after that prayer time and breakthrough at church.

> I feel like I am dying and Christ is coming alive in me. I am coming to realize that I cannot, but Christ in me can do all things. Back in January after I stopped taking my ibuprofen and my inflammation came back really bad, I felt impressed to call Carrie and have her pray for my physical body. From that point on I turned a corner in how I viewed myself and my body. I realized who I am in Christ and that I can do all

things through Him that strengthens me. This is who I am. I was able to let a lot of the old go as a result of walking in my true identity. I feel like I want to explode with this new truth in me!

God was using my pain to show me His strength. I must have stopped taking the ibuprofen for a time because it bothered my stomach. It is weird, because I cannot remember those details now. None of the other medication worked, and I was frustrated. I am such a lightweight that narcotics and heavy pain medications were out of the question—especially when you have two little children to care for! I began to see Jesus more than I saw me. For heaven's sake, I did not need to come more alive to me; I needed to die and just let Jesus live through me! I began to realize that much of my life was about me. The *me* in me was beginning to die for real for the first time in my life. God was using my circumstances to show me that He was God and that He was God in me. It felt really good and clean, like my eyes were being turned upward to Him and outward to others. I had a sense that I was being cleansed inside and purified. It felt like such a beautiful thing, and I did not sense God's condemnation at all. That is one of the many, many things that I love about God. When He does a work in us, He does not condemn us!

This was the beginning of me breaking free from me. God was using the pain in my body to show me that my old resources of fear, anxiety, shame, and lack were just not going to cut it here. They could not and would not carry me through. I am not saying that we should deny our circumstances or cast aside wisdom when we need to make good decisions, but faith lifts our eyes up to who we are and whose we are.

After the day of writing in my journal above, I began to walk around the house declaring Philippians 4:13 with more conviction than I ever had: "I can do all things through Christ that strengthens me." The focus was on Christ and who He was in me more than ever. I realized that I was not a wimp or weakling but that the same power that raised Christ from the dead dwelt in me. For years, like I have mentioned before, I did not believe victory and an overcoming life could be mine. We are mistaken if we think our greatest enemy is Satan. Oh, he is a big one, but for many of us, we are our own greatest enemy. For the first time in a long time, I could see that Jesus was bigger than my problems. I guess the months to almost a year of looking desperately to Him were starting to pay off!

I have since learned that the greatest reward is Him. What He does in our lives is just an added benefit. To be able to spend time in His presence and know that He loves us to the core of our being is so awesome. To be able to bless Him back by just being with Him is what we are made for! Things were really beginning to change for me, and I was encouraged to see more of Him in my life. I was experiencing more peace and rest. I even had more peace about my physical circumstances because I could see Him working and got a sense that He wanted to use it to do a work in me and to bless others.

This was all encouraging to me. He knew that I needed encouragement, because there was a lot more work to be done in me. God was laying such a good foundation of His love and security for me that the rest of the work that He wanted to do would be built on that foundation. I feared Him more and was made more aware of His presence. I was truly coming alive in Him and was realizing all that Jesus did for me and who He was in me.

Coming alive to who we are in Christ never stops. At least, it should not. With respect to many, many of the things He has taught me, He just continues to reveal and work with me on a deeper level. He is bringing even more freedom. Just today, a little over seven years into this journey, I was out on my patio early enjoying the coolness of the summer morning. I began writing out of some more freedom He is bringing me. He is speaking more and more about who He is, what He has done, and who that makes me—actually, who that *has made* me. Beloved, He sees us as we already are in Christ, not just who we think we will be someday. I was surrounded by my beautiful flowers and I heard the sound of the neighbors' pond. What I heard even more than that was what He was thinking of me. My Bible was open to 2 Corinthians 5:14–17 (NIV), which says:

> For Christ's love compels us, because we are convinced that one died for all, and therefore all died. And He died for all, that those who live should no longer live for themselves, but for Him who died for them and rose again. So from now on we regard no one from a worldly point of view. Though we once regarded Christ in this way, we do so no longer. Therefore, if anyone is in Christ, he is a new creation, old things have passed away and all things have become new!

In some of the same areas He made me realize who I am to Him, He is bringing those truths to a deeper level and causing me to walk in more and more victory. There have been times when the truth about who I am in Christ has come little by little and other times that it has seemed explosive on the inside of me. Today, like the day in my apartment at Bible college and the day at church, was explosive!

I had to let go of some more ways that I perceive myself that do not match up with this passage of scripture. Haven't you noticed that we keep trying to obtain something that has already been freely given to us? Silly little things that we are! God and I have been going around on a few things that I would like to keep holding on to and that He definitely wants me to let go of. So this morning, on my patio, I let go. How did I do it? Well, His Spirit is so gracious in letting me and us know how He already sees us. He specifically spoke to me through this passage this morning. So whatever belief system I have had that does not fit into this had to go. Oh, He has been working on it for a while, but the layers just keep coming off. They keep coming off as I realize what He has already done for me and in me and when I realize how He sees me (and that it is not how I often see myself).

Paul had such a beautiful revelation of this. He may not have been at the crucifixion with the rest of the apostles, but God so burned it on his heart and in his spirit that he may as well have been. He got what was accomplished at the cross. The Holy Spirit is amazing, isn't He? He can take something and make it so real to us. So Paul was able to see two things here. He saw a bunch of dead people. He also saw a bunch of alive people as well, people fully alive in Christ. We would do well to let the Holy Spirit show us both, that we are both dead and alive. Through my trials, I have been blessed to have my eyes opened to what is dead in me and what is alive. The old, sinful me that has been so used to living in shame and fear and any other self-torment is dead. I am alive to all the beautiful things God has to say that I am because of Christ.

My problem, and if you are honest, your problem, is that it is difficult to let go. We have this weird fear that if we let go of the old we will not know what to hang on to. I can relate. What He has also taught me is that He will never ask us to let go of something and not have something so much better for us to grab hold of. We may be used to people taking and taking from us, but God does all things for our good. What a beautiful tradeoff: He gets all our junk, and we get all His riches. That is really what grace is, isn't it?

During the time my body was racked with so much pain, the verses of 2 Corinthians 12:7–10 rang loudly in my spirit.

> And lest I should be exalted above measure by the abundance of the revelations, a thorn in the flesh was given to me, a messenger of Satan to buffet me, lest I be exalted above measure. Concerning this thing I pleaded with the Lord three times that it might depart from me. And He said to me, "My grace

is sufficient for you, for My strength is made perfect in weakness." Therefore most gladly I will rather boast in my infirmities, that the power of Christ may rest upon me. Therefore I take pleasure in infirmities, in reproaches, in needs, in persecutions, in distresses, for Christ's sake. For when I am weak, then I am strong.

These were the very truths that I began to live by out of the deepest places in my heart. I began to see how weak I was on my own, but by relying on Him, I was amazingly strong! Not only did I see how weak I was in body but also in my mind and emotions. Good thing that is not the only thing I saw. There is nothing like some good trials to show us what we are made of—good and bad! They really give God a chance to show off His power, though. I love it!

Again, little by little, being a conqueror became my identity. I discovered that I was an overcomer because He is an overcomer. By the way, these words were never in my vocabulary before. They were always in His. This is how He had seen me all along. Now I was getting to see it. And live it. And feel it. That is what coming alive is, dear ones!

That is what grace is. Grace is not Jesus just saving us from sin. Oh, it is that, but it is so much more. Grace is the power of God given to us to do what we need to do. At the time, my physical infirmities were being left in place to show me His overcoming power in me. His grace gave me the ability to walk out those days without losing my mind and to overcome. The same grace has touched this body to make it whole. As I began to think like the new me, I began to act like the new me and even feel like the new me. His grace is what enables us to let the old go, everything that does not fit into what His Word and Spirit say that we are. It is like we begin to wake up from a long, deep sleep and say to ourselves, "What on Earth have I been doing all this time?"

That is how it was with me. I would be walking around as the

Spirit was awakening me to Him and ask myself that very question. God would not allow me to walk in the new unless I first chose to let go of the old. We cannot walk in both at the same time. I began to catch on (not so quickly all the time) that if He was nudging my heart to let something go—some idea of who I was that He made aware that He did not agree with—I knew something way more amazing was heading my way. The trust that my Father and I had built by now had grown by leaps and bounds, so letting go began to be easier.

You know what? During this time, I saw my body heal more and more. Little by little. Layer by layer. Carrying around a dead person for all those years after Christ had made me alive took its toll on my body, especially on my back. Carrying around a dead person is just plain heavy and tiring! So many times we look at ourselves and identify with the person who died when Christ died on the cross. We look at and rock back and forth on the rocking chair of guilt and shame and regret, just rocking back and forth to all the stupid things we have done in this life. I am glad that on that day at Calvary Jesus chose a wooden cross over a wooden rocking chair, how about you? The cross destroyed all our sins and mistakes.

If this message is new to you or if you have never heard that if you're a Christian, you are alive, it would be good for you to get around some more good teaching on who you are in Christ. Get hold of some good Bible studies and open the Word for yourself. Ask the Holy Spirit to show you who you are in Christ. That prayer will not go unanswered. Surround yourself with people who know who Christ has made them to be and let them rub off on you! I am forever grateful for what He has allowed in my life so I could see the real me—the *me* He had seen all along! Seeing ourselves as He sees us affects everything in our lives, including our calling. What He has made us to do will be affected and even missed if we do not understand these truths.

One of the cool things that began to happen to me as a result of becoming aware of who He was in me was the ability to overcome my feelings of guilt and having a guilty conscience. I used to so identify with being wrong or guilty all the time, even when I had not done anything wrong. False guilt sometimes seems worse than true guilt. At least if you did something wrong for real, you can pinpoint it. With false guilt there is just always this vague feeling that you have done something wrong, but are not really sure. Well, as I was continuing to confess the Word out loud and believe who I really was in Him and who He was in me, I could overcome those attacks of guilt easier, and they would last for less and less time. I began to feel more confident and powerful as a person. There is just something that happens to your confidence when you always feel like you are doing something wrong or just not quite measuring up. Now, I was coming to realize that the One who did measure up just perfectly was living in me. When Satan would accuse me or when my own soul would go back into accusation mode, I would confidently declare, "I am the righteousness of God in Christ," or, " I am dead to sin and alive to God in Christ Jesus, my Lord." That will shut the enemy up pretty fast. He knows when we believe it for real.

For the first time in my life I felt clean. Oh, to feel clean after feeling ashamed and dirty all of your life! How utterly cleansing His blood is! How utterly freeing it is to believe that He is enough! Yes, I was truly coming alive to Him and in Him and for Him. It felt wonderful! It really is not all that hard to shake off the old stuff and the dead stuff when we gaze on Him and let Him lift our eyes onto who we really are in Him. When His Spirit is able to make us fully alive in Him, the old stuff just seems to fall off. We just like to roll around in the mire for a little while.

As important as coming alive to who we are in Christ is, there is another aspect that I feel like God showed me and taught me about, an aspect that sometimes as Christians we seem to neglect: coming alive to who we are as people. By that I mean seeing who God made us in every area of our lives, not just spiritually. Yes, Christ in us and our spiritual life is the most important part of us, but it is not the only part of us. What are the other things that make up *us*? What do we enjoy doing? What are our interests and talents? God certainly sees all of those things and cares about them. What just makes us tick? Do we love to cook, paint, or enjoy outdoor adventures? There are so many other aspects that make up who we are, so much more color to our personalities. As He was restoring me, He began to restore other things that had been lost in the craziness of my life. He will do that for all of us. New desires and old desires began to arise within my heart. I have always been crafty and creative in one way or another. I love to decorate my home and make things for it. I love to paint and rearrange, then rearrange some more. Any sisters with me, out there? My husband hates it. He says, "Can't you just leave it where it is at?" No, I cannot! My girls have the same streak running through them. They love to organize. Sometimes, if they have been away at a friend's house overnight or just away from the house for a longer length of time, they come home and start organizing. Most kids just want to come home and relax. Mine want to organize and decorate. Watch out, honey!

So as He was healing me, I began to decorate more, paint my walls all kinds of pretty colors, and spray paint anything that was not nailed down! Even being able to do things like paint the room and bathrooms by myself gave me so much joy! When I was coming out of the worst pain and could not stand to look at my white walls anymore, I went and bought a gallon of paint. I sat in my chair and painted a small little place on my wall. I wanted to paint my kitchen so badly that I took my lawn chair and placed it on a big counter we have. I sat in that and painted as much as I could reach, then I stood and painted for a little bit. Looking back now, I am lucky my chair did not fall off the island and break my neck. That would be another book! As I was able to handle more, I would stand for fifteen to twenty minutes and paint. Oh, I felt like I had just accomplished a huge feat!

Then, I gave my husband those puppy dog eyes and asked, "Will you help me paint?" He hates painting, by the way, but loves me, so he gave in. He could not stand looking at all the splotches of paint on the wall, as he calls them! He only gave in until he knew I could do it on my own! Right now, my girls and I (not my hubby) are painting their room lime green. Electric, lime green. Wow is right! Being able to fix up our home and decorate and, yes, redecorate gives me so much joy after not being able to do it for so long.

Another way that He restored me was by giving me the gift to bake. I had never really taken any classes other than a cake decorating class after my oldest daughter was born just to get out of the house. All of a sudden I discovered that I was really good at baking. People began asking if I would bake their pies, cupcakes, and cakes for money. This was a good way for me to use my creativity and to make some extra spending money. A few years ago my mother-in-law entered me in a pie-baking contest as a local historical event, and I won first place! They placed my pie recipe on our city's best restaurant menus! The girls and I went there for dessert, and they proudly announced that I was the one who won the pie contest. My girls were so proud of their mom!

It was really a beautiful thing to see parts of me come out that I never even knew were there. He had put so much creativity in me, but all the years of living in shame and bondage just seemed to bury them. He sees all the things that make us up as a person and so longs to redeem them all. He does not want anything to go unused or to go to waste.

What things are in you that your Father is longing to bring to the surface? Oh, they have been there all the time but just need freedom to be expressed.

Writing this book has been a huge, yes, huge, avenue for me to express my creativity and passion. Yes, it is work, but I love it and am almost always looking for a time to get away and write, especially after a long day at home with the kids this summer. Getting out to write equals a coffee shop and something sweet to eat!

I believe there is so much potential buried in all of us. So much passion. I am a passionate person, but it was buried under all the heaviness before. Now, I am freer than ever to express the passion that God has placed in my heart. I see this not only in my worship to Him but in sharing Him. There are so many more things that He has for us than we can even see or imagine are inside of us. He has seen them all the time. He wants to heal us so those parts of us are able to function as they were meant to. If we get so much joy out of discovering more parts of us, think about how much joy *He* gets in seeing what He placed in us used and discovered. God loves watching us and seeing the joy and amazement in our hearts as we do something new, even if we are not very good at it yet. He enjoys the process, and we should, too!

As much freedom as He has brought me into, He keeps speaking that there is so much more. My husband and I were talking last night, and I told him how I felt like there was so much of this book that I could not write until now. He knew that some parts of me, especially how I express myself, have not been freed up until lately to share all I have and in the way that I have. Even since the beginning of this book my ability and creativity to write have grown. That is the reality of coming alive to Him!

It really is sad that so many of the facets of His greatness that He placed within us go unused. They go undiscovered. Beloved, God wants us alive. Fully alive. Fully alive to Him. Fully alive within ourselves. Fully alive to be a blessing and bring life to others through how we express ourselves. God desires to uncover the buried treasures in all of us and use their riches to bless Him, ourselves, and others.

I remember when I began to laugh again. He gave me a pretty good sense of humor, and I can find humor in most things. Some things are so stupid and simple, but they make me laugh! When I was in the worst of my bondage, I was not laughing as much as I used to. Oh, I laughed, but I could not just cut up like I did before. My husband noticed as my journey progressed that I was laughing more. I was lighter. Getting rid of a lot of pain and heaviness made me much more lighthearted. Before, everything or most everything was so heavy. Now I cannot stand that. If I start going down that road, it is not very long before the Holy Spirit and I make a U-turn! His words in Isaiah 61:3 are so true: "He gives us the garment of praise for the spirit of heaviness!" (author's paraphrase). So you see, He wants all parts of us to be restored and redeemed—*and enjoyed*. All the work He does in us is so that we can enjoy the abundant life He came to give us (John 10:10).

Abundant life is so much more than church on Sunday morning and sitting around reading our Bible all the time. Oh, I love both of these things, but He came so that all of our life would be fulfilling. He wants others to enjoy the awesome things that He has done in us. I was only able to do that when He broke the chains of living to please others. Only by awakening to Him and His desires was I truly free. His face was bigger in my mind and my heart than anyone else. There is nothing more beautiful than coming alive in Christ, truly alive, where nothing else matters. He wants us to come alive in all the areas that make up who we are—body, soul, and spirit.

Our body does not get to escape the plan of awakening us to Him and to life. Oh, He is life. As we experience more of His life inside of us, it will flow through us. It has to touch our body as the power and life of the risen Christ comes forth. Lazarus being raised from the dead was just the result of being around life, being touched and commanded to come forth by life. Jesus was and still is that life. During the time He was healing my feet they still hurt. I was frustrated and asked Him and wondered to myself how long my feet would hurt for. I could see them getting better and changing all the time, but they still hurt. He gave me a dream. In the dream I was shopping (love it!), and I was pushing the cart. I saw myself, and I was not tired, nor did I have to sit down to rest my aching and tired feet. It was like He was giving me a vision of the life He was leading me into. I woke up from the dream encouraged and have seen that truly come to pass. I remember when my feet stopped hurting all the time. My mind went back to that dream. He was giving me the encouragement and strength I needed for the long haul. What He was doing in my soul and spirit were affecting my body. My body was coming alive to His power, just as Lazarus' body had to—yes, had to—respond to the power of life contained in the very words Jesus spoke as He said, "Lazarus, come forth!" His body could not remain lifeless and in that grave. Neither can ours! He died so we can be alive. Death had to submit to life!

He wants us to be fully alive to be the people He made us to be, fully alive to be able to express the beauty and glory that He created us with. Let's let Him breathe His life into us! Let's open our hearts and let Him make us fully alive to Him so that we can display all the beauty and color and depth of who He has made us to be. Our personalities are filled with so much more than many of us or others get to ever see. God Himself wants to awaken them and bring them to life. Our lives are meant to be awe-inspiring in displaying all of the unique ways that He has fashioned and formed us.

CHAPTER 10

HEAVENLY KALEIDOSCOPE

O NE OF THE most beautiful senses that God has given us is the ability to see. Oh, to see the sunrise in the morning in all of it's glory! It is there, just waiting to begin a new day. To see our children running and playing through fields of flowers and picking the perfect one just for us. To see them hit their first home run. To see our newborns' fresh, sweet little selves as they are cradled on our chests for the first time. Oh, to see is such a beautiful thing, isn't it?

When we become Christians, we also get a new set of eyes. Paul refers to them as the eyes of our heart in Ephesians 1:18 (NIV). Natural eyesight is truly a gift from God, but so is what God calls spiritual eyesight. These are the eyes God has given us to see Him, ourselves, others, and to live through His eyes. We actually get to see what God sees. Whoa! I often think of what God sees. Our family went camping last weekend, and the stars that began to come into view just before the sky turned pitch black were nothing short of amazing with a capital *A*! As I grabbed my husband and kids we talked about how God made all of what we were taking in. It was overwhelming! If what I was seeing was my view, what in the world is His view? Yikes. He sees every star and planet and galaxy from close up. Like, from way close up! He knows where everyone is located and could tell all of us in a split second. He does not need a telescope. Standing there looking up at those stars until I had a crick in my neck was worth it. Then I thought more of something that has been rolling around in my head for a while, something that He has been planting in my spirit for quite some time now. God grants us the ability to see what He sees. We may not be able to handle the fullness of it all at once, but as we grow in Him, we see more and more glimpses. Beautiful, isn't it?

Writing this book has been a gift to me. As I have said in other places in this work, God calls us to do things that will continue to work His purposes out in us. As I began this book I shared about the physical circumstances that propelled me into this season of healing. I thought I would mainly focus on that and not share too many other details of my life and what it was like growing up. That apparently was not His purpose for many reasons. One was for the very thing that we are talking about now: seeing clearly, seeing what He sees. Even after all the healing He has brought me, there were still some things that I was not seeing the way He wanted me to. He wanted to give me a new perspective about my life as I wrote about it. You have no idea how amazing it is to sit behind a computer or with your journal and begin writing as God gives you eyes to see what was truly happening all your life. It has been a gift to me. Thank you for being a part of God healing me, even now! It is such an honor to write and walk this life out alongside you all!

I would like to share about one particular area through which God has given me a new perspective about my life. It has to do with shame, because it was so prominent in my life. I just had to be broken free layer by layer. More layers have been coming off lately as I have been writing. My personality wants to just flat out get things done. So when I set out to write this book, getting it done was high on my list. Obviously giving you more than a few chapters to read was important to me. Having this work be excellent is really important too. However, as I was writing and as He is still using some things in my life to change me, He had more for me. He began leading me to share more about myself than I ever have. That led me to see things in a whole new perspective. He is causing me to see things about myself that I have never known. So, some of the things I share are new to both of us! Especially as I was writing about freedom from shame, He drove some things home to me. I could not believe that I was seeing things about myself and growing up for the very first time. Oh, it was me who experienced them, but part of my brain was still stuck in the past. I was still seeing it with blurry vision.

He showed me with many of the individual things I shared about myself in that chapter the truth behind each time I felt ashamed. He showed me that there was not something wrong with me, but that many, many things about life were not taught to me or modeled. I realize that sometimes I still enter situations that I feel like I am inadequate to handle, and He is reminding me of the reality of what was missing in my life that causes me to feel this way. There were just some beneficial and important things that I did not get to learn or experience, not only in the very early years of my life but into adolescence and adulthood. There was information about just living life and the basics of day to day life that I did not come to understand until much later. It took me a long time to understand that this lack of knowledge was not my fault, and in the process I have come to rely more and more on the Holy Spirit to help fill in the gaps, even today. That left me feeling like I was missing something and that something was wrong with me.

While much of the shame had been healed, writing this book has taken me to a whole new level of wholeness. It has been because He has opened my eyes to see my life more clearly. Now, as I am going through my day, He gently reminds me when I begin to feel insecure in an area that I never learned that particular thing before. Talk about taking the load off. I see that in so many other areas where I have felt inadequate. Seeing the truth has a way of taking loads off our shoulders. He does this while not condemning those who did not give us what we needed. He is awesome and so kind!

One of the things He spoke to me about the shame I lived in is that, as I shared, I looked my body as a young girl and did not like what I saw, not only because of my lack of Him in my life but my lack of nurture and care on a parental level. Oh, my mother was there, but we never really had talks about my changing body and what that meant. I felt at a disadvantage, and the feeling of shame was heaped on the pile I was carrying more and more. God has used writing about those times—which He would not let me pass over—to show me that the problem really was not because there was something wrong with me. Like I said, part of me knew that already, but He wanted to reinforce it. He has not only been faithful to give me a new perspective but to also come alongside me and to make up for the things that I did not have growing up. He truly has been a Father in every sense of the word to me. He is teaching me the day-to-day basics of living. He is teaching me how to be a wife, mother, friend, and minister. He truly does stoop down from heaven to make us great! I am so thankful He did not let me pass over all the things that I have written about my life.

Letting Him continue to heal my soul is bringing the health and strength back to my physical body. I am stronger and more healed today than I have been in years. He truly is bearing the weight of all that I thought I had to carry in this life. He truly is tending to the very areas in me that were never tended to. And He truly is making my body whole, the more and more I experience His love. You see, sickness, disease, and pain cannot stay in the presence of perfect love, in the presence of perfection. He is that presence. Here is my prescription for healing in any sense: just let Him love all over you. Let Him be your all in all. There is so much healing for all of us in His presence! He is continuing to give me new perspective. He is not only letting me see myself more clearly but to see Him more clearly. That really is what this journey for me has been about. Seeing Him. Knowing Him. Oh, and loving Him!

I love those long tubes that you look through called kaleidoscopes and the many images come up through them! When God sees us, the image that comes up in what I call the heavenly kaleidoscope is Jesus! Wow, for some of us that takes a lot of faith to believe that. I have gone through a season recently where I realized that at times I see myself the way God sees me, and then at other times I struggle to see who I really am. My soul seems to want to take over, and I live under a weight. Oh, I have grown so much in this area, but we are all still growing! As I went to the Father and asked Him about this, He seemed to speak to my heart the scripture in 2 Corinthians 3:18, "But we all with unveiled face, beholding as in a mirror the glory of the Lord, are being transformed into the same image from glory to glory, just as by the Spirit of the Lord." He whispered to my heart and spirit words I desperately needed to hear: *"You* are *being changed, look how far you have come!"* There I was, almost in the hook of shame and guilt again, and my Father came rushing to my side to save me from the enemy's grip! That is why I love Him so. He just keeps on saving us, and we have to let Him! I understood what He meant in that verse: the more we keep beholding Jesus, the more we in reality become like Him!

Back to the kaleidoscope. When God sees us, if we have accepted Christ, He sees the image of Jesus through and through. Every facet of the image in the kaleidoscope is Jesus. Every color, every angle. Any way you turn it or point it, there He is! He sees purity, righteousness, love, holiness, and all the other astounding things that make up who Christ is. If 2 Corinthians 5:17 is really true—that we are a new creation—why do we not see it? Why do we look in the kaleidoscope and see maybe one or two images of Jesus, and the rest are our problems, failures, sins, etc.? I hear the protests now: "But I *do*, do all these things. I do have weaknesses and problems in my life. Does God really not see that? Is He blind to that?" We have got to go to the Word for this one. Second Corinthians 5:16–17 says it plainly, but we have a hard time swallowing it.

> Therefore, from now on, we regard no one according to the flesh. Even though we have known Christ according to the flesh, yet now we know Him thus no longer. Therefore if anyone is in Christ, he is a new creation; old things have passed away; behold, all things have become new.

There it is in black and white. Wait—there it is in red. His blood. His very life was given for us so we do not have to live according the old man, the dead man of sin. We still very much identify with this old man because this is what we see when we look in the kaleidoscope. We need a new one to look through! God is waiting with a new one in His open hands right now. Will we take it?

Why can He look and see something very different from us? Because He operates in pure truth and reality. We think we do. We think we see, but He really sees! His view is the only correct one because nothing is blocking His view. How do we close this gap? How can we look in the tube and see the image of Jesus over our lives? By faith. By spending time with Him. By looking at Him.

Let's get what it means to look at Him. It is not like He is walking around here on planet Earth in flesh and blood anymore. We see Him when we read the Bible and let what He is saying speak to what is going on in our lives. We see Him when we sing a song to Him and the Holy Spirit opens the eyes of our heart to the One who is worthy of our every breath. When He whispers, "I love you," and we believe it, that, my dear ones, is when we see Him! Everything in His kingdom operates in faith—faith that is based on truth. His Word is true through and through. Everything He says is as pure as it gets!

We have to believe what 2 Corinthians 5:16–17 says. Paul was able to grasp it by revelation, and so are we. God is no respecter of persons! Had Paul always been perfect? Far from it, my dear! He actually murdered Christians and was fighting against Christ. Sounds like something changed His view of himself, or there is no way that he would be able to pen such beautiful revelations of who we are in Christ. Some may argue that at the time of this writing that Paul pretty much had it all together. He would say otherwise about himself in Philippians 3:12: "Not that I have already attained, or am already perfected; but I press on that I may lay hold of that which Christ Jesus has also laid hold of me." So since Paul had not arrived and was not perfect as he was writing this, there must have been something else going on in his head. Yes. He had seen Jesus. He looked through that heavenly kaleidoscope by faith and decided to believe God over the things he had done and even was still doing that were not perfect.

God wants us to know that when we accept His Son we are no longer in the flesh. What does that mean? It means that part of us is dead. I hear the protests again! But I just yelled at my kids or ate too much chocolate; surely that is the flesh. You are right, it is. Take a good, long look at the Book of Romans, where again Paul says through revelation of the Holy Spirit that we are dead to sin. Romans 6:11 says, "Likewise you also, reckon [consider] yourselves to be dead indeed to sin, but alive to God in Christ Jesus our Lord."

Back to faith. I actually like the word *belief*. If we really just flat out believed His Word and what He says about us, our actions and lives would dramatically change! We would start acting like the Word says a Christian should act. Our soul is the hurdle. It is what blocks us from seeing the perfect image of Christ in all the facets and images of the kaleidoscope. May we truly repent for believing ourselves and wounded souls over His Word. He came and did it all. Our sin nature was nailed to the cross along with all our sin and shame. Let us repent for making it all about us and not about what He has already done. Remember the words, "It is finished" (John 19:30). It really is finished. Let us stop regarding and looking at ourselves through the eyes of the flesh.

Remember back to the beautiful words Jesus spoke to me through my dear friend, *"The work is done, but I have allowed her circumstances so she will learn to let go."* Yes, letting go sometimes does not come easy, but He makes it possible. I am living proof of that! Look at 2 Corinthians 3:18.

> But we all, with unveiled face, beholding as in a mirror the glory of the Lord, are being transformed into the same image from glory to glory, just as by the Spirit of the Lord.

I love the "unveiled face" part! Nothing stands between Jesus and us. Sometimes we stand in the way, and He is still able to overcome that. When I see something other than Jesus over my life, I am still in the way. But there is grace and mercy. That day when I asked God to help me see who I really am all the time, He answered back the part of the scripture above that says "from glory to glory." That is really what had been happening in my life. The reality of my life was that I was being changed from glory to glory. I was entering into another glory.

OK, head out of the clouds! I hear some of you asking, What the heck does that mean? It means we are in our everyday lives changed little by little until we in our experience look like the Jesus. Because of what He has done in our lives we talk more like Jesus and love more like Jesus. Oh, and for heaven's sake, we are more patient like Jesus!

The Word says that God already sees us as new creations in Christ because that is what we are. He sees according to the truth. We often see because of how we feel. God is asking us to have faith that what He says is true no matter what we see. He is asking us to look through the heavenly kaleidoscope and see what He already sees. We have to see it by faith. The more we see it by faith, the more we will see it as a reality in our lives. We will talk like Jesus, we will love like Him, and we will obey like Him the more we believe that is who we already are. That was the message that God was trying to help me understand. I have to trust that I am a new creation and that old things have passed away and were nailed to the cross. I have to let go of the old me daily, as will you too. I have to realize the truth: I am a different person than a year ago, even a month ago. I am learning to celebrate that instead of just looking at how far I have to go.

As we behold Christ we become like the One we behold. As we spend time in His presence, read His Word, and let Him dwell in our midst, we are changed. My Father reminded me not to be so hard on myself or to believe the lies of the enemy, who says I am not any different than before because of how I feel. God is so much bigger than how we feel. And thank goodness, or we would serve a wimpy, wishy-washy God. Not so! As we trust in Him and what He says about us, we do become different.

My Father reminded me that day that I had changed. I had become more like Jesus. I looked more like Him, sounded more like Him, and had faith in My Father more like Him. I was being changed from glory to glory. The glory is when we see the change and experience all God has been doing in our lives between "glories"! The in-between is not fun, and sometimes we feel like we are going backward. If we are truly abiding in Christ, those times are so crucial to experiencing the glory of Christ. The victory, healing, and Christlikeness all come from our trials and purifying in those in-between times. Do not lose heart if you feel like God had been working in your life and you do not yet see the fruit or the glory or the result. Your heavenly Father wants to remind you like He did me that day that He is so proud of you. You are being changed from glory to glory. Cling to Him in those in-between-glory times! He allows us to experience times when we do not see so much progress in the natural so that we trust in Him and not in ourselves to change us.

He wants us to depend on Him so much. He also wants us look through that heavenly kaleidoscope and see Jesus. He wants every angle of our hearts and minds to be completely wrapped up in who He is; every view tainted with the vibrant colors of His love, grace, and mercy; every shape of our lives in the shape of the image of Christ. He sees it. Scoot in close next to your Father. He has an amazing view to show you of yourself. Let Him hand you the kaleidoscope and show you what He sees. What He has always seen. Let yourself drift away and be amazed. When you step away, may the image of Christ stay imprinted on your heart and mind, dear ones!

CHAPTER 11

FREE TO LOVE

Jesus said to him, "You shall love the LORD your God with all your heart, with all your soul, and with all your mind." This is the first and great commandment. And the second is like it: "You shall love your neighbor as yourself." On these two commandments hang all the Law and the Prophets.
—MATTHEW 22:37–40

OW. SIT BACK and meditate on that passage for a while. Every law (which are many) and every ounce of ink that was used by so many inspired writers of the Bible, and it all comes down to one thing—love! Jesus steps on the scene and comes to show us the way to fulfill it all. Love. We could say that love came to fulfill it all! Jesus did not come just to show us another way. He is the way. He showed us the way to love. I actually like to be a bit more passionate about it: He broke us free to love—to love Him, to love ourselves, and to love others. He broke us free to be like Him. Trust me, that day on the cross, and after His blood was applied to the mercy seat, it was all over, the war between God and man, man and man, and the war against ourselves. We just have to believe that it is already done. We also need to learn how to live it out. That is the fun part!

You see, the 1 John 4:16 says—along with the rest of the Bible—that God is love. It does not say *that* He loves, although He does; it says He *is* love. He defines love, and love defines Him. If you find your way all around and through the reality of what love is, you will find Him. Isn't He beautiful? Isn't He what we have longing for

161

all our lives? Yes and yes! God made us in His image, so love has to be the thing that defines who we are more than anything else. Keeping the commandment to love occasionally is not why Jesus had to come; bringing God, who is love, to live on the inside of us is. Wow, God and love, love and God live in us! So it is possible to love.

He is continually working in us to remove any and all blockages to that love flowing to us purely, flowing through us purely, and flowing to others in the same way. This Christian journey is not just a religion but living out the reality of God Himself loving us so much and wanting to be so close to us that He decided to come and live on the inside of us through His Spirit. He does not get much closer than that! He cannot help but love His creation, because that is who He is.

I believe there is such an immense and intense amount of love that makes up who God is that our minds cannot handle it. One day we will see Him face to face and fall down before love. We will see Him in all His fullness, and we will be able to handle it (1 John 3:2). Until then, one of His beloved apostles says in 1 John 3:3 that "everyone who has this hope in Him purifies himself, just as He is pure." So there we have it—our mission. To purify ourselves by letting Him work anything out of our lives that is not perfect, anything that is not love. Boy, He has a lot of work to do!

I love the fact that the apostle John in his writings teaches us so much about love, don't you? Where did He get that revelation? Where did he get the insight into God being love, His loving us, and our loving others? Of course, straight from the throne, but let's consider something else. On Earth, he walked with Love. He talked with Love. He got to physically handle Love, and He ate breakfast by the shore with Love. Yes, that Love is Jesus!

Here is something that I wrote one day while in my special spot out in the country where I spend time with the Lord:

"The Depth of Christ's Love"

Look into the face of one who has known
The love of God that He was shown.
He was an ordinary man like you and me.
He followed Christ, and He set him free.
He leaned against Christ's chest and heard God's heart beat.
The very blood that ran through God's veins,
It showed this man that our God reigns.
It changed his life and shook him upside down.
He was more than a man from Bethlehem town.
This man followed Him even unto death,
And now this man sees Him face to face.
The gates have opened to the fullness of grace.
The path God had for him, He has for us, too.
I want to follow Him. How about you?

This is something that I wrote about the apostle John as I was reading the Book of 1 John. I absolutely love those chapters. They are so full of the truth about the love of God. As I was meditating on the Word, I realized how much more John wrote about the love of God. The Book of John is just full of references to God's love for us and our loving Him.

The best way to share God's love with others is to be with love, to hang around love. Remember, Jesus was the fullness of God here on Earth. God was not content to stay in heaven, where mankind could not grasp the fullness of who He was and is, so love came to show us love. Kind of crazy, huh?

As I was pondering the guy who wrote all these passages, I realized why he could write so confidently about it. In 1 John 3:1, John has what I call an oh-my-gosh moment. He is in the middle of teaching about truth, and He just breaks out in to this praise of the God who loves us so much that He makes us His children. If we use our imagination, it is almost like he cannot contain the reality of what he has come to know about God. He spent three and a half years on planet Earth with Him. Those three and a half years turned into a lifetime of not only following love but overflowing with the love of God. It is as if Jesus was saying, "OK, this guy gets it. Let's put it in the book!" Jesus wants more than religious duty from us. He wants us to get it, to know for ourselves this endless love of God and then to go out and overflow all we have received.

I believe with all my heart the one that our love should overflow to and on is God Himself, the one that even gave us the capacity to love. I have shared much about the healing that God and I have come to know in our relationship, and it all came down to one thing, really: for me to be totally free to love Him with everything that is within me. Oh, He so wants to be loved.

I have realized in my journey with Him that He makes Himself vulnerable to us. Very vulnerable. He reveals who He is, and we can choose to reject Him and push Him away. Many do, sadly. Even as Christians, we do. I did in certain areas for years. He just kept opening His heart to me over and over. He knew that when I got it and truly saw Him, I would want Him. I would want to love Him. I truly believe that if every person on the face of the earth could see Him clearly, they would want Him and love Him. It took that for me. It took many years of coming to know who He really is. It really is hard to love someone you do not know, isn't it? He knew that revealing Himself to me in some really incredible ways would capture my heart forever. Honestly, I find it very difficult given the limited vocabulary I have to express just how much I love Him now. That is what He wanted all along. All of me. All of my heart. He means more to me than I could ever imagine or put pen to paper with.

Oh, the times He has picked me up out of the mire. The times He never shamed me, even when I shamed myself and even when others did. There were times in the past that I doubted His love in my life. Not anymore. I have joined the apostle John when he says in 1 John 4:16, "And we have known and believed the love that God has for us. God is love, and he who abides in love abides in God, and God in him." Oh, the hours of sitting at His feet weeping as I poured out my wounded heart to Him. The hours of pouring over His promises to love me and never forsake me. The times of Him whispering to my heart over and over, *"I love you."* His words are like the sound of the most beautiful and powerful waterfall we could ever imagine. They wash away all the debris of our lives that needs to be cleared out. This is what has captured my heart. This is who has captured my heart.

My life is becoming less and less about the rules I always thought I needed to keep. Now, one rule is coming into view more and more. It really is not a rule but a passion and desire. It is the reason we were made: to love God. Oh, I often think about Adam, the first man to dwell on the earth and to have uninterrupted fellowship with the God of the universe, for a time. I often wonder what that was like. Then God whispers to my heart and says, *"It is still possible."*

To be honest, many times He speaks these words to me when I am out in my garden. I love my garden. Roses, lavender, butterflies, hummingbirds. The bright blue sky of summer contrasting with vivid pinks, purples, blues, and yellows of the flowers surrounding me. They are all there. He is there. He is there reminding me, like He is even as I write this, that I was made to love Him. He was made to love me. To love us. Everything that comes out of my life should be the fruit of that intimacy with Him. Everything. I do not even think that He cares how many external rules and regimens we keep if we do not love Him. I lived there for so long. At times, He still breaks me free from those things. I think He is always freeing us more and more to love Him and to do away with anything less than that.

Believing Him now is not difficult because I know He loves me. Faith is not some formula. God actually says that faith works through love in Galatians 5:6. Everything else does too. He gently reminds my heart that if I am letting Him love me with everything, and I am loving Him with all my heart, my life is exactly where it should be—even though I am not perfect. Talk about freeing! Whoohoo!

Our hearts were meant to be filled and soar because of His love. They were meant to spend time communing with our Creator and simply loving Him back. He waits for us daily. He cannot wait until we get up in the morning to spend time sharing His heart with us. He does not want us to be so busy that we cannot hear Him just waiting for us. He watches us when we do not even know it or are aware of it. I was reminded of this camping last week. I snuck out behind our tent early in the morning to a meadow that opened up. Oh, it was so beautiful. We had the best campsite! I took my lawn chair and my Bible and just spent time with Him. For me, there is nothing like being out in nature to feel connected to God. There he was, a beautiful buck just standing in the field. The sun was beginning to shine on the prairie grass and small bushes around the meadow. I just looked at him and admired his strength and beauty, the beautiful colors of his fur and face. He did not know I was there until I moved. Then he bounded off into the trees just like an antelope. I was struck by the fact that God does the same thing with us. He watches us all the time. He admires us, His creation. He admires the beauty He made us with. Every one of us. He admires our face and longs to see it daily. Oh, He sees it alright, but He wants us to be aware enough that we will come close. That we will not bound off into the woods like the buck. He really wants our love.

All through the day He sees us and our busy little selves. Oh, I do not think I would like to see the tape replayed of me hurrying through the business of life. I would probably be embarrassed or just flat out laugh at the way I acted. But He waits. He waits and watches while we play with our kids, feed them breakfast, lunch, dinner, and the twenty snacks that they say they need all day. He watches and waits while we grocery shop to feed our hungry little troops. He waits as we clean our houses and run the thousand of errands we have. He waits as we head off to work early and kiss our families good-bye, sometimes to not see them until late into the evening. As He waits, He calls to our hearts. Will we hear Him? Will we slow down enough to hear Him? He wants us to hear His slightest whisper. He does not like to shout to us, but He will if He has to! He shouted to me through my circumstances with my feet. In all honesty, He could not get my attention another way. Things were blocking communication. What is blocking our communication today? What keeps us from giving and receiving His love the way He desires? He just wants to blow all those things out of the water. Let Him!

Even today, I am freer in His love than I have ever been. I used to live with so many do's and don'ts that I cannot even remember them all. Do this to be good enough for Him to love you. Don't do that or He will be mad. There is so much more to life than that. There is love. He is transforming my life with His love. Today I just want to love Him. I want to receive His love. I want to give Him what He is so worthy of: me and my love. All of it. I want to throw open the windows and doors of my heart and life to the one who did that for me. I want the wind of His Spirit come and teach me how to love Him more. That is why we are here. That is what we are made for!

Loving ourselves is a gift that only God can give us. Especially for someone like me—and I know, many of you—receiving this gift will not come easy. Jesus said that His yoke is easy and His burden is light (Matt. 11:30.) When we are able to begin to see ourselves the way God does, that is the beginning of loving ourselves. Oh, the freedom that comes when we embrace who He has made us to be and stop rejecting ourselves. Such healing occurs when we even change the way we think and talk to ourselves (our thoughts). Little by little God has been healing me in this area. Only as I have experienced His deep love for me do I even feel like I can love myself. All I saw before was guilt, shame, and a bunch of failures. I would look to others for my worth. Not a great thing to do. Many of them are broken as well, so when we do this we end up with a very fragmented picture and image of who we are. Only gazing into the eyes of Jesus do we find who we really are. All I have found there is such a deep love for me that it cannot help but change me.

In the beginning of my healing journey, God told me to be very gentle and kind to myself, because that would enable me to heal. Boy, was He right! If you are your own enemy, it is kind of hard to be *for* you. Little by little, God has been healing me. Lately He has been having me talk to myself the way He would. We all talk to ourselves, for crying out loud, in our thoughts and even out loud. I have just known inside that I needed to say things like, "Gabby, I love you and who God has made you to be. You have come a long way, and I am very proud of you," or, "I accept and embrace who God has made you to be." I sense such a smile on His face and such deep healing to my soul. All the years I have been hard on myself. All the self-hatred and condemnation have to bow at the feet of Jesus. I am seeing the effects of the Cross. I am free—free to love me! This is why He came. Everything hangs on love.

It is only His grace that can bring us to this place; not our efforts, not our strength. I say this is one of the greatest miracles that have occurred in my life: to be able to look at myself and love me—even on days when I yell too much at my kids or am impatient with my husband or do not exercise enough or get an attitude with someone. And the list goes on.

This love is so different than what we call love in our human sense. His love is so unconditional, and ours must be for ourselves too. It is easier to love ourselves when we are seemingly doing everything right. That is not the kind of love that Jesus came to bring us, unconditional love. No matter what we do, say, fail at, or do not do, that love remains. It is settled deep down in our heart, spirit, and soul. The battle is done. The enemy is defeated, and we are free!

I realize that much of my freedom now is a result of the seeds that I have sown over the last six years. God is so faithful to bring a harvest to all our seeds. So many times I would walk through the house and say scriptural truths out loud, like, "I am loved with an everlasting love," or, "God loves me, and I am good!" Half the time I think my family thought I was crazy, but I had to do it. My very freedom depended on it. It was so hard for me to open up and do that because I was so used to hiding everything, and because saying something like that is so personal; but through His grace, little by little, He brought me out of hiding.

I also have been at a place of repentance many times over how I have treated myself. I am His. He owns me, and I have treated His creation wrongly. I have sinned against Him and myself. Yes, this was the only way I knew how to treat myself, but it is still sin. I do not condemn myself for it any longer, but I do need to repent and go a different direction. I need to follow the path that Jesus has laid out for me. The path of love. The path of freedom. I also have to forgive and make things right with myself. Yes, we do have a relationship with ourselves, and we go everywhere with us, so it may be the most important after our relationship with our Father. I have had to say I am sorry to myself for how I have treated me, talked to me, thought about me, and condemned me. All healing comes from forgiveness. From releasing us from what we have done to ourselves. Right now, I am experiencing a fresh dose of healing, and I cannot wait to experience more!

You see, many Christians miss the commandment from Jesus to love our neighbors *as we love ourselves*. That is the problem. We *are* loving others as we love ourselves—and we are not doing a very good job of either. God showed me that the reason I was so hard on others and could not truly love them is because I was so hard on me and not really loving me. We really do what we are taught and what has been modeled for us. I never even heard that we are to love ourselves from someone that I actually saw doing it until the last few years. Amazing. And sad. You see, if we are going to fulfill what Jesus wants us to do and what we are designed to do in loving ourselves, it is absolutely imperative that we learn how to love ourselves from how God loves us.

Next to God, I believe godly parents are the greatest influence. Some of you may be asking, What if I did not have that? Can I still learn to love myself? Absolutely! I believe if we are truly hungry to walk in freedom and wholeness, God will provide the answers to our cry. Everything I learned about His deep, unconditional love for me I was now able to apply to me and to my view of myself and self-esteem. I would really not have good self-esteem if it were not for Jesus. Many parts of me were not able to develop properly because of all I went through. Aren't you glad Jesus is our Restorer? I am!

One of the reasons I could not love myself in a healthy way is because I was so busy believing lies about who I really was. Once His Word and Spirit started to uproot those lies, I could see the real me, the me that He had made, and it was much easier to love myself. If you are struggling with loving who you are, ask God if there are some lies you believe that keep you from His love. I remember going to the mirror and looking at myself and telling myself that I loved who God made. Wow, if you have never done that, it really is powerful. It may seem a little weird at the time, but it really brings healing to your soul when you look into the very eyes that He created and affirm who He made. As God restored a sense of love for myself, I experienced more healing in my body. It was and still is so cool to see your body be restored as a result of your life being restored.

Sickness and disease cannot stay in the presence of love! Oh, dear brothers and sisters, this is not condemnation for those of you who are still battling and dealing with very real physical problems. That is not His heart, nor mine. All I know is that the more I experienced His love, the more my body healed. His love brought it about. It was not some faith formula but just believing that He loved me and wanted me whole. That is always His heart, no matter what we see. The things that kept me from His perfect love actually kept me from receiving my physical healing.

Let God breathe afresh on you today and remove any barriers to love. The more weight that He takes off of you, the easier your body will function in the way it was designed. Our brain controls our body and all that goes on in it. If our brain is so busy and full of wrong and negative thinking, how could our body be that healthy?

My Father was tending to the deep, hidden places in me and restoring the little girl in me, the girl who should have been free to run around and dance like a princess in front of others. I never really felt beautiful and lovely, but now He was restoring that girl that He made me to be. One of the things that was frustrating during this season with my feet is that I had to wear sneakers most of the time. They are fine when you are working out, but good running shoes with a dress? Come on! So, my wardrobe was limited. I did not feel very feminine. I wanted to dress up and be the girly girl that I am. It meant so much to me that as He healed my feet I could gradually get out of the running shoes more and more. After I stopped wearing the arch supports in my shoes I bought some Dansko brand shoes. They had a good arch support built in them. Being able to wear more dressy clothes made me so happy! Then I was able to begin to wear dresses. They still were not my favorite shoes, but they were not running shoes. To you men, all this shoe talk may be exhausting, but to us ladies, it is exhilarating!

God knew it meant so much to me that I could express more of who I was through what I put on. Before I had tried to make myself happy from the outside in by what I looked like and wore. Now, my joy and happiness were coming from who He showed me I was, and I wanted the outside to reflect the inside. This is another huge area that He restored to me. I had never been there before in my life!

Pretty soon, after a while of Him continuing to heal my feet, the Dansko shoes began hurting my feet. I was not sure what was going on. They are very expensive and do not wear out quickly. Then I realized that because He was continuing to restore the arches of my feet I no longer needed as much support. Yippee! Gradually I was able to wear shoes that were made well and had good support but not as much arch support. I was able to (and still do occasionally) slip a Dr. Scholl's arch support in to my shoes. They really are not much but just give your foot a little extra padding. As my feet healed, I was able to wear sandals.

I save the best for last. Going barefoot! Oh, the years I waited to be able to do this! For a season, and many times—even now at times—all shoes began to bother my feet. Then I realized something so amazing. My arches were forming for the first time. He made me aware of something. I think I always had feet problems, even as a little girl. I remember lying in my bed at night and just crying because my lower legs hurt and ached so badly. My adoptive mother would come in and rub them and give me medicine for it. However, it was not until I began having these problems after giving birth to Emily that I put it together. Suddenly going barefoot felt the best for me, and it still does.

During this time I remembered back to when our babies were

first learning to walk. The doctors said that the best thing for their feet was to go barefoot as much as possible. This is so the arch and foot can grow and develop properly. So here God was restoring my feet, just as a child would develop a healthy foot. Jump up and shout! Geesh! Some things are too big and awesome to express with our limited human vocabulary and expression. This is one of them!

So for the last few years, Jesus and I have been walking around barefoot a lot! Running on the beach with the sand between my toes and the grass is so wonderful to me! I will never take it for granted again. Even now, the arches and all the surrounding ligaments and muscles in my feet seem to be getting stronger and stronger. As they do, at times I experience pain and what feels like stretching. It is not the same kind of pain from and injury, but a good, healing pain, if that makes sense!

Through all of this healing, God has given me wisdom on how to pace myself, especially in the early phases of the healing. The chiropractor I see really helped me know when to rest and when to push myself, and I just also seemed to know when to do this. When your muscles are in a certain position for a while, it takes a long time for them to be strengthened. He gave me grace and patience for this when at times I got frustrated. It wasn't that I was not grateful, but I just wanted the healing to occur quicker than it did at times. I was made aware that God has not only been healing me from something that occurred after my daughter was born but something that has always been a problem in my body. Only His perfect love can do that. When I realized that, it made me in awe of and love Him all the more. He was not only going back and healing the emotional scars I carried all my life but the physical ones as well. Through my life my lower back had bothered me, even as a teenager. God was making me aware and still is showing me that He is going back and healing all of me. As He has been healing me, sometimes it has been actually a little painful to my muscles and tendons and ligaments, which have spent almost thirty-five years in one place! There were times during my physical healing that I would get discouraged about some of the achiness, and He would remind me of this.

After each time of going through some soreness, I would be more healed and strong afterward. That encouraged me to go through some of the pain and strengthening that I was experiencing. I know He has a different method of healing for each person, but this is how He has chosen it for me. Some have a problem with God taking so long to heal someone. I did too at first. Now, I do not. There have been times that He instantly or very quickly healed me of ailments. Do not ask me to give you some theological discourse on it; I just know that I have been healed and am still receiving it. That's it! That is as deep as it gets, folks! All of His healing has come as a result of love—Him loving me, me loving Him, me loving myself, and me loving others and receiving their love.

Sometimes I would grow and heal a great deal and then get to see the huge strides we had made together. That was a trip! It was like it took my brain a little while to catch up to all He was doing. Another thing that was a trip was when you can actually feel Him restoring something to you. You see it, feel it, and see the results of it in your life. I may have been at home or somewhere, and I would react or think different as a result of His love in my life. Sometimes it seemed like I was looking at my life from the outside. It really is a beautiful thing when Jesus restores us! It is tangible. Looking down at what love has done to my feet, looking down and seeing muscles and bone raised and strengthened is nothing short of a miracle! It really seemed to hit me that He had done some truly amazing things in me as He was restoring me to walk in His love. This is when I began to see it come out.

At times, there was a part of me that wondered if all He had done was in my head! Oh, I knew it was real, but when you get to see how what He has done affects the ways you relate with Him, yourself, and others, the realization of freedom comes to a whole new level. I had experienced the reality of His love penned in Romans 8:38–39:

> For I am persuaded that neither death nor life, nor angels nor principalities nor powers, nor things present nor things to come, nor height nor depth, nor any other created thing, shall be able to separate us from the love of God which is in Christ Jesus our Lord.

Nothing. He showed me that nothing in my past that had happened to me kept me from His great love. No abuse, no rejection, no neglect. No sin, no shame. Nothing I had done could or did keep me from His love. Wow! To read that on the other side of my life and to know it is all the assurance I need of His love. I will never doubt it. Nothing had more power or has more power than His love.

I know many of you understand what I am talking about when you wonder if everything He did for you is real or not. I remember saying to myself, "It is not all in my head. I really am different!" It all started in my head and then affected the rest of my life! It will yours too. If you are somewhere in the process and you wonder if all the renewing of your mind and seeking to walk in freedom are worth it, I am here to tell you—definitely! Keep on keeping on, and you will see the harvest of the good seeds you are sowing. The heavenly Father will continue to rain down His Spirit to guarantee a beautiful and bountiful harvest!

As I began to learn how to love myself, I noticed something beautiful start to happen. I actually started to love others! What a great concept! It is sad to say, but I am sure that many Christians can agree with me when I confide that I never really majored in love before. It was something that I heard preached about or heard at a wedding as the preacher read from 1 Corinthians 13. We call it the love chapter, but I am sure that for many of us it is back where the pages are stuck together! How sad, how utterly sad. It is the very thing Jesus came to give us, and we so neglect it.

The enemy has deceived us that love is no big deal and nothing more than a word. He had me there for so long. He fights and wars so that we will not come to know the love of God. He knows that when we do his days are numbered. Satan really does not know what to do with a Christian who truly knows how to receive and give love, how to walk in love. This is the highest and most powerful spiritual warfare available to us. It is the greatest weapon. And so often we put it on a shelf, along with our dusty Bible.

Jesus breathed love. He lived love, and it flowed through His veins every day of His life. Still does. How can we neglect this? We have been deceived as Christians to believe that to love ourselves is arrogant and almost sinful. Listen to the words of our Savior again, "Love your neighbor as yourself." Who are we going to believe? Who are we going to follow? To believe His words and to follow them is the sign of a truly humble person. I really did not have a frame of reference on how to love others until I received His love and learned from Him how to love myself. Then I was able to learn and understand what it meant to begin to love others. That is why we are here. It is pretty simple, and we have made it so stinkin' hard. Religion is hard. Love is not.

On my journey of learning how to love, I remember asking the Lord how to do it because I was having a hard time loving a certain person. His answer came instantly. He said, *"Just let me love them through you. Surrender yourself to me, and I will love them through you."* His grace made it much easier to love that person. It was not such a huge task anymore. I am not saying that love will always be easy. Dying to ourselves and letting Him live through us is not always easy, nor is it fun. But I refuse to buy into the lie that the alternative—living for me—is easier. We are designed to love, and we function at optimum effectiveness when we do. When you are broken and beaten up, you cannot love the way we were meant to. I believe that He literally heals us to love, so that we can love.

During my journey I remember I began to look at people differently. They were no longer as much of a threat to me and my safety because He had and was dealing with that. Now I could look at them and actually wonder what was going on in their life and how I could help them. I remember one day driving down the road and seeing a young mother with a few kids waiting at the bus stop. I stopped and thought about her, about how hard it is to load my kids in the car some days, much less on a bus! About how hard it is to wait with fidgety kids pulling on your legs then loading a stroller onto a bus. It may sound like a small thing to think about to you, but for me it was huge. It meant my mind was off of me and my own problems long enough to think of someone else. That was nothing short of a miracle! I felt compassion for her and for others I saw. I would think about what they were facing in their lives. That is love, my friends. The day-in and day-out, love in everyday life.

All He had done in me was starting to come out of me. I began thinking of how I could love those around me. My husband and children were of course on the top of my list. This is where what God has done is lived out. Our families see us—the good, the bad, and the ugly! It is not like I did not love my family before, but when you are broken, your capacity to love is just not the same. We cannot love as fully and freely as He made us to. Loving the way God made me to love began to bring me so much joy that I wanted to see how much more I could love people. I like being a happy person. Serving at home and church took on whole new meaning for me.

Serving and doing things out of love is so refreshing, rather than doing something to be loved. All my life I had been in that rat race of doing and striving so people would love me and approve of me.

Suddenly, I was free to love. I remember as a little girl, I would frantically do things like clean and work so that my adopted family would approve of me, so that they would want to keep me. But for the first time, I knew I had been set free to receive the love of others. This was huge for me. Before, without knowing my value as a person and who I was to Him, I was just not able to receive the love of others. Many times, God loves us through others, so without being able to receive His love we cannot receive others' love.

I would like to begin with sharing how God began to really show me how to be loved. It is the story of how Andy and I met and fell in love. As I shared before, we met at Bible college, where we were both studying and preparing to be in ministry. Maybe some were there to find a spouse, but we were not. Actually, it was the furthest thing from my mind! I had a few fleeting thoughts about possibly finding the man God had for me, but not much more than that. So, in the summer of 1997 my roommate went to Ukraine on a mission trip. The team was very close as they spent time preparing and praying before the trip. They were even more bonded when they returned, as they had just spent three weeks in a foreign country together. My roommate invited me to come and hang out with them as they went out to eat, went hiking, and watched movies together. One of the guys on this team was none other than Andy Heusser!

As soon as I joined their group I noticed something was different about this guy. Oh, there were godly men at college, but it was not too long before I felt an attraction to Andy. He was sensitive and kind and loving to everybody. I noticed how he went out of his way to give people rides to work if they did not have a car. One of them happened to be me! He later told me that he had *noticed* me awhile before I noticed him. He watched me as I walked out to the track where I would have my quiet time with the

Lord, and He prayed for me. We spent time with his friends that went to Ukraine. Then came the time when He asked me out on a date—just the two of us!

While I was so excited to date Andy, I also experienced fear of getting too close to anyone. Before coming to Christ some of my worst sins revolved around poor choices with guys. I found that I was still afraid of making more poor choices, even though this time was very different. Part of me did not understand the new, righteous nature Christ had given to me.

I was also afraid of him rejecting me. The old lie of people rejecting me if they knew me smacked me upside the head. I was really afraid of something bad happening to ruin my chances at true love. I am happy that I did not push him away!

We continued to date, and when he would come to my apartment my roommates would squeal with delight. He took this as a good sign. We dated for about one year before he asked me to marry him. Of course, I said yes! Even through the fear and some of the issues I still struggled with, through much prayer and thought, I knew this was the guy that I wanted to spend the rest of my life with.

The worst of my fears in relation to Andy and I came to a head shortly after I had returned from a mission trip to Morocco, North Africa. One week after he proposed to me I boarded a plane to Africa to begin to fulfill the dream that God had put into my heart of going there as a missionary. As I was there, my heart came alive again to the passion God put in me to travel and to minister. I began to get fearful because Andy had more of a pastoral heart. He had traveled, but that was not his main passion. When I came home from my mission trip, my old fear began to be aggravated. Thoughts like, "What if I am missing God?" or, "If I marry Andy, will I miss my calling?" began to come very frequently. I was tormented by fear. My fear rubbed off on Andy, who is not someone who walked in fear.

At the time we were attending a wonderful church near our school. We were going through the marriage class, and our teachers were Joseph and Mary. Really! One afternoon we were so emotionally drained because of my fear that we called them to see if they could talk with us. They prayed, and Joseph said something to me that was right on. He asked me if I had a problem trusting God in this area as a result of all I had experienced in my life. I broke. Joseph and Mary prayed for us, and here we are! Starting that day, God began healing my fear, not only with His love but with the love of the one who has been my husband for almost fifteen years now! Andy has been the one that God has used to teach me how to receive His love in the most powerful way.

When you spend most of your time performing and then you are put in circumstances where you feel so depleted and like you have nothing to give, something has to give. That something is whatever keeps us from receiving others' love. For me it was my insecurity and lack of value as a person. As He healed me and I grew to know my value as a person, I believed that I was loveable. I learned that those who came and helped with my everyday tasks when I could not do it loved me. Those who prayed for my healing, both physically and emotionally, loved me. I let my guard down and just received. That brought such healing to me. It brought healing to let people get that close to me, like, all in my business. He was not going to let me get through this season any other way. It was part of my healing and wholeness.

It felt so awesome to be loved by people! It is not like I had never been loved. I was. I just could not always see it or receive it. God had removed the blockages keeping me from receiving the love from Him and others. My heart is so full of His love right now! That is how we were meant to live. Oh, He has brought me such a long way, but I still have so far to go. This last season just awakened me to His love. Now He is teaching me to live it out and to strengthen me in it.

None of us ever arrive but are always growing. It is like love is this huge, beautiful cycle that just keeps going: love goes from Him to us, back to Him, to us, from us, from others, then back to others. This is what life is all about. This is something that He so longs for us to get. He longs for us to live. Love is what I was restored to. Love is what we are made for. It is what He died to restore and what we were broken free for!

CHAPTER 12
UNWRAP THE GRAVE CLOTHES

*Now a certain man was sick, Lazarus of Bethany, the town of
Mary and her sister Martha. It was that Mary who anointed
the Lord with fragrant oil and wiped His feet with her hair,
whose brother Lazarus was sick. Therefore the sisters sent to
Him, saying, "Lord, behold, he whom You love is sick." When
Jesus heard that, He said, "This sickness is not unto death,
but for the glory of God, that the Son of God may be glorified through it." Now Jesus loved Martha and her sister and
Lazarus.... These things He said, and after that He said to
them, "Our friend Lazarus sleeps, but I go that I may wake
him up." Then His disciples said, "Lord, if he sleeps he will get
well." However, Jesus spoke of his death, but they thought that
He was speaking about taking rest in sleep. Then Jesus said to
them plainly, "Lazarus is dead. And I am glad for your sakes
that I was not there, that you may believe. Nevertheless let us go
to him".... So when Jesus came, He found that he had already
been in the tomb four days.... Then Jesus, again groaning in
Himself, came to the tomb. It was a cave, and a stone lay against
it. Jesus said, "Take away the stone." Martha, the sister of
him who was dead, said to Him, "Lord, by this time there is a
stench, for he has been dead four days." Jesus said to her, "Did
I not say to you that if you would believe you would see the
glory of God?" Then they took away the stone from the place
where the dead man was lying. And Jesus lifted up His eyes and
said, "Father, I thank You that You have heard Me. And I know
that You always hear Me, but because of the people who are
standing by I said this, that they may believe that You sent Me."
Now when He had said these things, He cried with a loud voice,
"Lazarus, come forth!" And he who had died came out bound*

hand and foot with graveclothes, and his face was wrapped
with a cloth. Jesus said to them, "Loose him, and let him go."
—JOHN 11:1–5, 11–15, 17, 38–44

*L*OOKING AT THE story of Lazarus is fascinating in many ways. Can you imagine being there? Can you imagine being Mary and Martha and experiencing the death of your brother, and yet in the middle of grieving your loss, Jesus comes and raises him from the dead? Talk about a roller coaster of emotions! Wait a minute, can you imagine being Lazarus, who was raised from the dead? What a trip! I wonder what he felt like as his body, which had been dead for four days, was instantly raised by three words, three of the most powerful words that Jesus ever spoke over Lazarus's life! There are so many things that we can learn from this story, but there is a lesson that Jesus wants us to learn that maybe we miss as we read the story. I will share with you how He made it very real to me in the journey He has led me on.

Jesus had all the power on Earth to raise someone who had been dead for four days, but He chose to use a human to unwrap his grave clothes. I do not know if it was one person or many, because all the text says is that Jesus told those who had witnessed this miracle to unwrap the cloths from around Lazarus. I do not know about you, but I would be a little taken back at this command. It sounds a little creepy to just walk over to this guy and begin unwrapping his body.

There are some parallels between Lazarus and us that would be good to look at. First, only Jesus could raise Him from the dead—and not only raise him from the dead, but raise him after four days. I am so glad that Jesus does not take into account how long we have been dead. Dead in our sin. Dead in our defeat. He just comes and shouts for us to *arise*! I love it!

Next we see Jesus use flesh and blood to help undo the effects of death, what is still hanging on because of death: grave clothes. Lazarus could not have kept wearing those stinky old things around. Actually, he would not be able to live while still wearing them. He was bound hand and foot. How was he going to unwrap himself? That is what we do in the body of Christ so many times. We walk around like Lazarus, who was freshly raised from the dead. Some of us have been raised back to life for years before we get those stinky old grave clothes off! Jesus has done everything to raise us from the dead, and we are still walking around smelling like death. We stand before God perfectly righteous and holy, but we see ourselves as being dead. We still carry the same baggage, hurts, and defeats that we did before we knew Christ. We are walking around bound hand and foot. The only difference now is that we are headed for heaven.

Just as I shared how God used people very dear to me in His body to help me walk out the healing and life Jesus already provided, He wants to use others to help unwrap your grave clothes too. We need to discern who it is that the Father is providing to do that. Not everyone is anointed by God to help us. Jesus has given the command to some around us, just as He did that day to those who witnessed the miracle of Lazarus to unwrap our grave clothes. He has called people to help us out of the old things we have walked in and to go free. We need to pray and seek Him as to who He wants to bring into our lives to help unwrap our grave clothes. If they are truly anointed by God they will know His timing and have His heart to bring freedom.

We must remember, though, that those He brings into our lives are not our savior. Only He is our true deliverer and healer. We can trust Him to use His body to see that we do not have to continue to wear the dead things of our past—all because He first set us free. We can trust Him that He is using His body to get us to stop hiding behind the grave clothes.

For many reading this, I realize that trusting and letting others in to your dark areas is quite scary. Here is my advice: look to your Father and trust Him with all your heart. When you do not know where or to whom to turn, you can trust Him. Proverbs 3:5–6 says, "Trust in the LORD with all your heart, And do not lean on your own understanding; In all Your ways acknowledge Him, And He shall direct your paths." When we trust Him, we can then trust those He brings to help us. We need them. There are times that God has us walk without the help of people, but it is not the way He designed us to live. When He brings people in our lives, we need to be careful not to put too much trust in them but to allow God to do the work He wants to do through them. It may be a word in due season, a prayer, a hug, a listening ear, and sometimes a loving rebuke!

Unwrapping grave clothes takes skill and patience. Imagine Lazarus trying to walk around with tight pieces of fabric all over his body. He would have fallen face down and not been able to make it back up. Beloved, God does not want us to be disabled. He wants us to be free! In fact, we are free; we just need to see it. God has used so many people to help me learn to walk in the freedom that He already died to give me.

Imagine Lazarus' response after Jesus raised Him from the dead. Stop for a minute and think was he was thinking about. He may have had memories of what happened just before he died, what he was doing. As He came out of the grave he may have wondered what on Earth was going on. Why is Jesus here? And why are these people here? And why am I wearing these clothes? I am sure that he was grateful for whoever began to unwrap the clothes at Jesus' command. Freedom. His skin could breathe, and he could move. This was the last thing to be done before he could get back to normal life. He could not have functioned normally wrapped in those clothes, and neither can we. Jesus simply commands His body to love like He loves and to unwrap each other's grave clothes. If we are listening, we have the privilege of seeing someone who was once dead learn how to walk in the life Jesus came to give. He does not call us only to physical life but to abundant life, like we read about in John 10:10.

Many in His body are not living in the fullness of the life He died to give us. That grieves Him. His voice is still calling to us, "Come forth." Many have responded to that voice but are not sure how to truly live. That is why He came. He fully expected on that day when He called Lazarus forth that he would be alive and completely restored to abundant life. That is His heart for us.

Let's let our brothers and sisters grab the loose end of the grave clothes that are wrapped around us, which remind of who we used to be, and begin to unravel them. Many times it is one cloth at a time. One layer at a time. Our tender Father knows what we are ready for and when we are ready for it. Before you know it, more of us you revealed to the light as the clothes come off, and you are freed. You may not know how it happened or when, but you will be free—free to function, free to move, and free to live. It came as the result of someone obeying the voice of Jesus to begin unwrapping! Let Him do it! Let Him use His hands to free you. Surrender to the work of the Holy Spirit when He wants to use His servants as His literal hands. You may feel irritated at people poking and prodding you, but it is all a part of the process. Anything done in love will ultimately heal and free you!

I remember that I felt irritated and just honestly wanted to be left alone after receiving a word that was meant to be encouragement from a friend. In spite of my attitude, God was not really up for leaving me alone! Do you ever get that feeling? He is stirring things us so He can free us from them. As I prayed and spent time in His presence, He helped my attitude. It honestly took me a while to understand and perceive what He was saying to me, but I made a leap of faith to believe Him because I knew He loved me. We will have to do that. Some grave clothes seem harder to come off than others. Thankfully, we will not be left unclothed, because Isaiah 61:10 says that He has clothed us with the robe of righteousness. The clothes He has for us are light, and we can move freely!

I would love for you to see how this process works itself into our lives and what this looks like on a practical level. The friend I spoke of who shared some things that were on God's heart for me really irritated me at first. Mind you, she never said anything negative. She just simply shared with much passion who God had made me to be and what He had called me to do. Why on Earth was I so irritated? I will tell you one thing: I really never had many people that close to me in my life, people who knew so much about me. I was used to hiding and living my own private life. Then God went ahead and shared some of the plans that He has for me, and I felt a little embarrassed. I was embarrassed that others knew and were beginning to see the real me, the me that His hands had made. There went another piece of the grave clothes. Shame. Fear. Hiding. OK, maybe it was more than a piece! I was used to growing up with shame and ridicule and had learned those defense mechanisms as a way to keep others from rejecting me. These things were not a part of the new life Jesus came to give me, so they had to go. They were the clothes that He wanted to be removed. God was using His body to unwrap them.

All sorts of things went through my mind. I was just not so sure that I could live out His plans for me. My God and my friend seemed to be very sure. She not only shared this word with me but spent much time then and since then interceding that His plans would come to pass for me. That is the body. They hear the call of the Father's heart for us and war for us even when we cannot do it for ourselves. His people pray, believe, and fight the good fight of faith for us at times when life has us too wounded and weak to do it for ourselves.

As I shared about my friend Carrie in the beginning of this book, the friend who had the few timely words from the Father for me, you can see a great example of how God continued to unwrap me from the death I was still living in. Those words that He chose to speak through His daughter loosed me from a lifetime of death. It was Jesus' life-giving power through her that brought freedom. This is how it works. Looking back now, I am so grateful that He does this with us. I am so grateful not only that He heals us but for *how* He does it. It is so intricate and beautiful for each of us!

Another beautiful friend of mine comes to mind as someone who really helped me walk in God's fullness and love for me. Love is what comes to mind when I think of her. She simply loved. She loved me how Jesus had loved her, and it began to set me more and more free. She listened to the pain inside of me and did not belittle me for it. That alone greatly showed me my worth and value and brought great healing to me. She had been through many similar things and struggled with many of the same issues that I had. Jesus had set her free, and now she was doing the same in His name. I remember the first time in the beginning when I had so many physical problems, and I asked her for prayer. She could tell that I truly did not know the love of my Father. She was bold enough to say that but gracious enough to show me how to receive His love. Her kindness and gentleness for the next several years would help free me into more and wholeness. It was His love through her for me that helped change me. She was just faithful to express it and give it out. She heard the command of Jesus. God used her to unwrap more of the grave clothes around me.

Was it always easy? Absolutely not. Was it worth it? Absolutely! It is a growing process on both ends, for those undoing the clothes and those being unwrapped. When we are covered in grace the process is so beautiful! God can use any means He wants to in order to heal us. There have been many, many times that I felt like there were some things that could only occur directly with God and not with people. Part of the reason for that is that all He taught me during the process of healing and freedom would be used for me to teach others *how* to walk this out.

Like, I said, there is no single formula for each person. He knows what each of us needs and when we need it. All we have to do is to trust. Trust Him if you cannot yet trust people. I understand what it is like to fear rejection so badly. Living there developed very hard places to penetrate in my mind and my heart. I also understand what it is like to fear opening up. So often I asked myself, "Why on Earth would I allow myself to be rejected again? No thanks, been there and done that!" But only when we open up about pain can it ever really be healed—whether with God directly or through people. I am a living testimony that those who trust in the Lord will never be put to shame (Ps. 25:3). That was one of my worst fears, being rejected and then ashamed and embarrassed by it. Oh, He gently and patiently pried my tight little fingers from around my life. He brought just the right people into my life.

My husband should be listed first here in the people God has used to help me heal. I saved the best for last! I just have to say that I have been truly, truly blessed by my Daddy with the best husband. He has really lived out the scripture in Ephesians that says for husbands to love their wives as Christ loved the church (Eph. 5:25). Poor guy, little did he know what he was getting into when he married me. I joke that I am pretty high maintenance and he is low maintenance. It is just so true! He has been the one who has seen me at my lowest lows and my greatest victories and everything in between.

God really knew that I needed someone as stable, loving, sensitive, and as caring as him. Those were all things that I never experienced on a constant basis. Andy has been the one to hold me when I cried and hurt so badly as I was being healed, and he was the one to listen when I needed to talk. The one thing about him that stands out above all is his love. He has been the single greatest teacher about God's love to me in human form. He just simply loves people. I have only heard him say something negative about someone a handful of times, if that, in almost fifteen years of marriage. Oh, he puts me to shame! He will go and has gone to such great lengths and sacrifice to love people. I have learned more about who my God is through him than from anyone else. Just putting all this out there on pen and paper makes me all the more grateful for him. He was the first one to hear and follow the command of Jesus to unwrap my grave clothes.

You really can trust your Father. Let Him undo those grave clothes any way He sees fit .When you feel someone from His body start tugging on a piece, let that thing go! You cannot move with it on, and you don't need it anymore! You will be free to move and to breathe and live. Those around Lazarus that day were a gift to him. Those around us who help us walk out our healing journey are a gift to us too. Allow Jesus to unwrap the clothes that have served as reminders that we were once dead. Allow Him to show us the way to walk in total freedom, not bound by anything. Not bound at our hands. Not bound at our feet. The only thing that will be left as a result is our heart bound to His. Let those grave clothes go, dear ones! Let your life be exposed to the light of the Son!

CHAPTER 13
BORN INTO WAR

*I*F YOU NAME the name of Christ and follow Him, you follow Him into a war. Thankfully He has given us great assurance in Revelation 12:10–11 that we overcome the evil one by the blood of the Lamb and the word of our testimony. Notice that in verse 10 where it says, "The kingdom of our God, and the power of His Christ have come...[and Satan] has been cast down." Any time God comes near, Satan is defeated!

There are many examples in the Bible of the enemy coming against people early in their lives and trying to destroy the plan that God has for them. Ultimately, it is not only them he is after. He is after anything that would help advance God's kingdom—and we are part of that.

I think of Esther, who was left as an orphan at an early age. Thankfully God raised up Mordecai to care for her and to teach her in the ways of the Lord. Look what became of her life: something beautiful. It could have ended much differently if God had not stepped in. She became the queen of a nation and saved her people. The enemy could have used the absence of her parents to cause all kinds of conflict in her that she would have never recovered from to do anything worthwhile in her life. I think we see something much different painted in Scripture. I just have to stop right here and say how much I love the story of Esther. If you are not familiar with it, go back and read it, either for the first time or to see again how God weaves Himself into the redemption story of her life and people.

Next we have Moses. Moses was born into war. Do not be deceived. This was not merely a political war; this was a spiritual war that would extend until the times of Jesus, even until this day. The Pharaoh in Egypt wanted all the baby boys to be put to death because the Hebrews were growing too strong and mighty. Let's look at the passages of scripture that tell this story. Exodus 1:7–9 says:

> But the children of Israel were fruitful and increased abundantly, multiplied and grew exceedingly mighty and the land was filled with them. Now there arose a new king over Egypt, who did not know Joseph. And he said to his people, "Look, the people of the children of Israel are more and mightier than we."

Of course they were! They were God's chosen people. They were fulfilling prophecy written on God's heart before time began. Moses' parents put him in a basket by faith, hoping that he would be saved from this terrible fate—and he was. God heard the cry of His people for deliverance, and He sent Moses to answer not only their cry but the cry of His heart as well. Exodus 3:9–10 says:

> Now therefore, behold the cry of the children of Israel has come to Me, and I have also seen the oppression with which the Egyptians oppress them. Come now, therefore, and I will send you to Pharaoh that you may bring My people, the children of Israel, out of Egypt.

Moses, like Esther, could have been destroyed by the things that happened to them early in life. God did not allow that to happen because when He breathed life into his nostrils, He also breathed a destiny. A purpose. They both could have been destroyed either through death or through such pain that they were never able fulfill God's purpose. I have a feeling that some of you reading this can relate.

Maybe the enemy planned to have you aborted, but God reached in and saved you with His mighty hand. You may know or not know what the enemy had planned for you, but today you are here. You have a pulse, you have breath, and you have a purpose!

Jesus is another example of what the enemy tries to do to destroy our lives at an early age. Think about it. Satan tried to destroy God Himself! Did he actually think he could succeed at this one? He would have a serious death blow, though, because as he tried to destroy Jesus, Jesus destroyed his dominion over us. We will talk more about that later. Let us look at Matthew 2:3: "When King Herod heard this he was disturbed, and all Jerusalem with him" (NIV). What things? That the King of heaven had made His way to this earth. Not only was King Herod troubled because of the political ramifications for him, but the kingdom of darkness was troubled. Satan knew that in a very short time, the one who would shepherd us back to our Father would also redeem us from his clutches. Praise Jesus! Satan's war was against God, who would soon disarm powers and principalities over people (Col. 2:15).

Notice that the enemy does not wait long into Christ's life to wreck havoc. He was behind the decision of Herod putting to death all the male children under two in order to get to the Christ child. Let's look at the scriptures that tell this riveting part of the story.

> When they had gone, an angel of the Lord appeared to Joseph in a dream. "Get up," he said, "take the child and his mother and escape to Egypt. Stay there until I tell you, for Herod is going to search for the child to kill him." So he got up, took the child and his mother during the night and left for Egypt, where he stayed until the death of Herod. And so was fulfilled what the Lord had said through the prophet: "Out of Egypt I called my son." When Herod realized that he had been outwitted by the Magi, he was furious, and he gave orders to kill all the boys in Bethlehem and its vicinity who were two years old and under, in accordance with the time he had learned

from the Magi. Then what was said through the prophet Jeremiah was fulfilled: "A voice is heard in Ramah, weeping and great mourning, Rachel weeping for her children and refusing to be comforted, because they are no more."

—MATTHEW 2:13–18, NIV

Remembering back to Moses, this sounds like a familiar scheme, doesn't it?

What I observe is that even though Satan had a plan to destroy Jesus, at every turn God was there to protect and preserve Him for His purposes. I bet many of you can relate in your own experiences as a child. Your mind may vividly remember a time or many times when you felt like God Himself was protecting you. Something out of the ordinary happened that kept you safe.

I have one time that comes to mind. I was about four or five years old and living with my birth mother. I was at home alone. It is hard for me as a mother now to even imagine my children or any child at this age being left alone to care for themselves. I knelt down on the floor, scared, because I was alone, and we had no food in the house. I reached for the phone and dialed the long-distance phone number of one of my foster families. How I even called that number or had the number I do not know. I basically have a photographic memory; if I see something even once, I remember it. However, I do not believe that this was the case this time. I called the foster family that I lived with the most and told her that my mom was gone and that we had no food in our house. I remember where I was at in the house and calling the number. To this day, I do not know how I did all of that as a very young child, besides God protecting me. He really did. This was the last time that I lived with my birth mother, because my social worker came right away and took me to my foster family, who has raised me ever since. What a day. What a God.

Not only did He do this for Esther, Moses, Jesus, and me, but if you look closely enough, He has done it for you, too. Maybe there were different circumstances, but He has come to rescue us, and more than once. I think we can stop and give a shout of praise here! Just as Christ's life and ours may have started out early with Satan opposing Him, if we look we can see His hand of redemption.

I pray this next truth would hit you hard (in a good way). What the enemy counts on is that we will never recover from the wounds that we received. So what are we gonna do? Let him win? *I do not think so.* Even if you do not know how to start or what to do, commit to God and yourself that you will never give up on the journey to find your blood-bought freedom in Christ!

Take a minute and look at the parallels. While I make absolutely no claims to any of us being Christ or even coming near to Him, there are some ways that Satan works that have never changed. He starts by trying to destroy us when we are young and to steal our innocence. He works before many of us can even comprehend what is happening to us. He wants to disguise himself through the painful and sinful actions of others, whatever it may be—abuse, rejection, neglect, etc. He wants to so deeply imbed distrust, mistrust, insecurity, and rejection in us that he can gain a stronghold in our soul. He is good at what he does and takes much time planning circumstances so as to trap us in a net for the rest of our lives. I think about my life, and how I never knew or met my birth father, was taken from my mother, I had to care for myself, experienced sexual abuse at the hands of neighbors, and endured many other circumstances. Satan's ultimate goal was to destroy me. I am sure that by this time a few or many people and circumstances are flooding your soul too. But—yes, I said *but*—God's word to us in Psalm 91:3 is, "Surely He shall deliver you from the snare of the fowler."

Put yourself in the story. Satan's plan actually goes beyond us. He is at war with God. Since we are made in His image, every time a precious baby is born into this world he is reminded of God.

Everything that is beautiful, pure, and capable of being restored to God and displaying His glory is thrown into his face—again and again, every second of every day, all over the world. Stop and think about that! You bet your enemy would want to get back at you! You bet he would want to create a war so fierce and so early in life that we might never recover.

Boy, has he really underestimated his foe this time! Let's talk about our Redeemer! I remember God telling me over and over in the beginning of my healing journey, *"I am restoring you to the beauty and glory that you were created with."* Isaiah 61:3 says, "To console those who mourn in Zion, To give them beauty for ashes, The oil of joy for mourning, The garment of praise for the spirit of heaviness; That they may be called trees of righteousness, The planting of the LORD, That He may be glorified." He speaks over us the hope that because of the work of Jesus on the cross, our lives will be beautiful and bring glory to God, show God off, if you will. Oh, beloved, I so want you to believe this. Maybe some of you are hearing for the very first time that you were created with beauty and glory. Since these have been His words to me, I feel so humbled to pass them on to you. More than that, I cannot wait until you get it! I can leap for joy!

I am also reminded of the words in Ephesians 2:10 that say that we are God's handiwork, His work of art! Jesus made it possible for us to live this out. Regardless of whether or not we feel like it or even see any evidence of it in our lives now, it *is* true.

Yes, the war has already been won, but the battle for our soul is on. We have been born into this war that has been going on for thousands of years between good and evil, dark and light, bondage and freedom. The huge component—the game changer, if you will—is that the One who has already defeated death, the power of hell over us, and the grave is standing next to the Father making intercession for us. Yes, *the Victor* is standing in full glory and all victory declaring that over our lives. He believes in us! Oh, God, give us eyes to see that our General, our Victor, has gone before us in the battle. Give us eyes to see what He has already won for us!

We are entering the battle, this war, from a place of victory if we have trusted Christ. There is nothing that He has not overcome! If you have not trusted Christ, give your life to Him right now where you are, and you will experience victory—actually winning at this thing called life. We were made to overcome. It is in the fabric of our DNA and being. We are made in His image, and He is not a wimp! It does not take reading too much of the Bible to see how much power God has.

The problem and the blockage to living in victory is what I call funky thinking. The Bible calls them strongholds, and I am guessing that those who translated the Scriptures did not have *funky* in their vocabulary! All my Christian life I never remember believing that I could live out the victory I heard about in the Bible. Maybe everyone else could have it, but not me. Maybe the really special and spiritual people. Funky thinking at its finest! Some of you can relate, I am sure!

It was not until God allowed these crazy circumstances of the last seven and counting years to occur that I could get the focus off of me. He wanted my sights set higher. Way higher. Victory in any battle or war comes from following orders. Go out and do your own thing in enemy territory, and you're bound to be a casualty of war in no time. Follow the orders of your commander or general, and odds are you will make it out alive. He has walked these dusty roads before. He has escaped the mines that were laid out to destroy His life. Will we walk in Jesus' tracks? Oh, they are big enough for all of us to find and to follow. They are not for the few "spiritu-ally elite"; they are for you and me! Let's open up the Word and our spirit to see what He has already done and to follow where He wants to take us. I promise it ends in victory every time. It does not matter how or where your life began.

The circumstances surrounding your conception, birth, and early years do not matter in this battle. Oh, do not get me wrong; it is not that He does not care what has happened to you. But as far as if they indicate whether or not you can live in victory, they do not. Just look at those who were born into war and won: Moses, Esther, Jesus, and many, many more. Good news, isn't it? God wants our eyes fixed on Him long enough to see and to hear that victory belongs to us! Keep your eyes on Him and your ears open to His Word long enough to hear Him declare victory over your life. He certainly has a way with words! He knows the power of our thinking.

Before I could actually start seeing some honest-to-God freedom in my life, He had to change my thinking. I needed a new battle plan, one based on Him and not on me. As you read the pages of my story, you will see how He did this for me. We will see that His love for us makes us more than conquerors and that nothing can separate us from His love and His plan for us (Rom. 8:37, 39). Nothing. Let me say it again. *Nothing.* Even though my life began in war, my strong Deliverer came for me. He is coming for you too. He has come. Hold out your hand and let Him pull you out. Many of the ways that God brought me freedom are universal principles that any Christian can follow to experience victory. Some are personal between Him and I. You will have the same experience because He loves you so much and so deeply cares where your precious feet are planted in this life. He knows you so well. All He asks us to do is, by faith, follow Him into victory. He is already waiting there on the other side. Let's grab hold of His hand and enjoy the spoils of war!

CHAPTER 14

PASSED OVER

I N THIS CHAPTER we will see our glorious deliverance. Actually, my prayer is that we all see our glorious
Deliverer up close and personal. I so long for this to be more than
another informative book. There are many helpful books written
today, but I pray that His anointing be upon this work so that you
are changed. I am being changed even as I write it. I pray again and
again that people would fall more in love with Jesus as they experience Him through the writing of this work. Seeing Jesus, our Deliverer, in a new light often brings us some much-awaited freedom.
This is what happened for God's people several thousand years ago.
They were slaves in Egypt and were looking for a way out. Sound
familiar?

In Exodus 12 we read about the children of Israel getting ready
to go into the Promised Land. Let's look at this amazing passage of
history and scripture together:

> Now the LORD spoke to Moses and Aaron in the land of Egypt,
> saying, "This month shall be your beginning of months; it
> shall be the first month of the year to you. Speak to all the con-
> gregation of Israel, saying: 'On the tenth of this month every
> man shall take for himself a lamb, according to the house of
> his father, a lamb for a household. And if the household is too
> small for the lamb, let him and his neighbor next to his house
> take it according to the number of the persons; according to
> each man's need you shall make your count for the lamb. Your
> lamb shall be without blemish, a male of the first year. You

may take it from the sheep or from the goats. Now you shall keep it until the fourteenth day of the same month. Then the whole assembly of the congregation of Israel shall kill it at twilight. And they shall take some of the blood and put it on the two doorposts and on the lintel of the houses where they eat it. Then they shall eat the flesh on that night; roasted in fire, with unleavened bread and with bitter herbs they shall eat it. Do not eat it raw, nor boiled at all with water, but roasted in fire—its head with its legs and its entrails. You shall let none of it remain until morning, and what remains of it until morning you shall burn with fire. And thus you shall eat it: with a belt on your waist, your sandals on your feet, and your staff in your hand. So you shall eat it in haste. It is the LORD's Passover. For I will pass through the land of Egypt on that night, and will strike all the firstborn in the land of Egypt, both man and beast; and against all the gods of Egypt I will execute judgment: I am the LORD. Now the blood shall be a sign for you on the houses where you are. And when I see the blood, I will pass over you; and the plague shall not be on you to destroy you when I strike the land of Egypt.'"

—EXODUS 12:1–13

This is such a wonderful piece of history of the people of God many years ago.

All of the things written in the Word are all to tell us of the coming One who would save us from death. Everything that has been written is to point us to one person—Jesus. God painted so many beautiful pictures of Him all through the Word so that when His time came to reveal Himself in flesh and blood we would recognize Him. Sadly, many have not, but let us not be among them!

Fast forward thousands of years later from the time of the Exodus story, and we can see that someone has been coming for us. This time the angel of death is not the hand of God allowing evil but Satan himself. In Exodus we read how God commanded the angel of death to go through all the homes of the Egyptians and take the lives of the firstborn children in their homes. This is a very vivid picture that God was painting to show us the power that Satan can have over us. God was foretelling the consequences that would occur *if* we enter the battle and are not covered in the blood of Christ. The effects of the death angel, or Satan, who God was trying to paint a picture of, are the same for us today. Death. And lots of it. Death to our identities, our dreams, and our futures. Death to having an intimate relationship with God. Haven't there been times when you sensed death on your heels or at your door-step? Thank God we do not have to answer the door! Jesus has already poured out His blood so we can be free to be passed over, just like our brothers and sisters thousands of years ago.

When we receive Jesus, His blood completely covers us and removes death. Death is anything that has tried to destroy us. It is the opposite of God Himself, who gives life. Death no longer has dominion over us. It has to pass us over. We can be confident that whatever curse of death has been in your family line, the blood of Christ makes it so that the curse *has to*, yes, *has to* pass over us. Here is the catch: we have to apply His blood to our lives. This means that we need to trust and cling to all He has done for us with every ounce of faith and belief that we have. We have to trust that if we have mental illness in our family blood line, His blood will draw a line for us. His blood says, "This one must be passed over." The curse of death will pass us over.

Satan was able to effectively use his weapons of fear and intimidation on me because I did not know what I am sharing with you. I did not fully understand how powerful the blood of Christ really is. His blood is not human blood. It is the blood of God Almighty! Whoa!

The enemy tried to make me fearful of going back to my old, sinful lifestyle and told me that it would eventually be all I could do. He also intimidated me with the fear that I would develop mental illness because it had been present in my family. That is where I had to hold up the shield of faith and believe His sacrifice and blood were more powerful than any mental illness or any sin and bondage that held me down. There were many such sins, some that I have not shared here. Praise God, the curse of death has passed me over. There were things that could have been passed down from previous generations that have not been. *I have been passed over.* Praise God!

In the Exodus story we notice that the children of Israel had to do their part to receive protection. They had to obey the voice of God, or they would have suffered. Sometimes I think we take grace too lightly. Instead, what God has done for us should make us *want* to be obedient to everything that comes out of God's mouth. We will have to obey God to see the curse of death pass over us and our children and their children. When God passes over us He also wants to pass over our descendents. He gives us all we need and frees us so we do not have to walk in and pass down destructive thinking patterns and behaviors to our children. We are not the only ones to walk in freedom here. Those coming after us can too! Listen to this in Exodus 12:25–27:

> "It will come to pass when you come to the land which the Lord will give you, just as He promised, that you shall keep this service. And it shall be, when your children say to you, 'What do you mean by this service?' that you shall say, 'It is the Passover sacrifice of the Lord, who passed over the houses of the children of Israel in Egypt when He struck the Egyptians and delivered our households.' So the people bowed their heads and worshiped."

God did not just want His miraculous deliverance to be contained in the memories of those who experienced it. Oh, He has not changed. Everything within Him wants what He has done in us to flow through us to touch the next generation.

According to my family history, I really should not be as good and as healthy of a mom that I am. I am not perfect. My kids are well aware of that. Just yesterday they reminded me. Both of them. More than once. They said that I am cranky all of the time and mad. This was all over asking one of them to change a shirt before we picked berries and asking the other one to practice some math problems. I just had to laugh, which made matters worse, by the way! You parents have your own stories in your own homes.

God is big enough to take care of any of our weaknesses. Not only did mental illness not get to have its way in my life, but not lust, not the eating disorder that I struggled with, none of it. He knows all about them. I am finally more righteous-conscious than guilt-conscious. Praise be to Jesus! I get to give out of what He has filled me with: love, grace, patience (most days), mercy, kindness, and gentleness. I learned all of this from my perfect Father. He is really the one who broke the power of my past and the bloodlines that came before me, all that sin and bondage that was just waiting to find an empty soul to latch on to. He taught me how to walk in victory, and now I get to teach my girls.

God reminded me more than once that my journey was not only for me. It was for them. It was so that none of the sins of my family line would touch them and so that all the freedom I was now experiencing would be passed down to them—and more. My desire is for them to find so much more freedom than I ever find. And I want a lot!

Sometimes I forget how much He has done in my life, not because I am ungrateful but because it has been so abundant and radical. At times we do not see the fullness of our freedom until we come to a place of decision and realize we are not reacting like the old us.

Here is another area of freedom for me. I am at a place where I can actually look at my body and not hate it. My body is His creation, and I have learned to accept it. No longer do I have to hate what society may tell me is a flaw or imperfection in my body. I can look in the mirror and like who I am and what I see. When I exercise, I do it mostly because the older I get I realize I want to have energy to keep up with my girls and to feel good. That tops looking good. My desires are totally different now. I want to feel good and take care of myself by exercising, getting good sleep, and eating healthy foods so I have energy to do what He has called me to do. It is no longer a vanity thing. It is no longer an all-consuming obsession. That, my friends, is being passed over! Many times, it is not until I go to try on a swimsuit that I realize I like the body I have. It is not perfect, but it is the one I have to work with! Then I remember all the years I spent hating what I saw in the mirror. Only He can change that! Not only do these things affect my girls but also all those I influence on a daily basis.

When it comes to our children, I think it goes deeper than just telling our kids to do the right thing or to be godly people. He wants it lived out before them. He wants them to hear our stories. Oh, some things may be inappropriate or too much for them to hear, but we can share much of it and emphasize His faithfulness.

It means more than anything for me to have a sound mind after coming from the background I did and suffering from the bondage I did, to not have mental illness and to be able to take care of my girls day in and day out—and to thrive in it! I love being a mom. It is one of my greatest joys on this earth! I love being a wife and giving to my family. They are the most important people to me in all the world. He has brought me out of so much, but this is really where it is lived out. Day in and day out. Oh, we have our days, I tell you, like yesterday, when my kids informed me I was not perfect. Like it was a news flash!

Having been a stay-at-home mom for almost ten years now I can honestly say that nothing gives me more pleasure than being with them. I have loved every phase of my girls' development. Maybe

I haven't loved every moment of every day, but I have loved every phase! This is part of my destiny and one I take very seriously: to raise two beautiful daughters who know they are princesses to God and to their father and me. I am overjoyed that He has healed me to the point that I can love them the way they are worthy of love.

When they wake up in the morning the first thing I often say to them is, "Good morning, my beauties," or, "Good morning, princess!" What a way to start the day! I am not depressed and living in the leftovers of my early life anymore. I am free to express to them what He has told me about myself over and over in the quiet places of my heart.

We are called to give life to our children, not just to feed them dinner and do their laundry but to bring life. We are called to help them walk in all the freedom of who He made them to be. We cannot do that if we do not know it for ourselves. That is why it is so critical to break free. It is not just for us but for them. They are desperately waiting for us to rise up and give them what they need and desire. If we are not free to love them fully and even to receive their love, growth is stunted. Let your little ones love all over you and give them so many hugs and kisses a day that they walk around rubbing them off their sweet little cheeks! Being passed over means just that!

If your parents were not able to express that kind of love to you, let God work in you so that you can do that for your kids. Let Him just love all over you like the perfect Father that He is. This will give you the tools to do the same with your little ones. It is never too late, by the way! Our kids are looking to us. My girls are looking to me to show them how to be a woman. In so many ways I feel I am still being restored in this area, and they help motivate me into more wholeness!

I am keenly aware that some of you precious brothers and sisters may be struggling in the area of mental illness. It is serious, and it comes in many forms. My heart is tender toward the stigma that surrounds mental illness, especially amongst Christians. Many do not understand it. Yes, some is caused by demonic forces that are alive and well in the world. Some come from injuries. Others come from chemical imbalances. Let Jesus take the load off of you. He does not shame you. I believe Jesus can heal anything, including mental illness. Let Mark 5 build your faith for what He desires to do. I also believe He has given us the Holy Spirit to lead us in our individual situations. Seek God first but do not rule out medication and counseling. Solid biblical counseling can give you the tools to get healthy. I went through deep healing with God without medication, but that may not be the route for everyone.

When God passes us over, anything that kept us back from giving all our heart to those who need it gets dissolved. Christ makes the difference in the generations coming up behind us. He breaks the chains of fear and embarrassment over expressing our heart to our children and to anyone close to us, for that matter. Anything that is less than love, He came to destroy. Being passed over means just this. We are free to be us. That sets our children and others in the next generation up to be who God made them to be. We can boldly display the work of His grace in our lives. We were meant for this.

Think of Moses leading the children of Israel into the Promised Land. Think of the heritage he was passing on to Joshua, who would lead them in. Moses never got to go in, but he knew Joshua was going. Moses poured everything he had into the one who would lead this huge group of people to where God was taking them. Will we do that? Will we show the next generation how to tarry in the presence of God to be changed and have the wisdom to lead, like Moses did with Joshua? We have to. We must. If we do not, a whole generation of people hungry not only to see but to lead people in His presence will be dry and thirsty. Void of any power in their life. We must break free ourselves to actually believe that we have something to offer, that our testimony and all He has done in our lives matters.

People need us to believe in them even when they are not able to believe in themselves yet. Being passed over means that He has worked so powerfully and beautifully in our lives that we can see the beauty in others. We are free enough ourselves to lend a hand to someone who is still in the ditch. What He has done in you matters. Your family, children, friends, and those coming up behind you *must* see and hear what He has done in you and for you. They must hear how He passed you over. If your memory gets a little rusty from time to time like mine does, just think of all He saved you from. Think of all the things you could have done and could have been right now if His mighty hand did not swoop down and save you. We are all a work of His grace.

It saddens me to hear some Christians say to me, "I wish I had a testimony like yours." That cheapens the work He has done for each one of us. I love to hear testimonies such as, "I was always a Christian." Believe me, honey, those who have always had faith in Christ have gone through many things in their lives and have a huge testimony not only to His saving grace but His keeping grace. I never get tired of hearing people's testimonies! I love Him so much more after hearing what He done with others! So, my dear brothers and sisters, lift your head high and declare what He has done for you! The blood of Christ covers you. The death angel has to flee. God has passed over you!

CHAPTER 15

BE THE ONE

THIS CHAPTER HAS come together as a result of many things. The first and foremost reason is that Jesus has done so many incredible things in my life that I have to be *the* one. You are probably asking now, *the one?* The one for what? Let's dive into the Word together and see it for ourselves!

In Luke 17:11–19 we see ten lepers who were made whole by Jesus. I believe our Father had something else in that passage that He wants us to see.

> Now it happened as He went to Jerusalem that He passed through the midst of Samaria and Galilee. Then as He entered a certain village, there met Him ten men who were lepers, who stood afar off. And they lifted up their voices and said, "Jesus, Master, have mercy on us!" So when He saw them, He said to them, "Go, show yourselves to the priests." And so it was that as they went, they were cleansed. And one of them, when he saw that he was healed, returned, and with a loud voice glorified God, and fell down on his face at His feet, giving Him thanks. And he was a Samaritan. So Jesus answered and said, "Were there not ten cleansed? But where are the nine? Were there not any found who returned to give glory to God except this foreigner?" And He said to him, "Arise, go your way. Your faith has made you well."

I want to be like the one who came back to Jesus to say thank you. I think that the ten being healed was certainly awesome, but the one coming back was more awesome to Jesus.

Today I feel like that one. My heart is overflowing and full of praise because I am continuing to see all the things that God promised me during this season come to pass! He is healing me simultaneously! He is worthy of all of me.

I was reading this story with my daughter in one of her Bible story books, and that is another reason I am writing this chapter. As we were reading, it all began to come together—all He has done in my life and the truths of this story just exploded in me! I hope some of you are starting to experience the same freedom as a result of His work in your life. If not yet, you will!

This story means a lot to Jesus too. He told it because it touched a deep and tender place in His heart. He has such compassion on the ten lepers who were not only sick with a terrible disease but were outcasts. There is a special place in the heart of our Father for the outcasts. I believe we can say that Jesus was moved to heal not only the physical disease but also the scars it had left on their lives. Jesus was never repelled by what He saw. Or smelled. Or heard. He was moved with compassion to do something about it, to remedy the situation. It was not enough to see the sick and lost and suffering and to turn and continue to walk down the dusty roads in Jerusalem. He stopped. He listened. He felt the losses of those He was around. And then He did something about it! He is just that good! He sees it all.

I am so grateful that He not only saw my physical pain but the pain in my heart and life. He saw theirs, too. He saw what being an outcast had done to them and their lives. Their lives were stopped in their tracks. He knew how this terrible disease had affected them—mentally, emotionally, and yes, physically. Oh, I remember the times when I was in such pain and turmoil because of my feet that I sensed Him so near. I sensed His desire to heal and restore and cure me, to heal me physically.

I do not know if we understand fully His desire to have us be whole and to have us live pain free. How many of us want our kids walking around in pain? Just as He did two thousand years ago, He still reaches His hand to those in physical pain and disease. We may not have leprosy, but if we look around we see all kinds of suffering from sicknesses and disease. I believe one of the greatest ways we can be a witness to people and show them Jesus is to care for, love on, and pray and believe God for healing just like Jesus did when He walked this earth.

Surely, these ten lepers were excited—not only to be healed but also to be able to enter into normal life again. They could go back to their families and friends and eat and be inside their homes. They could pick up and embrace their children. They could freely walk the dusty roads of the city again and go to the market. They could take care of their animals and businesses.

For those with leprosy, they were by the Law considered unclean. To be unclean in those days was equal to being punished by God for something you had done. Cursed. Cut off by God and people. But Jesus removed all of that! I do not think that Jesus wanted the ten to go back to life as normal before they had leprosy. He wanted them all to be changed, not just physically but inside. He desired that the touch in their physical bodies would produce a new way of life for them.

I am not saying they did not believe in Him or even follow Him in some way. But He wanted their hearts. He wanted closer fellowship with them because of what He did for them. That is what He is after whenever He does anything in our life. Only one responded to the call of Jesus' heart to come back, fall at His feet, and give Him thanks. Jesus wanted a simple thank you. Don't we all? When we do something for our children, wouldn't a simple thank you be nice sometimes? Why is our heavenly Father any different? I do not think He was just looking for the words.

I think that this man who came back was changed by Jesus because of his second encounter with Him. You see, it is not God's plan to go around having us experience miracles all the time and never mature or change. He wants us to be the one—the one to not only come back and say thank you but to thank Him with our lives. To be the one to hear the cry of the hurting and broken and refuse to do nothing. To see the lost and tell them about our gracious Savior. To love like there is no tomorrow.

Here is a scripture that is just screaming to become flesh in our lives:

> And my soul shall be joyful in the LORD; It shall rejoice in His salvation. All my bones shall say, "LORD, who is like You, Delivering the poor from him who is too strong for him, Yes, the poor and the needy from him who plunders him?"
> —PSALM 35:9–10

Here is another one just waiting to be shouted from the rooftop:

> You have turned for me my mourning into dancing; You have put off my sackcloth and clothed me with gladness, To the end that my soul may sing praise to You and not be silent, O LORD my God, I will give thanks to You forever!
> —PSALM 30:11–12

Wow! This is what God wants when He miraculously works in our lives.

I am so grateful that those God has placed me in the middle of get to see His miraculous intervention in my life often. Daily. My neighbor across the street remembers when I had to sit in my lawn chair and pull weeds because my feet hurt too badly to do it. There were about two to three years after having Emily that I would have been in too much pain to bend over for a few minutes, even in a lawn chair to pull weeds. She gets to see God's touch firsthand. She got to see as I began to take walks with my little ones. First, one block, then two, then a half an hour. I remember the first time that I walked up to the end of our street. Oh, I thought revival was going to break out! I remember looking up at the street sign feeling like I had just finished a marathon! She just commented today how I am always running around doing stuff. She gets to see most of it.

Since our ministry is based out of our home, there is something always going on: a clothing giveaway, Tuesday youth art days, school supply giveaways. These all take my physical body to do. I prayed that God would heal me so that I could fulfill His plan for my life. I know that He has called me to missions and to travel. Oh, people can do so much with physical handicaps, but I knew He had more for me. I so admire those in the body of Christ who have overcome so many limitations and still have many of them. I admire that they have not given up on His calling and their faith. I have been personally blessed by many of them and their stories.

My husband and children get to see firsthand the healing power of Jesus on a daily basis. It was just a month or two ago that I was able to do some things that I had not done in seven years, since Emily was born. Like I said, the healing has come very gradually. Cleaning my shower and bathtub was my husband's job because bending down at that weird angle was just too much for me to handle. So, a few months ago, to be able to clean my tub was the ultimate joy for me! I said, "Honey, I just cleaned the shower and tub for the first time in seven years!" I am not sure if he is more excited about not having to clean the shower anymore or me being healed.

The first time I was able to do new things physically I let everyone know. Oh, the first time I ran and played hide and go seek with the girls was such a joy for us all! By the way, I hid, and they could not find me for a long time. Yep, I still have it in me. We were running around the house and laughing. They said, "Mom, you're up and running!" Jesus was there laughing with us. Friends and family get to see what He has done for me.

My close friend Carrie, who I mention through this book, is still amazed at what He has done. I remember having a family picture taken at the beach, and I was barefoot. She just about fell out! Coming over to her house and kicking off my shoes was so cool. We rejoiced and still do in amazement at what He has done. There is nothing like rejoicing with one who has walked with you through the fire when He brings you out on the other side and you are not burned up! And your garments do not even smell like smoke. I make sure to give Him all the praise because I know He has done it.

Praising Him is not only what I say but also how I have been changed by His glory. He wants all of us to praise Him. David certainly got it. From the psalms we just read, his heart was changed by the God who reached down from heaven and delivered him from his enemies. Even when God did not deliver him, God gave David such amazing strength not to let go of his faith. David let God's work and miracles in his life draw his heart closer to Him.

How can He come so near to us and we remain unchanged? Sadly, it happens. God, in His mercy, performs many miracles for us, but many people are never changed by them. Just within the last few days I have been meditating on this thought. I have seen God do something so amazing and meaningful for someone that I know and love. It really is a miracle. He has been glorified. My mind has also wondered if it will really produce any lasting changes in this person's heart. So far I do not believe that it has. This person's relationship with God is seemingly unaffected. Is this what He desires when He does something so big in and for us? Forgive me if I am judging something that appears one way but really is another. I believe He can still use it to change this person's life, if they let Him. He is super merciful and does miracles for us, even when He knows they may not draw us closer to Him, at least not in the near future. I do not think doing away with believing for miracles is the answer. Having a humble, grateful heart is, but that begins with letting Him give us that kind of heart.

Everything we do and are comes from what is going on in our heart, from our attitude, our thoughts, and beliefs. The man who came back to say thank you bowed down at the feet of Jesus. I think this was an attitude of humility and recognition that he had been touched by God. I do think that this man was changed and received even greater blessings because he went back. Fellowship with Jesus was one thing he received. Jesus being proud of Him and wanting to tell this story for all to hear is another. God wants to do the same with us. He wants to work so miraculously that our whole lives are changed!

God's heart for me was not only to be healed physically but to walk in the wholeness that Jesus came to bring and to share that with others. This book was born out of what He has done in me and for me. I used to live much of the time for me and what I wanted. Since I have gone through this season of healing and change, I realize my heart has changed. For me, this is the greater miracle. Because of the way I was raised I grew up thinking that I had to take care of me, and because of that I got used to living in a bunch of unhealthy, fleshly ways that needed to be uprooted. This season provided what I needed to be whole.

My heart and motivation are very different now. Thankfully, God loves us no matter what condition we are in but desires so much more for us. One way we see His desire for us is in Isaiah 61:3: "That they may be called trees of righteousness, The planting of the LORD, that He may be glorified." All the work of Jesus outlined in Isaiah 61 before this one were so that we would be strong in Him and see Him glorified. The scriptures following verse 3 say that those who have been touched by God will go and rebuild the old ruins and help repair the things that used to be broken. I believe this is speaking of our responsibility to help others find the hope and healing that we have experienced. This is my heart in writing this book. I felt Him calling me to do it. I would not have had much to write about the way I used to live. I am forever changed, and I want you to be, too. I feel responsible to give to you what He has poured out to me so abundantly.

Not all of us are called to write or to speak, but *you* can do something. You are made for so much! Ask Him what He would have you to do. When you begin to experience His love and healing in your life, you will naturally want to give out—you will *have* to, or you will explode! When your heart and life are so full of Him, He will use you in mighty ways. The greatest miracle you could ever experience is the reality of knowing that we are not our own but have been bought with a price (1 Cor. 7:23). Our life does not belong to us anymore, and we are free to make decisions based on that truth.

I used to think that God just wanted to take from me and not add much to my life. How wrong I was! My life is so full now. I have the blessing of sharing my testimony all the time now with people, especially women, who are hurting and need Him. I am so grateful for the hard times because I can relate to where people are living. They feel like they can relate to me and trust me. Many times during my healing process I was made aware by the Holy Spirit that the things I was learning and how He was teaching me were not only for me but to help others. This motivated me. God knew that would keep me going when it seemed like an uphill climb.

I remember when my heart began to change so that instead of just wanting to be healed I desired to see Him glorified. As I saw and experienced Him I was made aware that He really was worthy of all of me. This is the story that He wants for all of us. Leave the other nine, if you have to, and go back to Jesus and tell Him thank you. Thank Him for all He has done. Tell Him you give Him your heart and life out of the gratitude of what He has done for you and in you. Let's hold nothing back. Let's leave it all on the line, where Jesus can pick it up and use it and us—all of us. Let's not go back to life as normal. Let's let that Man from Galilee change our normal. Can you hear Him calling for you to be *the one*?

CHAPTER 16
FOLLOW ME

And Jesus, walking by the Sea of Galilee, saw two brothers, Simon called Peter, and Andrew his brother, casting a net into the sea; for they were fishermen. Then He said to them, "Follow Me, and I will make you fishers of men." They immediately left their nets and followed Him. Going on from there, He saw two other brothers, James the son of Zebedee, and John his brother, in the boat with Zebedee their father, mending their nets. He called them, and immediately they left the boat and their father, and followed Him.
—MATTHEW 4:18–22

WHAT A BEAUTIFUL passage of Scripture. It is one that leaps off the pages of the Word right now because those are the very words I have been hearing quite clearly and concisely in my spirit for the last few years. If I thought following Jesus out of some things in my life was throwing my life for a loop, more loops were coming!

Following Jesus is not safe. We can trust that we will be safe, but if we want comfortable circumstances and a trial-free life, then the journey will not always feel or appear to be safe. It will not be free from having to make some hard choices to follow Him rather than man or any other thing. When we live in the natural we are following flesh, but when God calls us to follow Jesus we are walking in the Spirit.

For me, making the decision to let God heal me and set me free meant that I was going to have to continue to follow Him down a path that included some difficult choices for my family and I. Just wanting God to heal us so we do not hurt anymore is not His will; He has so much more. To follow Jesus means that He is the purpose for our lives. Seeing His kingdom come on Earth as it is in heaven is our new desire.

Let me throw out a thought: if you are not having to make some life-altering decisions, then you may not be truly following Christ. Ouch! I know that may sound harsh, but it is the truth, and the truth sets us free! We all have times when we are in what I call a lull. When we are truly following Christ we experience times where life may seem a little mundane, but things do not seem to stay that way for long. Have you noticed? Look at those who followed Him in the Bible. Their lives were crazy! It seems like sometimes they never knew if they were coming or going. One day they are watching Jesus heal people; the next, they were doing it! He seems to enjoy stirring up our lives enough to keep us very dependent on Him. I have actually gotten to the place where I expect to live like this and know that it is necessary to keep me humble and leaning on Him. So take heart, beloved, if your life feels like it is being turned upside down right now or you feel a little jolted. It is for your good! Little did I know how much my own life and that of my husband and children would be jolted in the middle of my healing journey with the Lord.

The first series of jolts came when He allowed the circumstances with my feet to occur. Then more change came when I realized what He wanted to do with it all! In about the middle of my healing journey, as I call it, God began to call me into ministry. This was a fulfillment of the knowing the Holy Spirit almost immediately gave me when I got saved at fifteen that I was called to work in missions and evangelism. For me this was truly a supernatural thing, because I was one of the most selfish and self-centered people you would meet. Some people who know me are surprised to hear this now. That just testifies that Jesus is truly alive and well!

When I was first saved and first heard that call, I began to go to the streets with a dear older man who discipled me and taught me about Jesus and who I was in Christ. Ralph Cruz truly made a huge impression on my life. He was the one who told me about Christ for the Nations. He taught me how to minister and pray for the lost to receive Christ. He stirred a passion in me to tell others about God's love. He was the boldest person I know. At times, he would carry a big wooden cross on the streets of Salem to tell others the message of salvation. I am having a full-circle moment now because I am realizing that I am seeing a harvest of all He planted in me almost twenty years ago. I am flying back from Dallas, Texas, now and am twenty-six thousand feet in the air. I feel a little closer to my friend since He went to be with the Lord many years ago! I wonder if he is among the great cloud of witnesses looking down on me running this race called life. If I could use my sanctified imagination I bet he is waiting and cheering with my Jesus to see that I make it to the finish line.

When God renewed that call He gave me so early in my life, which was about three or four years into this season of God healing me, He began to meet me many times in my home and speak to me about what He had for me in ministry. It actually shocked me, but I could handle it because it was coming from His Word and His heart! He began to fan the flame of passion that had been long buried in my heart and to also place new ones in my heart. Things that I never imagined or saw myself doing started to become a reality with my eyes of faith. I felt like a sponge, just soaking it all up.

In all honesty, it felt so good to be at that place. Many times during the intense season of healing what I went through felt like I was in the intensive care unit. That's not a bad place to be. I joked that it was like I was just hooked up to an IV of His love! We are not meant to live in the intensive care unit, though! So for Him to be propelling me forward, even into more freedom and victory through using my gifts and callings, felt wonderful. It felt so freeing to be getting my mind and focus off of me and what I was going through. It was needed for a time, but this was the beginning of a beautiful new season.

During the years of serious bondage I was not able to function the way He wanted me to. I remember the time that God spoke to my heart about Him releasing me into ministry. What in the world did this mean? Didn't I need some elders or something to come around and lay hands on me and release me? I certainly believe in that and have experienced that, but this time I felt like what God was doing was so much deeper. I realized that my Father had seen all the bondage and brokenness I had been in and yet still believed in who I was and what He had made me for. Now *He* was calling that forth, not any man.

There is a good lesson here for all of us. Many times we just flat out trust in man more than God. We want them to tell us who we are and approve of us, but our Father, I believe, wants us to know so much more about ourselves through our deep and intimate relationship with Him. Him believing in me began to help me to believe in myself. You see, when you walk in the amount of fear, shame, and defeat I did, you start to lose confidence in who you are. God does not want us to have empty self-confidence but rather confidence that is completely dependent on who He is. As He was telling me that I am was leader and about the gifts that He had given me, I began to believe it—for real and for the first time in my life. The old doubt and insecurity was gone, and I was free to believe Him. It felt so good! By that time He had proven that He was completely trustworthy, so why not trust Him in this area? Believing Him brought so much healing to my soul, which in turn brought more and more wholeness to my body. My body was able to continue to heal and strengthen from all of the damage. All of me was beginning to praise Him more and more, including my body! As the lies get washed away in His faithfulness, we are free!

He began to mentor and lead me in being a leader. He was so tender and gentle and told me many things about the gifts He had given me that I never knew about myself. All of the passion and love that He poured on me during this season began to explode in my heart for others. For His purposes. For what He wanted. He had always given me a burden for those who do not know Him, but this was different. Without all of the stuff blocking it, His Spirit was freer to move in me and through me.

He also gave and is still pouring into me such an intense love for His bride, the church, for those who have heard His call. I began to weep and pray that all would come to know the freedom that He had so graciously poured out on me. I knew it was not just for me and was not content to just keep it to myself. Parts of me were being uncovered that neither I nor anyone else had ever seen. He had seen them all along. He was showing them to me like a beautifully wrapped gift just waiting to be unwrapped and used and enjoyed.

This is true restoration. Think about when an old piece of furniture is stripped down, sanded, and then restored to its original condition. Oh, but our God goes beyond just restoring us. He restores us in excess of anything we ever knew, could know, or thought possible. That is His nature!

God released me into ministry during a time in my life in which I was really content. Oh, He still had some healing to do in me, but we were on the right path! I loved (and still do love) being a mom to my girls, I was enjoying our marriage (and still do), had great friends, and was just happy with life. I was not looking for some leadership position, but apparently God was looking for me! That is the way it should be. We should be led by God and not our own aspirations. Oh, we should always dream big and not lose sight of the vision He has given to us, but we must let Him fulfill it in His own time. Everything we do should come out of love and service to Him and then to others.

One thing He really put on my heart during that time was His role in giving gifts and releasing for ministry. He taught me that man can affirm what God has already put into us, but the focus was on God for me now. God was removing the effects of false teaching from controlling leaders, and little did I know was preparing me for some things in the future. I desperately needed to be free through the truth He was revealing to me. All my life my unhealthy view of men and women caused me to be very insecure or to idolize people, especially leaders. I know that much of this came from a lifetime of hurt and abuse from the hands of people.

I am grateful that He continued to free me from those thought patterns in my past. It felt so good. During this time, I felt more and more peace wash over me as my eyes were continuing to be lifted to my Father. By seeing Him as my leader it was like He was just closing me in again—just He and I. He is so wise and made sure that my life and, now, my ministry would be based on all the truths that He had taught me. I did not know how much they would be needed over the course of the next few years.

As I mentioned before, during the season in which God was healing my feet we had been attending the church we were at for about ten years. We had built many great relationships there and were ministering more as God was working in our family. When our pastor was gone, I would teach and preach for him. My husband and I served as deacons, children's ministry workers, and in any other ways we could serve. Our pastor was feeling the call to do more traveling and ministering away from our church, so out of the blue he took my husband out to lunch to ask if we wanted to assume the role of head pastors of the church. Talk about God rocking your world!

This was one of those times where in the natural we would have said, "Heck no!" Pardon my bluntness, but it is true! Our church had been through some very trying times, some of which we were still recovering from as a body. Every time we prayed about leaving we felt like God said to stay. Sometimes it did not make sense in the natural, but we obeyed. At first my husband said there was no way he would have us pastor this church, but after praying about it, God said, "Go for it!" We let the pastors and elders know that we would assume that role. It seemed like such an easy transition at the time. We thought that our pastor would continue to mentor us in ministry as we assumed this role. We assumed there would be all kinds of support for us and our family as we launched out.

This is the part where following Jesus closely for the last few years saved my life. The only way that I can describe the situation we were entering into would be to compare it to walking into the Amazon Jungle with no light—no light from the moon, nor a flashlight—and trying to navigate your way through it. That is what it felt like in the natural. The situation we thought we were entering into turned into something quite different than we expected and quickly declined. It was difficult to see in the sheer amount of division over issues and lack of communication. What we went through for the next nine to ten months would prove to be some of the most difficult in our lives.

As you already know, we had been through difficult times. But the things we were experiencing were not only grieving our heart but the Father's heart. All the while we kept questioning God about His will in us pastoring in this nuttiness. Each time we would seek Him again for reassurance He would give us peace about pursuing it. It was not about a position or status for us. We truly had a heart for the people. I never knew that I was called to be a pastor, but He was revealing to me that, that was how He saw me.

This is what He had been preparing me for. I saw His heart in the Word for His sheep. For His people. Then He graciously allowed me to share in the heart of the Great Shepherd. It was forming in me before my very eyes. Even in all this craziness of our church, He was still speaking to me and giving me more and more of the intense passion that He has for His church. These people were so precious to the heart of God, and we were so humbled that He had called us to lead them. We felt like the lucky ones!

During this time of what seemed like such an upheaval, we felt like our God was holding us steady in the palm of His mighty hand. It really is weird to describe to you. We were affected by all that was happening, but He was also working in my heart and in my husband. We were in the Word and were learning how to walk in the Spirit more and follow Jesus. Everything that I gleaned from the last season just seemed to pour into this one. Good thing! Walking with Jesus when life is going smooth is like a walk in the park. This was not walk in the park! We began to feel like our very spiritual lives and sanity depended on walking closely with Him.

Soon we also felt the weight of the spiritual welfare others were experiencing depended on it too. We began to learn how to be shepherds in the middle of a flock needing it so very badly. The people around us in the congregation were not being led to safe pastures but were launched into an intense spiritual war that they had not signed up for.

My heart was so close to the people and their pain and confusion. People were coming to us more and more to explain what the heck was going on, but we had no clue! We were still in the season where God was giving us a peace about being pastors. Looking back now I see it was a window of time where God wanted to bring humility, love, truth, correction, and then a renewed vision for His plans for that ministry.

After about five grueling months of waiting and praying to see if this was still something God had for us, my husband said to me one morning while cooking breakfast, "I hope you do not get upset with me, but I feel like God is telling us to stop and not go forward with the pastor position." Funny thing is, within the last few days He had used those very words to speak to me. The very words. It is almost as if He put a Stop sign out to keep us from going forward. This is the importance of walking with Jesus very closely. He will save your life! Either we need to be at His heels, or He needs to be carrying us.

There were times during the season that I felt like both were true of me. He carried us through the dark times of not understanding what in the world had happened and through our own disappointment of possibly not being able to lead these people into the very things that God had put on our heart for them. We had to be held in the arms of our Shepherd as we watched the enemy destroy our church. Sometimes it does not fit into our belief system that Jesus would ask Him to follow us into situations like this. Well, at times He does. He wants to use all of us to bring reconciliation. We watched as some of the leaders who were following God and trying to help and love others the best they could were devastated that their dreams were being crushed also. Some were just not in a position to do anything to remedy the problems, which had much to do with the way the leadership of the church was set up.

After God had given us the Stop sign, we were not sure at what would come next. We did not know if we would ever get a green light or if this was permanent. Both my husband and I were put into severe testing, which caused us to have to listen to the Holy Spirit more than ever before. It is one thing to hear God for yourself, but when He begins to put you in a place of leading others, it is a whole new ball game! God seems to have a knack for making us desperate for Him. I do not think He minds me saying that.

After praying about what God said to us, we knew we needed to communicate it with the leadership of the church. That proved to be a trial in and of itself. We heard from the Lord on a Sunday, and on a Monday, which was Labor Day, we called our pastor and his wife over to our home. We were up front and honest about all that was going on, our concerns, and what God had spoken to us. We also wrote some things down for him to take back to the elders and their wives. My husband and I knew that God wanted us to be obedient to Him no matter what we saw others doing around us and even if it did not make sense to us. This is what it means to fear the Lord. If He said stop, we could not go forward.

It did not take very long before all the elders and pastor were questioning our decision. They simply could not understand it. Some were just simply inexperienced in situations like this, and others were not seeking God like they should have been. I say everything I say simply to shed light on the situation, not to condemn.

Not only did God stop us from pastoring at that time, but He was separating us from the ways of man. There was not only much demonic influence in this situation but also a lot of man's wisdom. Neither got us very far. If I could tell you all the times that I was facedown in tears and torment over what pressure was put on us during this time, I could write a book on that alone. Many of you, sadly, are shaking your heads at this one. You have been there, too. How sad it was for me to see those I had loved and served with be affected by the pressure of man and spirits of darkness.

During this time I really did not realize fully that God was continuing to set me free from the fear of man. I am all for godly leadership and now know how much it is needed. But to follow man into sin and away from God is just plain foolish. The relationship with our pastor of many years began to be strained during this time. Both my husband and I felt like the direction he was desiring for us to go was not what God was leading us to do. This was a difficult place for me, because this man had been used so much by God during the season of physical challenges in my life and because I looked up to him so much.

Friends, my Bible college was awesome, but I felt like nothing could prepare me for this nuttiness! Looking back now, I was unhealthy in some ways and depended too much on our pastor and not enough on God in some areas. God has a way of putting an end to that. I began to depend on and trust in my Father so much more during this time. I now see that He was continuing the healing process in me and was using this situation to do it. God can and will use anything to see His will accomplished in us and through us. During this time, I came to really know the presence of Jesus.

A little before this season I heard of a book by Mark Rutland titled *Launch Out Into the Deep*. I felt like I should read it. I not only read it but devoured it! I did not realize how hungry my spirit was to actually do this! God was preparing me because He was, in fact, getting ready to launch us into the deep. Reading this book by a man whose life was turned upside down by the Holy Spirit was so life-giving after all I was seeing and experiencing at my church.

We spent much emotion, prayer, and tears seeking God and His will and encouraging others to do the same. We believed that we had a place of authority to speak some of the difficult words of truth and correction during this time because they had asked us to pastor, but we told them that we would not pastor unless some very specific things were dealt with. God taught me how to do all of this in love. It was tricky. He softened my heart with His mercy, and even though at times we had to speak truth in very difficult circumstances He gave us His love and mercy for those around us. We loved them with all of our heart even though we had seen so much. These are the families that we led and worked with for years.

Another church took over our church. Some of the members of our church continued to attend, but many left. This was a dark time for me. I had doubts over if I had been crazy enough to pastor the church or if I really heard from God. Some people around us did not help us with that struggle. They told us that all of this happened because we were not ready to pastor. If what we saw was true pastoral ministry, then yes, you are right; I am not called to that. Others said we did not hear from God, and it was not His plan. Everyone was trying to scramble over what the heck just happened. It was difficult. Now I realize that they were just hurting themselves and were looking for answers, as we were.

All during this season God led us to His Word in some very powerful and healing ways. He became my teacher and showed and taught me how to lead like Moses, who feared God so much. He reminded me that Joshua tarried in the tabernacle in the presence of God, and that is where he ultimately got his courage to lead the children of Israel into the Promised Land. He showed me that this is what a leader should be and was continuing to form my heart. He directed me to take out some things and place some new things in there.

We stayed at the church that our church merged with for a while to see if the Lord had anything for us there. We, for the first time in eleven years, felt released from that church. It was no longer our church. It had different leadership, different people, and a different vision.

Through that process Jesus daily taught me how to forsake all and follow Him and how to love and lead like Him. He was continuing to mold me into His image. I definitely felt molded—actually, beat up too! I was being molded by Him and beat up by others.

On the other side of those trials I can actually tell you how grateful I am for them. No, I am not some sicko who loves trials and pain. I would prefer to ditch them just as much as the next person, but I know that I need them. And He uses them. They are a part of life.

Something that gave me a little comfort during this time was learning about how Jesus was treated as He entered public ministry. Luke 4:28–29 says that the religious leaders tried to run Him off of a cliff. I felt like I was in good company. The Holy Spirit was such an amazing Comforter and Counselor during this time. We did have a few wise counselors and friends who walked with us through this time that we are so grateful for. They prayed that His will be done in our lives, ministry, and family. They prayed and interceded that we would be safe in the palm of His might hand. And we were. We are!

As I began to see His faithfulness more and more, my head began to lift above the clouds. It took a while, and some love and healing from the body of Christ and leaders in some other churches to bring healing and restore wholeness and my faith in godly leadership. I regained the ability to believe that He does have godly leaders that are pure. He must have preserved that in me all my life, because I have seen many terrible things happen in my life, all in the name of Christ.

Driving by the church now does not invoke feelings of pain anymore but gratefulness—gratefulness that Satan was again not able to destroy me or my family through bitterness and resentment. Jesus had shown me how to navigate through the trials and snares of this life and continued to teach me how to walk free from the enemy's plans. He is so good! Quitting ministry did not occur to us but actually launched us out into it more and more, as I will share in a bit.

On this side of the healing from all that happened about two to three years ago, I see that not everything that happened at our former church was bad or evil. We loved our pastor, and he helped me tremendously during the beginning of the season with my feet. He was one of the few who understood and could perceive what God wanted to do with the situation. My family and I are forever grateful to him for this. He helped me understand the love of God and ways of the Spirit in many wonderful ways. Not everything in him was bad. I just got to a place where to continue to follow him would mean not following Jesus for my life. What my heavenly Father was saying was different from what my pastor and spiritual leaders were saying about the direction of my life. Separating from that and continuing to follow Jesus instead of this man that I loved and looked up to was difficult.

Having all of this happen in our church during a time in my life where I felt like my church family was way closer to me than my natural family was very difficult and scary. I felt like the rug was being pulled up from under me again. That was the place where so much of my healing occurred and the place I felt safe sharing it all. It was the place where He healed me, delivered me, and called me into ministry. Our babies were born in that church. But something changed for me. We could no longer minister the truth in the atmosphere of what was happening. The enemy got a foothold and made sure that others would not find freedom. We built so many wonderful relationships with so many people. So much good fruit in my life and others came from that ministry. I am happy to say that a few relationships, including our family's relationship with my dear friend Carrie and her family, have continued and have been strengthened through it all. To let the rest go and have them not want to talk to you or return your phone calls was tough. But He was faithful to be with us in every step. He truly does weep with those who weep (Rom. 12:15).

After being released from our church we began to visit other churches to see what the Lord had for us. We knew we really needed time to regroup and heal from all the hurt of the last season. Many relationships were severed. I tried to hang on to some longer than God wanted me to, and that was not fruitful. He was so gracious in His words of healing and helping me to grieve and let go of the hurt. And forgive. Oh wait, He was using all the things that I learned in the last season, while adding a little more, to help me through this one! When you feel like all is being shaken in you, go ahead and let Him just turn you all the way upside down! Do not give up halfway. Keep following Him.

Let's look at what Jesus Himself has to say about following

Him. Go with me back to the text that I began this chapter with in Matthew 4:18–22. Who is this man who could say two seemingly simple words to mortal men and women and turn their lives upside down? Can you think of anyone you know who can say these two words to you and have the power to change your life? These words that were spoken by the one who created the universe led to the true riches of life. They were spoken not by some selfish God trying to control His subjects but by a loving and all-wise God who knows what is best for us. He knows that when we follow Him our deepest longing for why we were placed on this planet at this very time in history will be fulfilled.

So many times we do not even know the purposes He has for us. During this season I could not see it all yet, but I had a sense that by following Him out of some places and situations He was unlocking the destiny He had for us all along. Following Jesus does not always mean we only enter new places, but sometimes it means leaving things and people behind. Much of the time we walk so much in the natural that we cannot see His purposes. The story of these verses is really pretty simple. His words are not ordinary words. Because He is God His words contain power—power over our heart. Without Him stepping into our lives, we live pretty aimlessly. We may do some good deeds but nothing that will outlast this life or really have much meaning in the grand scheme of things.

I pray our heart would hear Jesus say, "Follow Me!" Our heart and life were made for these two words. He breathes life on us and in us when He speaks them. They give vision to our eyes and direction to our feet. No other person can accomplish so much in saying so little. When He says, "Follow Me," it means something different for each of us. The funny thing is that when He speaks them to us, we do not need anyone to interpret them to us. His words are like a perfectly crafted key that unlocks our heart and our potential. Jesus knows what we are made for.

This was true of His disciples. His voice was heard by ordinary people, and they were transformed into new people. Notice the words in verse 18: "They *were* fishermen." In verses 20 and 22 the text says that they immediately left where they were and what they were doing and followed Him. Then they came alive to their destiny and purpose. He does the same with us today. He did the same thing regarding my husband and I following Him out of the situation at our former church.

He came to make us fully alive to His destiny and purpose, not any ones else's or even our own. How about we just drop the old stinky fishing nets like those disciples did and pick up a whole new net? He wants our heart and life to be the net that He uses to capture people for His kingdom. All of us get to be a part of that! If Jesus wants us to follow Him, He may lead us out of some places and away from shores that our lives will wither in. If He wants to put us in an environment where we can grow and soar to become the people He meant us to be, He can do that—and quite drastically, I might add! He can and will arrange some circumstances for us to be able to use all He has done in us and taught us to spread our wings and fly. Where we were at was hindering that. We were not free to soar. We had to continue to follow the one who had been so faithful to us. I had to get into the boat and let Him take me into the deep waters that He had for me.

We must go as He launches us in the deep and we are over our heads. We cry out for help and He comes. He comes in the storm and the raging waters all around us. He does not come to save us and take us back to shore; He takes our hand and leads us deeper, if we allow Him to. He takes us deeper because that is where the big fish are, my friends! It is where we cannot feel the sand beneath our bare feet, but we can look up and see the hand of our Savior taking us where He destined us to live—in over our heads!

CHAPTER 17
OVER MY HEAD

As the Lord released us from our former church, our family began to visit other churches to see if He had a place for us to go and serve. We were happy to go and serve someone else and the vision that God had given to them. We were used to that, and that was *safe*.

He does not even seem to like that word! As we were at these churches looking around and seeing where we could fit, it all seemed empty. We prayed and did not sense it was because we were still hurting but that God had something else for us. These desires stirred in our heart until we could no longer shake them. He was forming a vision for what He had for us right before our eyes! Oh, being in God's will truly is the safest place for us, just not for the parts of us that like comfort or predictability. Unfortunately, my personality seems to enjoy both of those things!

It was during this time that my husband and I started feeling a stirring and calling to start our own church. Never in thousand years would I have ever, ever seen this coming. Yes, it has to do with the whole following Jesus thing. I certainly could not go back to fear, so the only logical thing seemed to be to go forward.

None of the leaders we served with at our previous church were with us, nor were there many people to go to for wisdom or counsel about this. The emotions of fear—especially fear of being disappointed again like in our last situation—seemed to flood my soul. Why on Earth would I want to go start something and be disappointed all over again by people? No thanks! There were a few wise counselors in our lives that I am grateful for. But poor me, for the most part all I had was the Holy Spirit and the Bible. Our family took about six months to seek the Lord and pray about what we were feeling before we began our church. We knew we desperately needed healing from all we experienced, and God really used all that I had learned through the last season to continue to bring healing to this area of my life.

It became apparent to me that everything He had done in me was preparing me to lead in this capacity. He was continuing to form the heart of a shepherd in me, even through the pain. I could see that those men and women who knew us well and asked us to pastor saw something in us that we did not see in the beginning. They saw that we were equipped to pastor and to lead. The longer I walked with Jesus, I began to see it also. God removed us from our old environment so that He could use us and so that we could fully walk out what He had placed in our heart.

On May 28, 2011, we began Awaken Fellowship! We are currently meeting in our home. What excitement and anticipation filled our hearts as we took the plunge. All through the season of waiting on Him, He placed so much vision and passion in our heart. His words to me continued to heal me as He gently reminded me that although I was disappointed about how the last situation unfolded, He had new things for our family. He reminded me that all He had placed in me would be fulfilled, only with different people and in a different setting. Oh, how His words of life brought great release and healing to my soul! One day as I was folding laundry He comforted me as I was still mourning the loss of what we thought we would be doing at our previous church. He spoke that I did not have to leave behind all the gifts, passion, and vision, but rather they were something that *could* still be fulfilled. That set me free to continue to seek Him for what He wanted to do with us right then.

How naive my husband and I were to think that all would

be easy once we started a church. In the beginning we had some people come to our church that attended our former church. We in no way began a church to bring them with us. They left before us and were still looking for a place to worship. The night my husband and I were sharing the vision God had given us for this church that couple looked at us and said, "Pastors cannot have vision; only apostles can have vision!" The righteous anger of God rose up in me that evening, and I addressed the error head on with Scripture. Yes, all those grueling months of strife and false teaching at our former church caused me to see God's heart and passion for truth. They also caused me to see His great need to fiercely protect His bride from false teaching based on man. After that the couple never came back. Oh, they are precious people, but they were not called to be a part of what God is doing with us. It seemed like we were still trying to shake off the residue from the religious bondage that was attached to our former church.

We also had some people who had caused me and my family great hurt in the past come and want to speak into our ministry. I knew God was asking me to be bold and not only to confront this on a personal level but now on the level of a leader. Boy, finding courage in this situation was difficult! Eventually they stopped coming as well.

There were others who simply did not understand why we were starting a church. They reasoned that there were so many other churches and that our city did not need another one. I guess I was not prepared for that question, and all I could say was, "God told us to." Sometimes faith has to be enough. It was not enough for some around us. They gave us a hard time about doing something as simple as loving God and loving others. We felt more pressure from others who used to have authority over us. Both my husband and I finally had to put our foot down and walk away from some relationships from our past church that were a distraction to what He was calling us to do.

The thing that shocked my husband and I the most was that some people thought meeting in a home was not church. Oh, you can have Bible studies in your home, they protested, but *not* church! God was using all this opposition to continue to free my heart to follow Him and Him alone. He was freeing me to not care about what people thought of us, about what He had asked us to do, or about the way He called us to do things. One of the things that God placed on my and my husband's heart was that what He would have us do would not be traditional. Of course it wouldn't! I felt like I could not look around at what some churches were doing and follow them. He was laying out a unique course for us, as I believe He wants to do with each ministry and church. He is way more creative than we give Him credit for!

The Father really put a passion in my heart that His desire is to bring many people into His kingdom and that He does not want them led into more traditions of men but toward His Son, Jesus Christ. He did not want them led to more denominations but to freedom in Christ. This passion still burns in me today to have what we do be more about His kingdom than my church or set of beliefs. Oh, as a teacher and Bible school student I have such a passion for truth and solid biblical doctrine. I just cannot do the whole thing without love anymore!

The Father is waiting for us to cast the net into the waters. It is time to go to the other side of the boat. We have been fishing long enough on this side. You see, when God created me, He not only made me a pastor but an evangelist. This runs through every fiber of my being. It is my passion to see those God made be reconciled to Him through His Son, Jesus Christ. It is the thing that I wake up thinking about in the morning and the passion that drives me to share Christ with others. He has placed me in just the right setting to do the very thing He has designed me to do. What He has called me to do stirs all those passions up. It propels me into my destiny!

We live in Salem, Oregon, which is one of the least-churched areas in our country. People would rather hang out at Starbucks than attend church! How encouraging it is when people tell you they have no need or desire to go to church. As much as I believe in the church of Jesus Christ, I can at times see where they are coming from. After all we experienced at our former church, for the first time in my Christian life I could understand why they would not want to be a part of that. Instead of seeing the situation as hopeless, we bring Jesus *to* them!

The passionate heart of God for the lost and broken has caused us to do some things that may seem nontraditional to some. He has shown us that for many who have been so wounded in their lives it takes time and trust to open their lives up to anyone, much less God. He is showing us *how* to love them and show them Jesus in some very practical ways. We provide clothing, school supplies, and other outreaches that meet a need but ultimately will show them that they can trust God. Letting the Holy Spirit direct all that we do is so life-giving. Jesus led us out of the war zone of strife and debate at our former church straight into the harvest field. He took our hands and said, *"The fields are white for harvest."* (See John 4:35.) He led us past those arguing over what elders, pastors, and apostles *can* do and into what He *was* doing! How exciting! I would never in a thousand years trade where we were for where Jesus has taken us and where He *is* taking us!

I have learned more about the heart of our Shepherd during this time. I learned from sitting at the feet of Jesus—and, at times, weeping at the feet of Jesus—what it means to be a true shepherd. I should say, I *began* to learn. Do you ever notice the more you learn, the more you see that you need to learn? The fierce love that

Jesus has for His bride is so incredible. I have experienced it and felt it not just for myself but for His people. For His flock. Out of the love He has given me for His people, I have sincerely prayed that I would not hurt others as we have been hurt. He has called us to reach out to the very people who have been hurt by spiritual leaders and in churches. We have learned how precious each one is to the Father. This is why He has called us to something that is not traditional.

Oh, the message of Jesus never changes, but often we need to be sensitive to His Spirit and how He would lead us to share it. Many, many times Jesus and I have hit the streets together. He has had me drive or walk up and down the streets of our neighborhood and city and pray for those who do not know Him. Many I know by name; many I do not. They are precious to Him. He is calling them! We get the privilege of partnering with God to see them come home.

God allowed us to go through that season for many reasons, but one was to learn how to treat people. Paul hit the nail on the head when He wrote 1 Corinthians 13. This is where it is at and what love really is. If we think we can come to church and sing, dance, prophesy, or whatever and then lie, gossip, and lead people astray, we have a rude awakening coming! Go back and read through the prophets (especially Ezekiel 34) to see what happened when shepherds led God's people astray. God wants to so restore us so that we lead out of wholeness and not our flesh and brokenness. Too many people want to lead before God exalts them. Experience with the Father causes us to love; love is how we treat people. Period. If we do not treat people the way God does and the way He lays it out in His Word, we fall short of love. And yes, I am talking to myself too!

Often God has us go through the school of life. This is where His Spirit teaches us things we could never learn from anyone else.

He had been continuing to uproot the fear of man and pride that plagued me all my life. I so wanted to be like Jesus, who had no fear of man and was free to obey God. God was using my circumstances and Isaiah 50 to continue to free my heart. All I had been through with my physical circumstances really freed my heart and laid a good foundation of trusting God, but apparently God wanted more of me! He died too powerful a death and lived to obediently to God to give us partial freedom. He truly is relentless! He had been untangling the bondage one string at a time, and this was another string to be cut from around my heart. I realized what a huge bondage it was for me to allow others to control me and to follow what others wanted for my life, even in ministry.

All that God taught me before, what we went through with our former church about Him giving me the gifts and the calling I had, was strengthened during this time. God did not let any of what He taught me go to waste. Through all of this I was seeing what He had for me and hearing His plans. He had to separate me from others I was serving with at our church to do this. This was scary for me. Nonetheless, God would use all of this to completely free me and to tell me who I was in Him.

I do not know if I can express with pen and paper the agony and grief these situations produce and how it hurts when we are forced to continue following Christ over man, those who are closest to us. It hurts our soul, which has ties to those people. I am forever grateful for the things that our former pastor taught me and my family about following Christ and His Spirit. He walked with my family and I through the season I was in with my feet and helped us tremendously. There were not many others that we knew at the time that would have had the perspective that he had on what God was doing in my life. Sometimes, though, we get to a place where certain people can no longer help us. At times, through tears and grief, we come to realize that they can actually hinder us. It is painful. I know this, and I am sorry that many of you have been in this place. However, Jesus will heal every disappointment and hurt that comes from spiritual leaders.

Getting free in this area is tricky because it involves our faith in God. Although our faith may get shaken, He wants our faith in Him to be strengthened during these times. He truly is the only perfect one who will never harm us or let us down. And yes, sometimes, we have to learn that the hard way! Even if you have followed man, it is never too late to get back on track. He is so merciful!

God had brought me too far to abandon Him for anything on this earth. There was no position, title, or praise of man that could replace my Jesus' precious voice telling me how proud He was of the tough decisions I was making. Trust me in this, hearing these words and feeling the approval of His presence is worth more than anything anyone can give you. Anything! I now know this, and nothing can take it away from me. You may be saying, "I could never get to that place; I am too bound." Beloved, if I can break free, He can break you free too! He so loves you. Just throw yourselves at His feet and ask Him for this. This is a prayer He will answer!

As I continued to yield to His voice, a new boldness began to rise up in me. Little by little, good decision by good decision. This is often how freedom comes—a little at a time. I spent much time with my Father during this season because I was beginning to feel like He was all I had. We had lost many close relationships. We lost our spiritual leaders, our mentors, the ones I thought God would use to mentor me in this ministry He was calling us into. Oh, but the tears of pain began to turn into tears of joy in His presence! He was washing off the hurt and disappointment from dreams not lived out and was doing away with the guilt and shame that we had done something wrong. Many told us during this time that we were simply not ready to pastor or that we missed God. They said He never had a plan for us to pastor that church. That hurt.

We just had to stay in step with what God had told us and knew that if nobody on Earth understood us, He did. His love began to wash off all we had been through, and I knew I was safe in the palm of His mighty hand. He also loved on us through a few people who walked with us through this time, and I do not want to forget to honor them and their love, wisdom, and understanding. One is my dear friend, Carrie, who I have already written about! May God richly bless you, my friends and family!

It was out of this place of desperation and season of craziness that God really seemed to launch us into what we believe God had for us all along. What I had not planned on was that I was not only going to experience external pressures as we began our church but that He would use this time in my life to finish the work He began in me seven years ago. Let's just say that Jesus and I have wrestled with my identity issues more than once! Him calling me to lead unearthed the residue of shame and fear that were still lurking in the secret places of my heart. He had freed me from most of it, but He has this relentless quality about Him that wants it *all* gone! Him putting me in situations where I had to tell others what we were doing, even when many did not understand or seemingly care, forced me to choose who I would believe about my calling—Him or me. By this time, I had learned that I might as well agree with Him!

Being few years into this church planting business and still only having a few people really bothered me at times. It did not seem to bother God, because when I would pray and seek Him He would remind me of the promises He gave me that many would be coming into His kingdom and our church and that this was a time of sowing, loving, and planting seed. Often I would get discouraged and want to give up on it all because I was not seeing the results I thought we should be seeing.

When this happened, there were a few things that kept me going. The first is my love for Jesus. I just cannot quit on something I know

He has called me to. The second is my love for the people. We may be small in number, but God is up to something big! Those we are called to reach and are in relationship with are some of the most beautiful people. I wish you could meet them!

As a result of the shame I lived with, the enemy was able to, at times, convince me that there was something wrong with me and what we were doing. This sounded all too familiar. It caused me to seek my God until He completely set me from shame. It was like the rope of shame that held me down all my life was loosed and broken little by little. He was breaking the last threads of it through what He has called me to do. Let me tell you graciously that He did it for me.

Recently He gave me a dream. In the dream two men were talking to me. One was listening while the other was telling me how he began a church that lasted one and a half years. In the dream I turned away from the men and began to cry. A huge load came off my shoulders. I woke up and wondered if God was trying to tell me that we would no longer have a church like the man in the dream. After much prayer and seeking Him, He showed me what He wanted to communicate to me through the dream. He showed me the word *failure* was sitting on my shoulders. God nailed it, as usual! Suddenly I realized that by carrying that shame I also carried the sense that I was failing at the very thing God was calling me to. I felt like I failed at this whole church planting thing because we only had a few people coming.

This was one area in which the enemy could always belittle me. He often used people, and sadly at times myself to agree with him that whatever I was doing was not good enough. This was no different.

God, apparently, was not going to let that trend continue. After this dream and after letting God continue to free my heart as I let go of that big old lie, I have been completely free from shame. I do believe it was the last thread to go. Praise God!

God put on my heart one of the prophetic words that He gave our family as we began this church. He said that He had something for us; it would seem small, but there would be much fruit and what we were doing would make a big splash. At times that word seemed contrary to one that two of our Bible college instructors gave Andy and I as we graduated Bible college. They said that we would be like honey and an example and influence to many young people. They said I would be bringing in people off the streets and that Andy would be discipling them and establishing them as leaders in our church. They saw me bringing in many and him teaching them. That was fifteen years ago.

Often I would question God about not yet seeing this, and He impressed upon my heart that the season for a great harvest is coming. In fact, we have begun to see the first fruits of the harvest! Our church has been providing a summer youth art program for kids in the area. We tied in the truths of the gospel through the whole program. Little by little, week by week, we got further into the story of the Fall of man, which eventually led into us needing a savior. Well, the Savior did not just stay in the pages of history from thousands of years ago. He leapt off the page and into our garage, where we were holding the outreach! I just love it when Jesus shows up. The sweet anointing of the Holy Spirit was there. Before we knew it, three kids decided to follow Jesus. They heard the call!

I am so very proud of those young people. One is a beautiful young lady that I have been praying for and just loving on for a few years now. Some of that lovin' included going to the mall and out for ice cream. I told her if she hangs out with me, there will be lots of chocolate and ice cream involved. That is just the beginning for them. Just last weekend they were baptized. We talked more with them about following Jesus. They, along with us, will continue to hear Jesus call to us those very words—"Follow Me"—for the rest of our lives. He is definitely an adventurous God, and we will never have a dull moment following Him!

Just last night, we had our first baptism service. Five beautiful young ladies were baptized! One is our cousin, two were girls we led to Christ this summer, and two are our girls! There is nothing like getting to lead your own children to faith in Christ and then to getting baptize them. I am still floating! Looking out on the crowd and sharing the Word before the baptisms, I also had to share how I never saw myself being a pastor. Oh, it is one thing to lead people to Christ, but to disciple them and be responsible for a church and ministry is a whole other ball game. I gave Him thanks and praise before them that we get the awesome privilege to lead. He knew I was called to this all along. He is showing me that my gifts, temperament, and where I have walked in this life are what He is using to fulfill His plan for me. I love it and would have it no other way.

Even now He is stirring our hearts for more. He has reminded us that although our beginning is small, He rejoices in it (Zech. 4:10). He wants us to also! He has placed such vision and a passion to reach a greater multitude on our family's heart. We know He is preparing us to reach even more people with the good news of Jesus!

God and I have been having many full-circle moments, as I call them. I would like to share one with you. Fifteen years after graduating Bible college, in March of 2013, I returned to Christ for the Nations to attend a conference and to receive my minister's license. The young girl who arrived at that school on that hot and humid August afternoon when I did not know a soul and was scared to death came back at thirty-four years old. She is much more healed, free, and walking in her purpose than ever before! Taking a step of faith into more of what He has for me in ministry really proved to be life-changing for me—and healing.

One of my former roommates came down all the way from

Minnesota to attend the conference and to see me receive my license. Having her and Andy there truly humbled me, and their love and belief in me and what He has called me to do brought immense healing to me. During the years of my worst bondage, after Bible college, I failed to keep in contact with my friends I had met and built relationships with like I wanted to. I was too bound and tired from trying to survive. Can anyone relate? Now, even that was being restored, as I was. As God brought me out of this season of healing, I noticed that I had a new desire and energy to reconnect with old friends. It is funny how God uses many things to restore confidence to us, isn't it?

I believe that God is pleased with my decision to get my minister's license and to continue to pursue the call He has on my life. The messages that came through the people we were surrounded by, the worship, and those bringing the Word were all so timely for my husband and I. They not only affected our personal lives but our ministry. The credentialing ceremony was very significant in my life. I am such a softie. We did not even get through the introductions of the morning and I was in tears! Part of what brought me to tears was the fact that the leaders who were praying for us and giving us the licenses said they had been fasting and praying for us. This brought so much healing to me after all we had been through with our former church. It was like God was restoring the desire in my heart for godly leaders and influence in my life. He had brought me through the few years of what felt like isolation to completely free me from my need to trust in man. Now He was bringing back godly leaders who would continue to believe in us and bring healing to our lives.

My husband and I enjoyed going back to our Bible college. After all, it is where we met and fell in love! We met up with old friends we had not planned on seeing. We laughed, we cried (OK, I cried), we danced, and we were refreshed. We ate at Cracker Barrel way too much. (We do not have them in Oregon!) And we enjoyed time without our kids!

Most of all, He affirmed through the messages that we were on the right track. Now I was ready to receive affirmation from man, because God was in His rightful place in my life. No longer was I looking for them to tell me who I was. I knew. I remember going down to the altar in the front of the auditorium. I balled my eyes out. This time it was not as a Bible college student who was just trying to survive the deep work that God was doing in me, but it was because I realized His great faithfulness to me. None of what I had gone through in my life since Bible college (or before for that matter) was able to destroy me and keep me from the destiny He had for me. Nothing. He brought me back to the place where He planted such vision in my heart for His purposes in the earth. Now all I could do was weep in His presence. Sometimes there are no words to express the amount of gratitude in our heart!

After coming home from our trip, I realized I was more healed. My heart was more on fire for what He was calling me to do. Taking the step of faith by putting myself out there and getting my license and having to share with others what He called me to do and what I was doing healed me. He continued to lift off of me the shame that I always hid under. I noticed that my body felt better. God was putting much more on my plate, but my body was able to handle the weight of it all. I told Andy that I believed that God was continuing to heal my body as I surrendered my life to His dreams for me. How cool is that?

I personally am amazed that I am actually doing some of the things He has me doing. Waking up now is an adventure to see what Jesus has for me each day. Being led by the Spirit is exciting and new every day. It is funny how many years of regret and defeat over not feeling like you can do what God is asking you to do can all be washed away with just one look from the Master.

If there is anyone in the Bible I can relate to, it is Peter. I can relate to his walking in the natural tendencies he had before the power of the risen Savior changed his life. He seemed to have some fears and insecurities that were just all wrapped up in "Peter." One of my favorite chapters in the Bible—at least right now, because I have a new favorite all the time—is in John 21. Oh man, I feel like I could just jump out of my skin right now! I cannot tell you what this chapter means to me. I know some of you can relate when God is jumping off the pages of His Word into your life!

Let's look at John 21:15: "So when they had eaten breakfast, Jesus said to Simon Peter, 'Simon, son of Jonah, do you love me more than these?' He said to Him, 'Yes, Lord; You know that I love you.' He said to him, 'Feed My lambs.'" Jesus went on to say this to Peter two more times. What on Earth was Jesus getting at? It seemed like the more Jesus asked, the more it went deeper into Peter's heart and spirit. You see, we read in Luke 5 that Peter had originally been called out into the deep with Jesus to become a fisher of men, not a better fisherman. He became a totally transformed fisherman! Jesus certainly blessed him in that, but He called Him to something much greater. Peter was made to be a fisher of men.

Peter followed Jesus closely and was one of the closest to Jesus on this earth. Jesus allowed Peter to be sifted and tried so that all that was not true and authentic would be brought to the surface and washed away in the Master's love. Let's look at our Lord's words in Matthew 26:31–35:

> Then Jesus said to them, "All of you will be made to stumble because of Me this night, for it is written: 'I will strike the Shepherd, And the sheep of the flock will be scattered.' But after I have been raised, I will go before you to Galilee." Peter answered and said to Him, "Even if all are made to stumble because of You, I will never be made to stumble." Jesus said to him, "Assuredly, I say to you that this night, before the rooster crows,

you will deny Me three times." Peter said to Him, "Even if I have to die with You, I will not deny You!" And so said all the disciples.

After Peter denied Jesus, the Bible says, "He went out and wept bitterly" (Matt. 26:75). I think that I can hear the familiar sound of that weeping. Feeling like an utter failure at following Jesus and His plans for us. Feeling so sick of yourself and what you have lacked. One of the most amazing attributes about Jesus is His ability to forget. My personality and broken self just cannot do that so easily. I have a great memory, and sometimes that is not always a positive. How can Jesus just forget about all the nutty stuff we have done or not done and ask us to move on? Jesus is a restorer.

We break right into the middle of Jesus restoring Peter in John 21. Wasn't He going to rebuke and chastise Him for denying Him in the middle of His darkest hour? Instead, He gives Peter back his original assignment and tells him He believes that he can and will do it. I can so relate. I feel like Peter now, looking into those piercing eyes of love that have believed in me when I have not even been able to believe in myself. Our Savior is able to pick us back up, even from a fresh fall.

I am not talking about failing in the last few years, because Jesus and I have cleared that up. I am talking about feeling like I failed at my life. Do you hear that? I love testimonies of those who say Jesus set me free ten or twenty years ago, but what about when He is in the middle of setting you free right this very moment? I love that Jesus allows us in on such intimate moments between Him and His people, don't you?

Jesus says something next that just blows me away. In John 21:18–19 He says:

Most assuredly, I say to you, when you were younger, you girded yourself and walked where you wished; but when you are old, you will stretch out your hands, and another will gird you and carry you where you do not wish." This He spoke, signifying by what death he would glorify God. And when He had spoken this, He said to him, "Follow Me."

Stop and let that sink in. Little did Peter know that Jesus letting the enemy sift him would lead to Peter's greatest restoration and calling—to feed the church of Jesus Christ. There was no way that the old Peter was going to do this. The old Peter had too much flesh and too much pride.

As a youth I attended a church camp. At the camp during worship and man called me out of the audience and had a word from God for me. He said that many souls were weighing on the line for me to tell them about Jesus. He said that God did not want me to shy away from the calling He had for me to lead them to Him. How did I respond? I shied away. Like, big time. Oh, with all of my heart I wanted to obey Jesus, but I was so bound. Picture a leg that is broken. No matter how bad you want to run with a broken leg, it is just not going to happen. All the years of bondage and the effects of abuse took its toll on me, and the calling that God had upon my life suffered.

I cannot say that I have all the freedom that He wants for me and that I do not fall down at times, but I am far closer than I was when that word was given to me. God has given me a beautiful picture to explain this to me. He reminded me of when my children were learning to walk and they fell down. He asked if I got mad at them for falling many times, and I said a quick , "No, that would be terrible!" I sensed it was the same with me and my heavenly Father. I am truly, for the first time, learning to be myself and do what He has called me. Oh, those glorious seeds of His calling were there when I first accepted Him, and He has protected them all this time!

Now that He has brought so much healing to me, I am learning to walk in them—not perfectly, not without falling, but we are heading in the right direction. And oh, He is so proud of me! No man or woman on Earth can give me the approval and joy that I have from just flat-out following Jesus. This is what He wanted to accomplish in this season in me. I can say that with confidence. We have made such progress in our relationship.

Oh, you will have such hope when the eyes of Jesus look so tenderly at you and He speaks over you who you are and what you are called to do afresh. You may have heard the call years ago for the first time, like me, and have not been able to walk in it because of your own stuff. But after the testing and the sifting, lift up your eyes and your head, because Jesus is coming for breakfast! He is coming to sit down and get in the middle of your business again and call you back to what you were made for. You will hear Jesus tell you in His own way, like He did to Peter, "Follow Me." This time you will do it because you absolutely know that you are a huge mess without Him and that there really is no other option for you. You cannot go back, and the only place to go is forward. Do not worry. When you follow Him, He will lead you into the best!

In the process you will learn much, like I have, about the amazing grace of God. His grace is so deep and limitless and gives us the ability to walk out His plans for us. He desires us to come to the place of grace, to live in the place of grace. This is a place where we know beyond anything else that if He is not working in us and through us we can do nothing of eternal significance. Grace is getting to the place of death to the old us and walking in who He has made us to be. We see it by grace, and we walk it out in grace. I so love His grace!

God has me saying and doing things now that would have stirred up more unbelief than faith in me if you would have told me five or ten years ago that I would be doing them. I guess I could get really honest and say that God is propelling me into His plans for me more and more. A new boldness is coming to witness and share the gospel and to pray for the sick in public. As we began this church I was nervous about sharing it with people and what they would think. Sharing Christ with people, even a few years ago, was more difficult for me than it is now. Those are the things that God has been sifting out of my life, the old fear, shame, and hiding that came from my past. God is setting me free in the middle of what He has called me to do. All glory goes to Him!

I do not have all the freedom that I want or even all that He desires to give me. More is coming! I am looking so forward to it. He is continuing to teach me *how* to walk out being me. There are times when I see it unfolding daily. When I fail and do not do everything perfectly, He reminds me what a loving and merciful Father He is and just picks me up and sets my feet back on the path. He reminds me often that I never got mad at my girls when they were learning to walk but clapped as they walked on wobbly little legs until they were running. At times, I feel like I am in-between wobbly little legs and running myself. He is restoring me and teaching me how to be me and how to do what He has called me to do.

There are so many in our city and neighborhood who desperately need Him, and I am getting to share my testimony with them about how Jesus changed and is changing my life. I get to share how God has healed my body from so much. He is the focus now. My eyes are getting off of myself and what I feel I still lack and onto the one who told me to follow Him. Oh, what glorious freedom to get our eyes off of us. The Holy Spirit has such a way of glorifying Christ with our heart and mind! That is grace! At times I will be driving down the street and I feel I need to stop and share Christ with someone, and I do! There are many beautiful women who I get to listen to, pray with, and lead to Christ. That, my dear friends, is a miracle, because I could not do that for a long time. And now I get to do it out of who I am, not just because I do not want God to be mad at me. Now the fear of Him is healthy and in the right per-spective. Before, because I grew up in a harsh and legalistic envi-ronment, I wanted to do whatever I could not to be bad or wrong. Praise Him, now I do it because I just flat-out love and honor Him. I get the privilege of showing them Jesus with my life.

One of the early chapters in this book talked about healing with the Father. Joy fills my heart to know how much more healing has occurred in my relationship with my Father between the time of that writing and this, which has spanned almost two years! Peter experienced that healing the day Jesus restored him. We may read this as a one-time account, but I have a feeling that God's restora-tion process for him was just beginning that day. He was setting Peter's feet on a new path of freedom, like He is with me and you. Peter's life really began to change when he realized how deeply Jesus loved him through all the crazy things he said and did in the flesh, even actually denying he really knew Him.

We can never change the fact that God is love and that every-thing He does is out of love. We just can't. God knew what Peter was made for, and He continued to transform his life by the coming of the Holy Spirit and giving Peter a place of leadership in the church that Jesus was forming. Jesus believed in Peter, and I believe that simply knowing that brought such healing to him. If he is anything like me, that is what is propelled him to go on fol-lowing Jesus and not look back. We would all do well to follow his example!

Though at times what God has given us to do has made me feel like I am over my head, at this point in my life I would have it no other way. Jesus and I have traveled too far and climbed too many mountains to go back to the shore. He has shared His heart with me, and I have been open and honest with Him and shared with Him the many, many things He has placed in my heart about reaching the multitudes with the good news. If He has me lead these few people, as long as He is there, I want to be where He is. I am not moving on without Him. I am taking the Moses stance, who told God, "Unless you go with us, do not lead us out of here" (Exod. 33:15, author's paraphrase).

I am truly at a place now of being humbled and honored to serve Him and those He has placed in our lives. He is my everything. Being with Him wherever He is happens to be is my everything. My relationship with Him has gained so much intimacy by me following Him out into the deep. It took a while to get here, but the bumps, bruises, and scrapes were all worth it! Jesus is in the deep. I think He has been waiting there quite a while for me. He has been waiting there for you too. Dive in!

CHAPTER 18

CHOICES

*S*OMETIMES MOTHERS HAVE to say the hard things, things our children need to hear and that will make them grow. One of my greatest passions is to encourage and exhort others to go on in their journey with God and pursue all He has for them, even when it means being a little firm. Consider this chapter just that! I desperately pray that you would hear my heart and His in what may seem like a little firm, swift kick in the right direction! Goodness knows I have needed several in my life, because sometimes I drag my feet on some issues!

For some reading this book you may still not be sure about letting God into the places in your life that would really set you free. I know many, many of you are allowing Him in, and the results are and will be utterly astounding! Joshua tells us to choose this day who we will serve (Josh. 24:15); God will be faithful and do all He says in the Word, but we have a responsibility to live out the freedom that Christ died to give us. There are some things that only He can do, but there are some things that only we can do. God will encourage us to make good choices that line up with His Word, but only we can do that.

In all honesty, getting free from our past will force us to separate from things that have held us back from all God has for us. I have shared some of those truths through the testimony of what we went through in our former church. What about when those things are people that we have been in relationship with? Ugh, this is a tough one and one that does not have a blanket

black-and-white rule for each person. There are some Biblical principles that can help us navigate through some very choppy waters.
Sometimes seeing them in the Word is difficult because frankly
we do not want to see them. We are too scared.

I know this because I was scared for years. Let me share a bit of
my own experience on this and then dig into the Word so you can
understand how to apply it to your own life. I will mainly stay on
the topic of relationships, because for me, that is where I walked
in most bondage. However, these truths can be applied to any area
of our lives where we need to make good choices.

Sometimes we unknowingly make excuses for why we do not
set boundaries and say no to certain people or things in our lives
that are not healthy for us. I think those excuses are compounded
for Christians because we have believed lies and embraced legalistic thinking and teaching based on fear and not on love. This
is the kind of teaching that says we should never set boundaries
with people in our lives. Sadly, so many Christians, and Christian
leaders at that, are not walking in love. Not the love of Jesus. Not
the love the Bible talks so much about. Love is based on God and
who He is. It is that simple.

These lies have led us into bondage, and the enemy is having a
heyday with some of you. He keeps jerking us around on the short
rope he already has us on. We are looking for some miraculous
deliverance to appear from somewhere, and we may go to some
"miracle meeting" somewhere and expect God to bring deliverance from the things we still carry around. But His Word brings
us freedom, and it does it every time we obey it. We may not see
instant results, but we have to stick around long enough for Him
to get us out of the mess we got ourselves into.

While we desire freedom, we may fear making any decision that
will make us "bad." My husband has a saying that has helped me
and even made me laugh a bit! "You are already bad and wrong in

some people's eyes, no matter what you do or how you do it. Stop trying to be good and just go and join the 'bad' side!" Just get it over with! Some of you are trying to suck up to or gain the approval of people who will always fault you for something. So, just take the plunge and join those who are truly free to make choices that are needed without caring what others think. It is a lot more freeing over here! Stop trying to be so good all the time. With some people it is just a waste of time. Pursuing legalism will not ease the drive of your shame, guilt, or fear of being wrong or doing the wrong thing. Only following God's Word can do that for you. Stop trying to go to the ends of the earth to apologize just so your guilt is relieved for a moment. Do not worry; it will come back much worse next time, because it is a vicious, downward spiral. The enemy desires it to take you out, along with the people he is using to hurt it at you. Look at the face of Jesus. Forgive and do all the things His Spirit and Word tell you to do. But, for crying out loud, make the decision that if Christ died to give you total freedom, you will live in it, no matter the cost, no matter the choices that have to be made.

I am able to write such a copious amount of material on breaking free from unhealthy relationships because I have had to do it—and more than once. Now the tender part of me gets to come out. I am sure many of you reading this now are relating and thinking how this will be hard. You may be reading this through tear-filled eyes. I know. I lived it out and got to the other side with tear-filled eyes. It cost me much to gain the freedom that He has had waiting for me all along. It has cost my family much. But then again, the reality is that those who lose their life really end up finding it (Matt. 10:39). I would much rather be on this side of the pain and grief of what that would mean for me, letting go of what could never be, than to be in bondage to anything but the love of Christ.

Paul said the love of Christ compelled him (2 Cor. 5:14). He compels me to make the hard choices. His grace makes it not only possible but easy. I want His love, not fear, to motivate me and the choices I make. He wants that for you. Let Him hold your heart as you decide to walk away from some things or people in your life that are keeping you back from total devotion to Him. The Bible says that if we love anything more than Him we are not worthy of Him (Matt. 10:37). That *anything* means anything!

As I shared about our family's trying experience with the church we were at and looking to pastor, as we were getting ready to leave I sensed Jesus saying to me to follow Him. He is calling today just the same as He did two thousand years ago to some ordinary people. We are ordinary people, called and purposed to live extraordinary lives. So many times what separates people from living victorious lives are their choices. Think of those you know or know of who are living in victory and joy, and mark my words, they had to make some difficult and costly choices. They had to choose Jesus over all else. This is the way we are called to live for the rest of our lives. It does not get to be a one-time thing!

While it is wonderful to look at godly examples of faith and courage, let's set our gaze on the greatest for a few moments. Many assume that Jesus just flat-out hung out with and got along with everyone. Wrong. While He walked in perfect love toward all mankind, if we dig deeper into the Word we see that there were things and even relationships that He separated Himself from in order to fulfill God's plan for Him. Let's look for a few moments at His interaction with the Pharisees, who were supposedly teachers of His Word! Look at Matthew 23:1–4 (NIV):

> Then Jesus said to the crowds and to his disciples: "The teachers of the law and the Pharisees sit in Moses' seat. So you must be careful to do everything they tell you. But do not do what they do, for they do not practice what they preach. They tie up heavy, cumbersome loads and put them on other

people's shoulders, but they themselves are not willing to lift a finger to move them."

He just flat-out stayed away from these supposed teachers of the Law. I think they gave Him the willies! He gives you permission to do the same. The thing about following Jesus is that we actually have to do it. It is not just a saying we have as Christians. It is supposed to be a living reality in our lives. When He says move, we move. When He says stay, we stay—whether it makes sense to us or not. Sometimes it will not at the moment, but oh, down the road, we will see how wise our Savior is.

When we chose to leave our church, not in strife and anger but in obedience, it was hard with a capital *H*! But to keep following those who were there would have meant we were not following Jesus. None of us are perfect by any stretch of the imagination, but our lives should match up with our message. If the lives of your leaders don't, you have His permission to run! Do not follow someone who is not laying and is not willing to lay their lives down for Jesus, because they are not true Christian leaders.

There is another group of people that Jesus distanced Himself somewhat from: part of His family. This may come as a shock to you, and some of you may already be protesting that I am making this up. I know; it shocked me that it was in there too! I just never had to study it for myself because I was so busy trying to keep everyone happy rather than follow Jesus wholeheartedly. John 7 begins:

> After this, Jesus went around in Galilee, purposefully staying away from Judea because the Jews there were waiting to take His life. But when the Jewish Feast of Tabernacles was near, Jesus' brothers said to Him, "You ought to leave here and go to Judea, so that your disciples may see the miracles you do. No one who wants to become a public figure acts in secret. Since

you are doing these things, show yourself to the world." For even his own brothers did not believe in Him.

—John 7:1–5

In verses 6–8, Jesus responds:

"The right time for me has not yet come; for you any time is right. The world cannot hate you, but it hates me because I testify that what it does is evil. You go to the Feast. I am not yet going up to this Feast, because for me the right time has not yet come."

Later, He decided to go up, I am convinced, not because His brothers pressured Him to but because He chose to. You see, even God's own earthly family did not understand or believe in who He was. If we continue to study the Gospels, we do not hear very much about His family. Mary was the closest to Him, and He has such deep affection for her. I am not sure what happened to Joseph, and I would love to study more to see if there is more history on that. But Jesus does allow us to catch a few glimpses into His family—just enough, I believe, to maybe see a little of our own and maybe enough to hopefully set us free to follow Him, even when it comes to our family relationships.

Let's look at another interesting passage, and then we will talk about what this may look like for us.

When the soldiers crucified Jesus, they took his clothes, dividing them into four shares, one for each of them, with the undergarment remaining. This garment was seamless, woven in one piece from top to bottom. "Let's not tear it," they said to one another. "Let's decide by lot who will get it." This happened that the scripture might be fulfilled that said, "They divided my clothes among them and cast lots for my garment." So this is what the soldiers did. Near the cross of Jesus stood his mother, his mother's sister, Mary the wife of Clopas, and Mary Magdalene. When Jesus saw his mother there, and the disciple whom he loved standing nearby, he said to her, "Woman, here is your son," and to the disciple, "Here is your mother." From that time on, this disciple took her into his home.

—John 19:23–27

This is one of those passages that just needs to be pondered for a while, especially since it involves family and those Jesus grew up with. Maybe this is the first time you have heard this passage taught from this angle. Usually we focus on the Crucifixion, which we should, but God's Word is so multifaceted that He is able to teach us many things from just a few written words. In Jesus' final minutes breathing the air of this earth, what does He do? He loves others. He loves those closest to Him, making sure they would be taken care of. He talks about straightening out His affairs! He is so tender, even as He is enduring the worst suffering any human could and would ever go through. He wants to make sure His mother will be cared for. He knows her mother's heart is suffering with sorrow, sadness, and a whole host of human emotions. He still found it possible to show her His love for her.

While at times it appears that even Mary did not understand completely who Jesus was, I believe that they shared a good, healthy relationship here on Earth. Nothing in the Scriptures would say otherwise. And she was there. I am sure that thirty-three and a half years full of memories flashed through her mind during these last few minutes: Him being born that majestic evening in the stable. The quietness of the barn, after all the activity of angelic visitations, the Magi, and the anticipation of this miraculous birth. The first time she got to see Him, really see Him. There was the stir of the animals and the little one she bundled on her chest. His warm, sweet breath blowing on her chest. Now, at the cross, she looks up to see her firstborn Son breathing His last gruesome and pain-filled breaths. I am sure that nothing could have prepared her for this. Even divine warning and prophesies could not have painted a clear enough picture of what this would have been like. Nothing. I am sure she remembered the water being turned into wine at the wedding as her heart pondered such greatness as the miraculous intervention of heaven reaching down to Earth through her Son. Did her mind flash back to His first steps and His infectious smile? I am not sure. Now she was seeing His blood-filled face and body hanging on that cross.

What we are sure of is our Savior's tender love for His mother here. But notice who else is there, and Jesus' instructions to Him: the disciple who Jesus loved, John. I am not sure where the rest of Jesus' brothers were or if they were there at the time of the Crucifixion. Jesus chooses someone outside of His earthly family to care for the one closest and dearest to His heart.

While I believe Jesus wanted His family to be His closest relationships here on Earth, that was not possible; it is not possible for some of us either. It is just not. No matter which way we turn it or look at it, it is not. In a perfect world I believe that is God's plan to have close, healthy relationships with our families of origin. Sometimes our families fall into the category of some of Jesus' brothers. They just flat out do not get us or what God has called us to.

Let me open my heart and say that I know that this may be opening up some whole new thoughts and possibilities for some of you that you can and, at times, should look outside of your earthly family to share who you are and your most intimate moments. I say the previous statement with tenderness of heart. I remember, not so long ago, that this truth opened me up to some truly life-changing freedom.

This is where we have to follow Jesus. Did He sit down and have a big ol' pity party that His family did not get Him? I never see one instance where He did that. Oh, He was fully human, so I am sure some of His and His Father's conversations revolved around His family relationships, but He never let that deter Him.

Even the night before His death, at the Last Supper, we do not see a record of Jesus' family being there (Luke 22). In Jewish culture, the Passover meal was to be shared with family, each member having a role to play in the meal. Instead, those closest to Him are there during their last few intimate moments here on this side of the Crucifixion. They may not have been perfect or fully understood who He was until later, but they were the ones He chose, and they were together.

That night and at the Crucifixion, Jesus did not want with Him those who did not know who He was or believe in His mission, nor did He want to be surrounded by people who would have criticized Him and what He was doing. This was too important. Too intimate. He knew the fullness of the Father's will for Him and was living it out. He did not have time or extra emotion available for those who did not believe or for those who would even criticize Him.

Throughout His ministry, Jesus understood that those He surrounded Himself with were very important in order for Him to fulfill the Father's plan for Him. Notice who He spent the most time with: His disciples, whom God had showed Him to choose. He did not make His brothers the leaders of His ministry. Not yet, anyhow.

There is an instance in the Bible in which Jesus is talking to the multitude in Mark 3:31–35, and Jesus broadens His family to include those who listened to His message and did the will of God. We would do well to follow Jesus in this area. Jesus did not let anyone, not even His family, deter Him from the Father's will for Him. Oh, He loved His earthly family, but He did not spend emotion or have a pity party when some of them did not believe in Him or even when they said negative things about Him. He knew who He was, why He came, and where He was going. Did you hear that? He really did not seem to spend any time trying to convince them who He was. He knew it, His Father knew it, and that was good enough for Him. Jesus loved them but knew what His mission was. (By the way, His mission was not to gossip to fellow believers about them or to put them down, either. He did. however, allow these glimpses of His family life to be recorded so we would gain some insight and freedom too.)

Boy oh boy, have I had to grow up in this area big time. You see, when I began writing this book I was not yet prepared to write this chapter! This book has been a work in progress, like I am. I was beginning to make some good choices, but God had me start out small. Beloved, we find freedom because we have made not just one good choice but one good choice after another: the choice to forgive, the choice to let go, the choice to love, and the choice to fully surrender to Him. He led me to make smaller choices that He knew I was ready to make, followed by larger ones that took more courage. Isn't He a wonderful Father? I am so glad He does not just throw us out in the middle of a huge mess and ask us to choose Him without us being ready to do it. He never sets us up to fail, only to succeed! He is the faithful Father who watches us and our character grow as the result of choosing Him over all else.

Oh, He is there in our stumbles. We will have some stumbles—maybe even some flat-out falls. Each time our Father picks us up and dusts us off we get to see more growth in our life, and another link of the chain that was binding us falls off. He loosens the shackles that had our feet bound. His grace picks us up off that dusty old ground and places our feet on a rock, the rock of His grace and truth. We get to look into our Redeemer's eyes and see them full of radiant grace and mercy.

Let me share how He led me to walk in some incredible freedom in this area. I am still utterly amazed that it is me that is getting to live this out. It is for us all! Like I shared earlier in the book, God led me to make some decisions to lay down some healthy boundaries with some people I had been in relationships with. God had restored to me enough confidence in who I was in Christ that it began to affect my relationships. I felt a bit like Jesus. I still loved these people and did not speak evil of them, but I just was not drawn to them or their dysfunction anymore. His new vision for my life and what He wanted me to do and become were my focus. I just was not in their world anymore, and they were not in mine. Shortly after my husband and I made some decisions regarding this, there were some people that really came against me. Our decision to follow Jesus out of some situations that were not godly really made the enemy mad, especially because this is what he had always used to keep me in bondage to him and his schemes. I began to cycle through fear, guilt, shame, negative talk, self-doubt and torment, then back to fear, and guilt...OK, you get it!

Because Christ was literally breaking me free and because I was gaining tremendous freedom in Him, the enemy wanted to discourage and distract me from going on into more freedom. I was also beginning to help others find the freedom that had seemed elusive to me for too long. I knew that freedom was mine, and I was not going to let anything or anyone steal it from me. Tenacity is one of my strengths, by the way!

Let me tell you how gracious our God is! The very day—no, the very moment—I had received news of the negative things that people were saying about me because of following Christ, God provided a great victory for me. I was home by myself, and I just read what was said about me. This person could not understand how I could finally be making my own choices. Others had always made them for me. I was sitting in my dining room trying to process all I had just heard about myself. At that very moment I had my computer on, and a dear friend who lives all the way on the other side of the country sent me a very encouraging and affirming message on Facebook. My God had come through for me! I needed it. You see, God was saying to me that if I would continue to trust Him to handle this and let Him defend me, I would continue to see more amazing deliverance. You will too!

I was finally letting go of defending and protecting myself. I did not respond to the accusations but trusted in who I knew God said I was. God had already seen the real me for some time, but *I* was beginning to get larger glimpses of her and was simply amazed. *Strong* and *confident* were never words that I would have used to describe myself, but that day was different. There is nothing like a fiery trial to bring Jesus out in us!

I was amazed that day, and I still am. He knew I needed major encouragement as I stepped into some new territory. He knew I was facing my worst fears head on, and He was not about to leave me! That day I felt a little like David, who said in Psalm 35:9–10, "And my soul shall be joyful in the LORD; It shall rejoice in His salvation. All my bones shall say, 'LORD, who is like You, Delivering the poor from him who is too strong for him, Yes, the poor and the needy from him who plunders him?'" Yes, my bones were shouting that day, and I will thankfully never be the same! I did not cower to the fear of man but remained confident in who God said I was.

You see, I was becoming more like Jesus. I was letting my God tell me who I was and letting what others thought about me affect how I felt about myself. I could write a book alone on how I used to do that. You may be able to also. Thankfully, His love and grace had so worked themselves not only into my spirit but into my mind and belief system that I could remain steadfast and confident even in the face of disapproval, which had always made me bow to others and their desires and plans for me. Who they thought I should be and what I should be doing. Not this time. I was free to follow my Savior. The seeds that had been sown in me from the words penned in Isaiah 50 about fearing the Lord were beginning to take root in me. All the times of crying out for freedom from the fear of man and longing for the fear of the Lord were heard. Those tears and cries had not been in vain.

Beloved, when we get to see the fruit of our times of wrestling for freedom in the Lord come about, there is nothing sweeter! By the time we get to the place of freedom, we almost forget the pain of the battle because the victory is so sweet. Jesus is our prize and our victory. *He* is the freedom our heart has been waiting for all these years! Oh, we have come a long way, and I still have much to learn in living out freedom one day at a time. I know that as I continue to learn how to trust Him to deliver me and not defend myself He will come through for me every time. I am in all honesty saying that since I have made some of the most important choices in my life the last year regarding separating myself from unhealthy relationships. It has been a truly liberating experience for me, a very healing thing. It has not been without pain and hurt, but He has been faithful.

He has been faithful to continue to bind up my broken heart and life as I have looked to Him and trusted Him. My heart has healed, along with my mind, emotions, and body. I realize that what I was allowing others to do to me was putting a huge amount of pressure on me in all areas, including physically. My feet have continued to heal and strengthen as I have allowed Him to do the heavy lifting by trusting Him.

This last year has been the most liberating and healing year for me. I am seeing Him bring His Word to pass as I am living it out in my life and in my choices, trusting Him that what He says about me is true and trusting Him that what others say about me is sometimes false. This has been one of the greatest victories for me. If He can break me free from this vicious cycle, He is way more than able to do it for you. Nothing is impossible with Him. Nothing! Trusting Him like this and seeing Him come through for me in this area has so deepened my admiration for Him. He truly is my source of victory, strength, and confidence. I am so glad He believes in us when we cannot yet believe in ourselves!

All those in the Word and all those alive today who live in any amount of victory have done so one choice at time. They had to choose God over their feelings, circumstances, the opinions of others, and their own fears and doubts. Don't let them have all the victory when there are some big ones waiting for you! Don't sit around and complain if others are living in peace and joy and freedom and have fought their way to those things but you are not willing to. Ouch! Let's let Him set our feet on the steady ground of His faithfulness. Let's join Joshua as he boldly declares that he is choosing to serve the Lord. As we do, we get to enter our promised lands too. It is no longer a long way off, but it is right before our eyes! Who knows where the next good choice will take us. Only be bold and courageous, for the Lord your God is with you wherever you go (Josh. 1:9)!

CHAPTER 19
THE GOD WHO WAITS

Therefore, the LORD will wait, that He may be gra-
cious to you; And therefore He will be exalted, that
He may have mercy on you. For the LORD is a God
of justice; Blessed are those who wait for Him.
—Isaiah 30:18

THIS VERSE IS coming alive to me in new ways right
now! The thought that the God who made everything
has waited for *me* is just nuts! He has not only waited, but He has
waited to be gracious. Double crazy. I think so far I have mentioned about a thousand reasons why I love Him, but this makes
one thousand and one! He has been waiting to be good to me. He
has been waiting to be good to you too!

He was there when our heart first began to beat in our mother's womb. He was there when the doctor helped deliver us. He
was there to hear our first cries, and His heart was longing for
the day that we would choose Him, who gave us this life. He has
been waiting to pour out His grace on me. Guess what. After this
point in my life, after all we have been through together, I am just
a sponge soaking it all up!

Here is what I think God wants us to see: He wants us to reflect
back on our life not with regret and shame but with the knowledge that He has been there waiting. He has not been waiting to
punish us like we may think. I cannot tell you how many times
I failed, sinned, or whatever, that I came to God feeling terrible.
Many, many times when I came before my Father I was carrying

false guilt. Some of the times I did sin and needed His forgiveness, but even in that He is so gracious.

Actually, I look back and realize much of my life I carried false guilt. When I first started my relationship with God I expected He would be mad every time I came to spend time with Him. Like I shared before, that came from experiencing some harshness from people in authority in my life growing up. The more I experienced His goodness and how patient He was with me when I did come to Him, the freer I got. I wish I could tell you it happened overnight, but it took years of reading His Word and finally choosing to believe it.

So often we stay in bondage because of how we feel. Let's lay that whole thing down and just let Him be the God that He is. If we look close enough, we may see evidence of His faithfulness, love, and protection, even when we did not acknowledge Him. He is like the perfect gentleman pursuing the one He loves. He will do whatever He has to for however long it takes to get the girl! Or the guy!

I think He specifically waits for the right time to work in our lives too. He could have arranged this season for me along time ago, but He knew I was not ready for it .God knows when we can handle the pressure and when we are ready for it. He knows every hair on our head and detail of our life. I am so grateful that He waited to heal me physically when I was able to handle it. Some may disagree and say that we are always ready to handle what God has for us, but I am not one of them. His timing is seen in everything—from the amount of time in a day to the amount of time we carry our babies in our womb. Seasons all revolve around timing. His miraculous healing of my body needed my soul to be ready, for me to be ready to receive it and then share it. Remember how I shared that I was too afraid and insecure to tell the foot doctor that I believed God was going to heal me? Well, my Father was so gracious that He waited until He had done such a work in me that

I could and would shout it from the rooftops! Shame no longer held me back. The Bible has a whole chapter that talks of us not being ashamed when we have waited on Him. (See Psalm 25.) Boy, have I proved that through and through!

I would like something of you. Get somewhere quiet where you and God can reflect on your life. Ask Him to show you the places and times where He was waiting for you. All the places that He has been faithful to you. Yes, even the times before you even believed in Him. You may feel like your life has been a mess, but actually it is like a puzzle, and all along God has been there putting the pieces together. He has been so faithful to protect, heal, love, and provide for us. I really desire that the Holy Spirit would lead and guide us into all truth about our lives. I really want us to see how good He is and how much He loves us and has been waiting for us to come to Him.

If we already have a relationship with Him, He wants more of us. He wants all of us and our heart. He wants to continue to love, heal, and free us. Beloved, He does not want to destroy us but to heal us! It may feel like we are going to die in the process, but that is not His heart. He waits for us, even through years of our rejecting Him and turning to other people and things to ease our pain.

I remember when my adoptive mom came back to the Lord and started going to church after my parents' divorce. She was telling me about God and taking me to church. God started to show her some of the things I was doing that she could have had no way of knowing otherwise, mostly about trouble I was getting into. I vividly remember one day being in my room upstairs fed up with God trying to interfere in my life. How dare He! I looked up toward heaven and was angry. I remember the words as if they were yesterday, "If You just leave me alone, I will leave You alone." I am sure glad He can handle our anger and attempts to drive Him away. I am also glad that He waits to be gracious to us. He waited for me—and He got me!

Some of you have similar stories! These are the things God wants us to see. Maybe for the first time we can truly see that He was there, even through the pain and abuse. He was there waiting to be good to us.

So many people get stuck here. So many people blame God for the losses and bad things that have happened to them. The sad part is that they never give God a chance. God says that He waits for us, but the last part of Isaiah 30:18 reminds us, "Blessed are those who wait for Him." We really do need to give Him a chance. Give Him a chance to explain and give you understanding of what happened in your life and why. We may not get all the answers that we are looking for, but we will get the ones that *He* wants us to have. Give Him a chance to show you His purpose in all of your pain. You are seeing firsthand that my pain is being used by God to help others. Let Him use your story to help others. Get to know God through His Word. Listen for His voice.

Those of you reading this book who have never trusted in Christ or do not even know what that means, will you give Him a chance today? You really can trust this God who has waited for you. There may be some who have wandered away from following Christ and are now living in guilt and shame, wondering if He could ever forgive you. Hear these words from God Himself, "As far as the east is from the west, So far has He removed our transgressions from us. As a father pities his children, So the Lord pities those who fear Him. For He knows our frame; He remembers that we are dust" (Ps. 103:12–14). Also, in John 6:37 Jesus Himself says, "All that the Father gives me will come to Me, and the one who comes to Me I will by no means cast out." You do not have to worry that what you have done is too big for God to forgive. All you have to do is to believe that Jesus is God who came in human form to this earth. He came to die on the cross and be raised from the dead. He had to die on the cross and give His blood so God could forgive us. It was actually God Himself coming to Earth to take care of the sin problem. He was born in a culture where the worst punishment for sin was to carry a cross and then to be crucified on it. He took away all our sin and the punishment for our sin. We do not have to keep going around trying to do good things to feel better about all the bad things we have done. There is no more punishment, no more guilt. You must only believe that this is what God has done for you and confess it with your mouth out loud, and you will be a Christian. Continue to follow Him and read His Word and pray. Find Christians who can help you. If you do not know any, ask God to send you someone. He will not disappoint you!

I think if we quiet out heart enough to listen, we will hear the voice of the One who has been waiting for us. He is waiting right now. Waiting to be faithful to you. Waiting to heal and free and release us from all that binds us. Waiting to release us into our destiny. Yes, He is the God who waits with such patience and love for us. For some of us He is waiting for us to make some steps forward and some choices that will propel us into the purposes He has for us. Many times we are waiting for Him, but He is just waiting for us to get with the program.

He watched and waited as I was a little girl and even a baby who was neglected and rejected. He waited as I grew up and rejected Him because I did not know how good He was and how much He loved me. He waited as I struggled with guilt and shame after believing in Him. He waited and longed all the time for the day I would be His. I am forever grateful that He did!

Think of your life. What has He watched you go through? What has He had to turn His pure face from as you were sinned against and as you sinned yourself? It was all for a purpose. Let Him show you today. Better than that, do not let His waiting go in vain. Let

Him use all you have gone through to help others. Let what you have gone through draw you closer to Him and not further. He has waited because He has wanted us to choose Him, not to force Himself on us in any way. He gave us the ability to choose. That is why He shows us so much goodness in this life. With all that is wrong in the world, think of all that is right and beautiful, like our children, spouse, and home. Think of all our eyes have taken in, in this life. Glorious sunsets displayed for all to see. Waterfalls. Snow-covered mountains. He has shown us His goodness in this life so we will turn to Him, the One who fashioned it all. His face is warm and lovely and His arms open wide. He is the God who waits. He is the God who waits for each one of us today. Will we let Him in? Let's not make Him wait at the door of our hearts any longer!

CHAPTER 20

MORE PRECIOUS THAN GOLD

*In this you greatly rejoice, though now for a little while, if need
be, you have been grieved by various trials, that the genuine-
ness of your faith, being much more precious than gold that
perishes, though it is tested by fire, may be found to praise,
honor, and glory at the revelation of Jesus Christ, whom
having not seen you love. Though now you do not see Him, yet
believing, you rejoice with joy inexpressible and full of glory,
receiving the end of your faith—the salvation of your souls.*
—1 PETER 1:6–9

REMEMBER BACK TO John 21, where Jesus prophe-
sied to Peter that when he was older another would
carry him where he did not wish (John 21:18)? Yes, it was probably
not a promise that Peter claimed daily over his life or had posted
to his refrigerator! (Did they even have refrigerators, for crying
out loud?) I believe it was a promise sowed in his spirit by His
Savior. Can I throw out a thought here about Peter and his future?
History tells us that Peter, in fact, was killed for his faith in Christ
by being crucified. He was crucified upside down on a cross. He
may have missed the crucifixion of His Savior because of His sin
of denying to even know Him, but this time around there was no
escape. Here is the thought I want us to think about: by the time
Peter walked to that cross where he would give his life for His
Savior, he had already died many, many deaths.

I think this is something worth thinking about and studying a
bit more. Let's look at some Scripture and see some of the things

this amazing saint can teach us! Look back at the passage from 1 Peter that I referenced at the beginning of this chapter. What beautiful words penned by a humble and confident leader who had an amazing amount of love for God's people. Oh, yes, that is what the grace of God, the power of the Holy Spirit, and some fiery trials can create! Peter did not turn out so bad after all, did he? I actually really like Peter, and since I can relate to some of his struggles in his faith, he gives me hope for the things God has for me. I am sure some of you are nodding your head up and down because you feel the same way about yourselves.

In 1 Peter 1:6–9 Peter was encouraging Christians who were facing some hard times and persecution for their faith in Jesus. There is the distant ring of the words of Jesus to Peter as he undoubtedly went through one of the most difficult times of his life:

> Simon, Simon! Indeed, Satan has asked for you, that he may sift you as wheat. But I have prayed for you, that your faith should not fail; and when you have returned to Me, strengthen your brethren.
>
> —LUKE 22:31–32

Here we see the very words of Jesus coming to pass! Isn't it beautiful? I love how Jesus says, "And *when* you have returned to me, strengthen your brethren" (emphasis added). This is exactly what Peter is doing in these verses! Amazing!

I think about the other times throughout the Book of Acts and the New Testament where Peter continued to die to his old self and began to walk in who God made him to be. For the sake of time and space I will not share the whole passage, but in Acts 10, Peter gets another wake up call! He is already leading the church of Jesus but needs some major readjusting! Can anyone relate? Let's not be so quick to jump on Peter and his weaknesses, or we will quickly see many of ours come and slap us in the face! Peter had one way of thinking about who could have faith in Jesus, but Jesus Himself had a whole other idea! Ouch! Put that one down with some more trials he had to go through.

Then, not long after Jesus left this earth, His very words began to ring true in the lives of those who were still following this risen Savior. Persecution set in, and life got difficult. Peter was imprisoned for his faith (Acts 12) and then ultimately is crucified for his unwavering faith in the Jesus He knew is alive. I am sure we are just hitting the highlights and not seeing all that he went through. Suffice it to say, there were some trials. I do not believe that Peter would have had much genuine hope and encouragement to give us without going through some things. There is nothing like hearing about going through some things from someone who has lived a padded life in a castle who has never been touched by life's pains. Not this guy. He is the real thing. Jesus wants us to be the real thing, genuine.

You see, God knows that the difficult and painful things we go through have the ability to strip away all that is not genuine, all that is false and based on a lie. That is why He has to allow some of these things to touch our lives. That is where the whole tested-by-fire thing comes into play. You see, John the Baptist foretold that Jesus and His ministry would be just that in Matthew 3:12: He would come as fire. What the heck? Why does that have to even be in there? Am I the only one here? Regardless, it is in there, brothers and sisters! We are tested. We will be tested. Oh, our spirit is safe, but our soul—our mind, will, and emotions—are a work in progress. Yes, it started the moment we got saved and will end at our very last breath. In between is the fun part!

Can we look at 1 Peter 1:6, which says we are to greatly rejoice in our trials? I can honestly say that I have been going through more trials lately of stretching and growing, but I am not rejoicing like I should be. No leaping up and spinning around here. Just yesterday my husband and I were at the park discussing how much we are feeling stretched and pulled by what He is asking us to do. I can tell you I was not rejoicing. Well, not at first. After talking, lots of prayer to not poke anyone's eyeball out, and (some) laughter about it all, I could begin to see the bigger picture of what He is wanting to do, what I asked for Him to do in my life and in ministry. At the beginning of this healing season I was not rejoicing much either, as you remember. I am now! There are many, many genuine things that are left behind after the trying of my faith.

Let's keep in mind that the man who is writing these scriptures is also the one who denied Jesus not once, not twice, but three times. Well, I am glad God is not an umpire! Like you have read about Peter and the things I have had to overcome, some of our most fiery trials will involve just getting past our own self. You see, He began this journey with me as He allowed the circumstances with my feet to occur. That opened up so many things that He wanted to accomplish in and through me. This season has definitely been a fiery trial for not only me but my family. We have all walked through the fire together. What I really hope and pray we all see is through my story is that there is hope. That He is the God of all hope.

I pray that you see Him way more than you see me. I also pray that you see Him in your own life and circumstances even clearer than you did before. You see, He wants to use all of us. Not just Peter. Not just me. All of us. So what is or have been the trials and difficulties in your life that God has allowed to purify you? Do not take them lightly. The trials come to remove and burn up anything in our lives that do not look or sound like Jesus.

After all He has allowed in my life, I am truly grateful. There are not enough praise and worship songs or paper here to express my gratitude to Him. He truly has been faithful in my trials to never leave nor forsake me, even when I did not navigate every road just perfectly. He is the perfect One. Him alone. He has not forgotten His promises to me. My body is more healed now than it has been in almost eight years. I am doing things that at times were hard to imagine I would be doing. I get to go to the park and play and laugh with my girls. And yes, I get to push them on the swings! Now they just want me to get them started; then they do not want any help!

In the last one to two years I have been occasionally able to run with my daughters. Oh, I remember the first time we were at our neighborhood park, and I just had the urge to run. I hadn't done it in six or seven years, but I just took off. The girls laughed at me and said, "Mom runs funny!" I turned around and said, "You would too, if you had not done it in six years!" By the way, that was the first time my Emily had seen me run. In that moment, all the years of pain and living deprived of my physical body just melted away. For my little girl to finally see me run was so awesome.

Joy that I could not even express began to fill my life as I had more of these types of experiences. It was all worth it. Lying on the couch for almost two years. Doing only the things I needed to and being in pain all the while. Needing help to do everyday chores. Not being able to experience certain things with my family. The five summers of not being able to truly enjoy the outdoors. Wearing stupid sneakers that were good for my feet on the beach when I wanted to run barefoot. Wearing those same stupid sneakers instead of cute shoes I wanted to wear to show off my painted toenails. It was worth all of it to finally walk in the freedom God intended.

These are the things that really make up a happy, fulfilled life, people! Oh, last summer was the first year after five summers that my feet could handle wearing sandals. What joy I had as my family left the mall with my (expensive) pair of sandals! Painted toenails, here I come! It was about the same time that I could run barefoot on the beach. I have pictures of my feet and my little girls' feet the first time they dipped back into the very cold Pacific Ocean! I had so much joy getting to do the things I had missed out on for so, so long. You know what? It seems like just a moment to me now. The joy that has overtaken my heart and life are what I live with now.

What really fulfills me now is having peace in my heart and mind knowing that I am so absolutely loved by the One who made me. Knowing that I will never, never have to go back to living in bondage to fear and shame. Knowing that I am secure, and so is my future. I look forward even to the small things, like going hiking with my family, going camping with friends, and cleaning my bathrooms. Yes, cleaning my bathrooms! When my pain was the worst I could barely walk to the bathroom, much less clean them! I remember the first time I was able to stand and clean one bathroom, then shortly after that two. I thought revival would break out in my house! I must have looked crazy standing there with the cleaning rags in my hand praising Jesus. Oh, what a sight! Now every time I clean the bathrooms, I thank God that I am able to even do it. I tell Him that I appreciate Him healing me so I can take care of my family and serve others.

I could go on and on here, but I think you get the point. He has so restored me that I just cannot keep it all in. Oh, there is a little more physical healing and strengthening that needs to occur in me. I know that as He continues to restore what was so broken on the inside of me the outside will match. Even now He is still working and using me sharing my testimony in this book and in many other arenas to bring wholeness to me. To bring out the confidence of who I am in Him that has been buried inside. To force me to leave some more old ways and beliefs behind. I am convinced that all will be completely restored, just as He has promised. God's calling on our life does not just minister to those He sends us to, but it accomplishes His purposes in us. Trust me in this.

So what about you? What is on the other side of your trials? Healing? Freedom? Hope? Knowing and loving Him more? With all that is within me, I say, please let Him use the hard times, the times you feel at the end of your rope. His hand is waiting to grab you when you finally let go. Trust Him. He so wants to do amazing things with your life! Oh, I do not mean to give the impression that life is just about trials. I am up for fun and laughter and joy just as much as the next person. What I do want to say is that the times in between the trials are when we get to enjoy what God has done in us during the hard times if we have let Him have His way in us. Then the joy is deeper, the victory sweeter!

The peace of knowing He is truly in control of it all is what we get to enjoy. That is when we can truly just chill out and enjoy life. We may not know what is around the next bend, but we can enjoy life and live carefree knowing all is well. This is the abundant life Jesus died to give us. That promise is not just for when we get to heaven, but here. It is for our homes, at our workplaces, with our families. I have so much peace and joy now that I sometimes do not know what to do. It is still taking some getting used to! I can laugh and sing and dance now more than ever. I enjoy people and life more than ever. I find joy in simple things because He is filling me up on the inside. I can enjoy going grocery shopping as much as writing this book or leading people to Christ. He just fills my life, through and through! So, I thank Him for the trials. Maybe not always like I should, but I am grateful He loves me enough to allow some things to come into my life that will forever change me!

At the end our life we will stand before Christ. The trials of this life will have faded like a distant memory. The only things that will remain will be what the trials have left behind: genuine faith and that which is genuine, like love, joy, and peace. God wants us to see what is truly precious and valuable. When we look from His vantage point we are walking in faith. Faith sees the end. It is a gift from the God of heaven to bring heaven into our life. Heaven is where He rules and reigns. Faith brings that into our life.

We can be sure that faith will never perish. All the other things we have counted so dear to us may perish if they are not eternal. The same faith that began our journey with this beautiful Jesus will lead us right to His very feet. There, bowed down before such majesty, it will all have been worth it: all the difficulties of this life, all the pain, loss, and sufferings. The fire will have purified us until we stand before the One with eyes of fire. Oh, they are set ablaze with holy love for us (Rev. 2:18). The precious faith He gave us in the beginning of our journey will have led us back to Him. Now we get to see Him face to face. When we turn our heads and get a full-on glimpse of His eyes of fire, our faith will not be needed anymore. He will be there!

Until that day our faith gives us glimpses of our beautiful Savior on this side of eternity. We see Him in our children's smiles, in the sunsets, in the love of the body of Christ, and yes, even in our trials. He has been there. He has been walking with us every step of the way. As we learn how to live out our faith more and more we see Him more and more. This is how it has been for me. Little by little as I held on to my faith in Christ and His plans for me, I saw Him more and more. It will continue to happen until one day I stand at the feet of the one who created me.

It happened like this for Peter too. And it will be like this for us all, if we have trusted Christ. With each of Peter's trials, as his faith did not fail, He got to see Jesus more and more. His eyes were open to what is real in this life. Our faith tells us and shows us what is true and what is real. Anything that is not of faith is sin (Rom. 14:23). Peter's last trial on this side of heaven proved that to be true. After Peter denied Jesus his faith surely did not fail but rather grew stronger in the one who held all things, including his future, in His hands. As Peter was placed on that cross when it was his time to die for his Savior, his faith was so strong. He knew death could not win because he knew his risen Savior, and he saw Him taken to heaven before his very eyes. He knew that meant death could not touch him either. In a matter of minutes, he would again be reunited with his Jesus, the one who started real life for Him. The one who said, "Follow me," and changed everything for him.

Oh, how I would have loved to see an instant replay in heaven of that reunion, wouldn't you? He would again get to see the one who he walked with and talked with and ate breakfast by the sea with. Finally Peter would get to see Jesus risen, glorified, and more beautiful than ever!

Our reunion with Jesus will be just as glorious! Knowing that each trial we face brings us closer and closer until the day we see Him should give us great comfort and encouragement, dear ones! Let's let the Holy Spirit lift our eyes above the clouds long enough to see His warm and beautiful face smiling down on us! That is what faith does. That is why we cannot let it go.

You see, like Peter, we all have an amazing purpose and call on our lives. For those of you who have been wondering what your purpose is, here it is: to have your whole life praise, honor, and give glory to Jesus as we stand before Him. He wants our lives to shine forth these things progressively more and more the closer we come to the day of seeing Him face to face. This is what we are made for. This is what is rightfully His—all praise, glory, and honor!

The trials we experience come to strip away anything in our lives that does not give Him praise, glory, and honor and that does not show Him off. He works in our lives so that when people see us they get to see who Jesus is. He wants to be so worked into the fabric of our heart, life, and mouth that nobody is left wondering what this beautiful Savior looks like, sounds like, or how He loves. Once we have passed through the Refiner's fire and we have allowed it to burn all the unforgiveness and hate and pride and fear and whatever else we wrestle with away, we will look like Him. Our brokenness, sin, and inability to walk in His purposes have stolen the praise that should be coming out of our mouth. It has choked the honor we should be giving Him as God and the glory our lives were meant to shine.

Peter was willing to put his life in the only hands that could pick him up. Jesus wants us to trust Him like that, to know that He holds our past, present, and our future. He wants us to trust that no matter how many times we fall, He will always be there waiting to pick us up. Trust me on this.

I wonder if I have worn Him out from all the times He has had to bend over to pick me up. What about you? Can you relate? The same hands that formed it all hold our heart and our future so closely. Nothing slips by Him. Nothing. Jesus is our destiny. Standing before our God with only that which is genuine is our destiny. Only that gives Him all glory, honor, and praise that He is due. The saints, angels, and all the universe have already joined in. We will be and are being purified by all that has come our way. Let Him use the circumstances you are going through. Let Him use your life to show off! Oh, our lives have the potential to be absolutely beautiful. Our eyes need to see it. He already sees it as done because He is looking through that heavenly kaleidoscope!

Chapter 21

LOOKING UNTO JESUS

Therefore, since we are surrounded by such a great cloud of witnesses, let us throw off everything that hinders and the sin that so easily entangles. And let us run with perseverance the race marked out for us, fixing our eyes on Jesus, the pioneer and perfecter of faith. For the joy set before him he endured the cross, scorning its shame, and sat down at the right hand of the throne of God.
—Hebrews 12:1–2, niv

Wow, double wow! As we prepare to close our time together I am a bit emotional. I am also a preacher, so there will be a few closing statements. I am truly grateful and utterly amazed at not only what God has done but that He has allowed me to share with you so *He* can be glorified. I feel a bit like a cheerleader as I am writing this. Maybe it is the heart of our Father speaking to us so we can receive a little more encouragement for our journey. Need some? Me too. Let's look into our Daddy's heart for a fresh word! If I may take a little liberty here and use my imagination concerning these verses, I think we will see something awesome.

Sometimes my mind cannot wrap itself around the exact things that God allowed to be into His precious Word. Sometimes I sit and think of those who the message came through and wonder what it was like to know what you wrote or were inspired by would be included in such a beautiful, life-giving work of art. Though most scholars are not sure who wrote the Book of Hebrews, one thing is certain: it is alive! In fact, this book even says so in Hebrews 4:12: "For the Word of God is alive and active. Sharper than any double edged sword, it penetrates even to dividing soul and spirit, joints and marrow; it judges the thoughts and attitudes of the heart" (NIV).

To return to Hebrews 12:1–2, I'm going to ask you to use your imagination. I do not think that God minds if we do that. I believe Jesus, the Son of God, had a little to do with these verses being included in the canon of Scripture; let us imagine why. I think it is because He lived them. It is almost as if He said, "These need to be included in here because I have something to say about overcoming and finishing the race!"

Oh, can you see it now? It is almost like we can see Him standing up for this one to get a closer look. He is peering down from the throne making sure we got this message. I love it! Jesus is looking to make sure we make it, finish our race. He never left His throne, but I am certain there are times in our lives and in our race that He jumps up, shouts, and gives a good cheer for us and our beloved brothers and sisters! He is leading the great cloud of witnesses. He has been there. He had His own race to run and many things to overcome. He kept His Father and His plan ever before His face. That is how He made it, and that is how we will make it. Lord, open our eyes to see Jesus and the great cloud of witnesses He has provided for our encouragement!

You see, Hebrews 11 is often called the Hall of Faith. He wants to include our story in that chapter. This is not to say that He will go back and rewrite His Word, but He wants us to follow their examples of what He calls faith. Oh, I so want to be included, don't you? Last Sunday at a church our family was visiting the preacher said that those men and women were not included in Hebrews 11 because of their great leadership abilities but for their great courage, which takes faith. I agree and am glad that is the case. That is all He wants—our faith. He wants us to have faith for our journey.

In the introduction to this book I said that Jesus will do whatever He needs to do for us to finish our journey. We may feel like we will be drug, pulled, or pushed over that finish line at times. Maybe we feel like we will barely make it. God has done everything so that we make it. I love that Jesus is the Author and Finisher of our faith. I love that we have a leader who has gone before us and overcome. Who wants to follow a loser? Or a wimp? Someone who has no victory? Not I. Probably not you either! This is not who we are talking about here! Instead, we see Jesus, who kept His eyes on the Father and did not let what was going on around Him deter Him one bit from the Father's plan. Jesus had a race, and He finished. He finished strong! He overcame death and the grave. Beloved, there is no greater thing to overcome. This is who is leading us to that finish line. This is who is cheering us on.

Oh, and He has provided a little help in the grandstands. He says the great cloud of witnesses is there cheering us on too. You bet our Savior is at the front of the pack! May God open our eyes to the fact that there are more for us than against us. Let us quiet our hearts so we can hear the heavenly crowd cheering us on. Go on and close your eyes. See yourself surrounded by Paul, Timothy, David, your prayin' grandma, and Jesus! Add any of your favorites from the Bible. They are there too. Jeepers, if I were on the other side with this great cloud of witnesses, you better believe I would be acting like a crazy woman! Imagine if we could see from the other side. That is what faith is. Believing that what He said is already done.

Here is a story just begging to be told by one proud momma! My oldest daughter, Sarah, had a track meet in May 2013. She was running the two hundred meter relay for the second time. The first time she placed first, but I was not able to be there to see it. This time I was super excited and filled with anticipation because I know she is fast and, well, because she is my girl! The day of the track meet was hot. On top of that, she just had some pre-braces brackets put in her mouth the night before, and her mouth was in pain. I was a little uneasy about how she would do in the race. I just told her to do her best and let her frustrations go to her feet. I was on the sidelines, and she was keeping up with the pack but not in the lead. Then, all of a sudden, she came around the last corner and shot way out ahead of all the other kids—not just a little ahead but a lot. Every parent around me knew whose kid she was. I was jumping, shouting, and trying to take a picture all at the same time. The picture did not turn out, by the way. It is forever imprinted in my head though! I ran to the finish line and hugged her and told her that I was cheering for her like a crazy woman. Apparently she blocked my shouting out! Oh, by the way, she placed first again!

So, other than being super proud, why did I tell that story? If we are so excited and crazy over a race on planet Earth, how much more are our heavenly Father, Jesus, His angels, and saints cheering us on? It is the race of our life, and they would not miss it for the world!

Let me give you one more insight at why we will make it to end of our race: Jesus is praying for us! We all have people we know to call when we need prayer. We are not messing around here. When our babies are burning up with pneumonia or a family member has been in a serious car accident, we know these people are serious in their prayer and belief that God will and can do the impossible. There is someone else on that prayer chain praying for us that we may forget about sometimes. Jesus, the Son of God. The victorious one. The one who created the heavens and the Earth and can at any moment do anything anywhere. Yes, Him! If you do not believe it, turn with me to Romans 8:34: "Who is he who condemns? It is Christ who died, and furthermore is also risen, who is even at the right hand of God, who also makes intercession for us." I do not know about you, but the risen Christ who is seated next to God Almighty is someone I want to be able to call on when I am in trouble. The cool thing is, He already knows when we are in trouble before we do. He can see trouble coming way before we even know what is going on or going to happen. How awesome is that? Part of what the word *intercession* means there is "to close the gap between God and us." He has done that by way of the Cross. It also means to close the gap between what God wants to do in our lives and where we are currently residing. Pretty awesome, huh? You see, He may have the whole world to run, but He purposefully takes the time to make it one of His jobs to intercede for us. Let's go a step beyond *job* and say He makes it His priority and passion to intercede for us. He gets right down in the middle of where we are and goes to work. He looks at our lives from His perspective and desperately works to get us to see what He sees so our lives will line up with what He already sees!

I am so glad He prays for us from that perfect place of being all-knowing and all-wise. Paul was the one who, through the inspiration of the Holy Spirit, penned that scripture found in Romans. I am guessing that he had a revelation of Jesus being for us and praying for us because he was someone who so desperately needed it himself. I guarantee that Jesus praying for Paul had a huge impact on his eyes being opened on that dusty Damascus road. His life was turned upside down by a strange and miraculous series of events described in Acts 9. Jesus was in on this one! This is why Paul can share from a place of confidence. He has been there. He was on the other side of Jesus interceding for him.

If we still are a little hung up on the idea of God Almighty taking the time to pray that we finish our race, let me show you one more example from Scripture!

> And the Lord said, "Simon, Simon! Indeed, Satan has asked for you, that he may sift you as wheat. But I have prayed for you, that your faith should not fail; and when you have returned to Me, strengthen your brethren."
>
> —LUKE 22:31–32

I know I have quoted this passage in this book before, but here it is from a different angle. There is no other way to interpret this other than that Jesus is praying for us! Jesus knew the fierce trial Peter was about to enter into. What touches my heart is that Jesus wanted him to make it. He believed in Peter. He walked with this guy and watched his faith in Him grow by leaps and bounds. He was his friend. Now his friend was going to need Him more than ever. Aren't you glad that when we need Jesus most, He does not just up and leave? He is a friend in the truest sense of the word, and Peter would come to know Jesus in a way that he had not known Him before.

I guess I use this story so much in my writing because it touches such a deep part of my heart. I can relate to being the one that failed and should not be making it. But Jesus prayed for me. Jesus prayed for Peter. His prayers have worked. They have touched something in the heart of our Father that wants us to make it too. This may be the thing that I love most about God—that He just flat-out loves us and believes in us, even when we cannot do this for ourselves. Jesus prays from the place of all authority before God. He prays from the place of perfect knowledge of what should be. He prays from the place of perfect love—for you. For me. For us.

During this season of my life, I know Jesus Himself was praying for me. There were times that I was not sure that I would make it, but He knew. He knew that all the things the Father had for me during this season would come to pass. He prayed confidently and boldly. He prayed for me in perfect love, knowing this is what I needed so much of. I bet some of those times I sensed His presence so near, my spirit was just being made aware of His prayers and heart for me. I could feel it. I could sense it. There is nothing like sensing that the God of the universe wants you to make it and is there making sure you make it. He is unlike any other!

So, we have Jesus Himself making intercession for us, but there is one more Person of the Trinity who makes such a difference. Actually, He is God Himself, but He reveals Himself through His Spirit. Yes, the precious Holy Spirit. As much as I love Jesus and all He has done for me and all He has given for me to be free, the Holy Spirit is so dear to my heart. This whole journey has taught me to cling to and love the Holy Spirit more than ever. I never knew it was possible to be led so closely by the Spirit of God. It was not that I never believed in the Holy Spirit, but suddenly I needed so much more of His power and presence in my life.

Early on in my journey, as God began to reveal things to me by His Spirit, I remember questioning Him as to whether or not those revelations were Him. I was hearing things and seeing things and having things revealed to me that I never even knew existed. It was like a whole new world was opening up to me. As I thought on these things, this verse came to me from John 16:13: "However, when He, the Spirit of truth, has come, He will guide you into all truth; for He will not speak on His own authority, but whatever He hears He will speak; and He will tell you things to come." God was showing me that to make it all the way through to freedom I did not have to be scared of the Spirit and what He was doing and showing me, but I needed to trust and rely on Him more than myself. If it were not for the Holy Spirit leading me and guiding me, I would not be on the other side of my trials.

Oh, the days, the hours, the years of praying and listening for that voice to tell me who to forgive, what to do, what to let go of, what to grab hold of. There is no way that I would have been able to navigate through the choppy waters without Him.

As I was coming out of the darkest time of this last season, I remember fearing that the closeness I had gained with the Holy

Spirit would be lessened because I was not such a wreck anymore. I was less of a wreck, I guess! More peace was coming, and I could function more and more in all areas in a healthier way; but I did not want to go back to my life the way it was before. To be honest, I felt a little scared. I had never lived in freedom and did not want to lose all I gained. The Holy Spirit Himself came and assured me that He was not going anywhere and that in fact He would continue to walk closely with me all of my days. One thing that He did put on my heart is that if I wanted to walk closely with Him, I would need to make love the priority in my life. He is all over love, and love is all over Him.

He taught me something that day when He reassured me of His presence that has proved to be true again and again: in the middle of me loving God, loving myself, and loving others, He is so present. I sense Him and feel Him. Not all the time. I think if we felt Him every minute of the day or all the time we either could not handle it or we would get a big head. Oh, but He wants us to experience Him a lot more, I would venture to guess, than most of us do now—including myself!

The Holy Spirit has also prayed for me through others and even in my own spirit. Yes, here comes another scripture! Romans 8:26–27 says:

> Likewise, the Spirit also helps us in our weaknesses. For we do not know what we should pray for as we ought, but the Spirit Himself makes intercession for us with groanings which cannot be uttered. Now, He who searches the heart knows what the mind of the Spirit is, because He makes intercession for His saints, according to the will of God.

I so love the last part of that scripture: "according to the will of God." So many times we do not even know what that will is, but thankfully, the Spirit does. Early on in my journey, when I did not know how or what to pray, I would pray in the Spirit, in tongues, the language of heaven. That language is perfect and knows how to communicate with God so completely. Much of the revelation that I have now came to me as a result of doing that. Oh, God certainly hears us when we pray in English, or whatever our native tongue is, but there truly is something about praying from that deep place in our spirit. If He asked me to forgive, and I did not know how or what or whom, I would pray in the Spirit. His Spirit would remind me of the beautiful promises that were for me in the Word and make them alive to me.

The Spirit is the one who would keep my eyes fixed on Jesus, as we began talking about from the scripture in Hebrews 12:1–2. If I started looking back, as I was so accustomed to, He would gently lift my eyes back to Jesus. He kept me focused on Him and was the one who reminded me that it was all about Him. I have proven over and over that I have needed Him. Even now, He is the one lifting my eyes ever toward and back to Jesus when my vision gets blurry or distracted.

His Spirit prays for us through our precious brothers and sisters in His body. The times that Jesus and I spent alone were so precious and life-changing, but the times when others prayed for me are so dear to my heart. God has used a few people consistently in my life, as I have shared in this book. My dear friend Carrie has been used greatly by the Holy Spirit to see God's will come about in my life. We need the body of Christ. He changes us all as we let Him love and pray through us. We are powerful tools in God's hands when we do this.

Beloved, we do not have to worry that we will not make it to the end of our race. For crying out loud, some of us are wondering if we will even make it past the trials of today! He is there. He is in us if we believe in Christ, and He is not going anywhere. He is our constant traveling companion until we make it to our final destination.

He wants so much to be our friend and the one on whom we constantly rely.

I know there are many people reading this work with different beliefs on the Holy Spirit, but it seems pretty simple to me. Jesus left and said that we needed Him, so He gave us His Spirit to live in us and walk with us (John 16:7–15).

We can put our confidence, not in ourselves to make it to the end of our race but in the One who began us on this journey. Oh, how grateful I am that I no longer have to rely on myself to get me through the trials of life and to the end of my journey on Earth. You do not have to either. All the resources I needed and that we need to finish our race have been given to us! We just need to let go of the empty resources and ways of surviving that kept us from living in the resources of heaven. Now He has shown me that He has given me the tools and faith to make it through the rest of my journey. I am confident that until I see Him face to face His precious Holy Spirit will ever turn my eyes away from all this world has to offer and onto Jesus. He is the joy set before me! He is the joy set before us!

The joy that was set before Jesus was fulfilling His Father's will. I believe we were also that joy that kept Him going through the pain, through the rejection, through it all. He, through the power of the Holy Spirit, kept His eyes on His Father and on gaining us as His possession. With that in mind, He finished His race. Now He can tell us to do the same.

He is the Author and Finisher of our faith. If He set our feet on the track of life, surely He is going to and has given us everything that we need to finish the race. We do not have to fear stumbling because He will always be there to pick us up and put us right back on the track. Let's not lose sight of or let our hearing grow dull to the sound of the crowds in the grandstands. Let's allow the Holy Spirit to bring them to life, into full view.

That day on the track with my daughter gave me a glimpse of what is taking place over our lives in the heavenlies. As much excitement and fervor as I had over my daughter Sarah winning her race, He has so much more for us! Crazy, isn't it? He sees you. He sees me. He sees us. We are rounding the last bend and are heading toward that finish line! Don't give up, don't faint, and do not lose sight of the one waiting for you at the finish line!

CHAPTER 22

COMPLETE IN ME

For in Him dwells all the fullness of the Godhead
bodily; and you are complete in Him, who is
the head of all principality and power.
—COLOSSIANS 2:9–10

THROUGHOUT THE BOOK as I have told the story of my hurt and my healing you have likely wondered, "Did He really do it, Gabby? Did He do everything that He promised He would? Did He really heal your feet?" I know most of you are probably wanting answers to those questions, because I am just as inquisitive as you. The answer is, "A thousand times *yes*!" Would we expect Him to do anything less than to keep *His* word to us? Not in a million years!

I am writing this final chapter in the fall of 2013, seven and a half years after the birth of my sweet Emily. Last night our family went to the park. We enjoyed the crisp fall air after all the rain we have had already. Emily wanted to collect leaves so we could take them home for art projects. We love the fall in our family for so many reasons: the brilliant-colored leaves that just hang on the trees until the wind rips them down, pumpkin patches, drives in the country, cool mornings and evenings, and last but not least, crisp apple cider and sweet pumpkin donuts!

Last night as our family was playing basketball, fall brought some more intense joy to my heart. *I* was playing basketball. Yes, me! This body that could not have even bent over to pick up a ball without severe pain was running around shooting hoops (and making quite a few). As the girls went over to play on the playground I caught my husband, Andy, looking at me in amazement as I passed Him the ball for a shot. He was amazed that I was doing all I was—running, making shots (I told him I had been practicing), and passing him the ball with a fair amount of strength. There we were as husband and wife rejoicing at all He had brought to pass. Gone are the nights of lying in bed with tears streaming down my face wondering if I would ever do these types of things again. Standing on the basketball court that evening we experienced the glory of God in the sun shining through the vibrant red trees of fall and in His touch in my life. *On our life.* That moment will forever be ingrained in our heart and mind!

The last six months have brought what seems like a fairly rapid closure to this season He has had me in. Physically I have seen my body continue to heal and strengthen. I no longer regularly take ibuprofen for any foot or leg pain. Once in a while when I have been walking, running, hiking, or have just had a long day on my feet, I take a few. This is something that just sort of happened. Six months ago I was still taking two a day to keep the small amount of pain at bay; I did have a period within this time frame that my feet were very sore. But, after going through this healing process for as long as I have, I knew that my feet were changing again. Whenever God heals my feet and repositions them, they are more sore. Muscles, tendons, ligaments, and a whole body that has always been in one position will hurt if it goes into another. I rejoice in this because I know after the pain will come more strength and healing to my body. And it has. Running and jumping on the way home from the park last night were evidence of His touch in my body!

Today our family will head out to the pumpkin patch to pick out pumpkins, gourds, and Indian corn to decorate our front porch and home. It is so wonderful not to have to worry about whether or not I can stand longer than a few minutes without pain! Next week, I get to go again with Emily's class for a field trip to another pumpkin patch. The joy of being able to do these things when I was not able to for so long erases the pain and grief of all I went through. It was so difficult to have to stay home from field trips and seemingly miss out of so much of their lives for a few years. Looking back now, it was all worth it. The tear-filled days and nights, missing out on some things, and spending lots of time sitting—*that* is where I got to know Jesus better. *That* is where He met me and restored me. He absolutely knew what He was doing and used a great amount of wisdom in *how* He did it!

My body still needs a very small amount of healing and strengthening from all that it has gone through. But by this time I have come to absolutely trust that His word in the beginning that said I will be made complete in Him—body, soul, and spirit—*will* come to pass just as He said. I love how our God is the great romancer. We never know exactly how He will come and sweep us off of our feet, but we know He will. He has always seemed to leave me with that sense of awe, amazement, and wonder of just how He will bring all of these things in my life to completion. What a grand adventure! I so love trusting Him like this now.

As our family was standing there on that basketball court in awe of the fiery red leaves that the wind will all too soon rip from the trees, I was reminded that we are entering into a new season. With each change of season our family continues to be in the path of that wind. Do not be fooled. This wind that the Holy Spirit brings also rips some things out of our lives that should not remain. (I am sure you can attest to that already!) Yes, here we go *again*—more trials, more preparation for what is ahead, and more letting go of things we had no idea we were holding on to. By now I should be used to the wind, but sometimes the gusts still catch me off guard!

In September of 2013 Andy and I traveled to attend Mark

Rutland's National Institute of Christian Leadership in Florida. I felt a stirring to attend in early 2013 but was not sure why. As I came home from receiving my minister's license at Christ for the Nations in Dallas, Texas, I sensed God had something for me at these classes. He spoke and said that they would help prepare me to publish this book and help prepare me for other plans He has for me. I had no idea I could even finish this work over the summer while both girls were out of school. We had so much going on in the ministry with our biggest youth outreach and our first baptisms, along with our normal day-to-day commitments. But I have learned and am continuing to learn about the amazing grace of God; His grace is so tangible for us when He beckons us to do something. I think He likes to show off a bit when we are venturing out into something new. He loves to show who He is to those of us going a little—or a lot—deeper with Him.

This past summer was just that kind of show-off session! I literally felt like I was along for this wild ride that my God had me on. It felt so good to trust in someone way bigger and mightier and more awesome than myself. I learned so much about His grace that there were times I could actually sense the tangible reality of His endless and bottomless grace. I would never change any of the memories that He and I made this summer! Gone are the days of being too afraid to trust His hand and His heart for me. I now carry a knowing that He is for me and only has the best for me. It truly is a wonderful place to make my home, because where I resided most of my life resembled very little of this type of security.

That leads us to the National Institute of Christian Leadership. Andy and I boarded a plane and headed for Florida. The classes were held at the Charisma Media Center in Lake Mary, Florida. They were originally to be held in Dallas, Texas, but those classes were canceled. *Those* were the classes I signed up for. A few weeks later I received an e-mail informing me that they were going to be postponed. My heart sank for a few short minutes because I really sensed I was supposed to attend and that they would help me with this book, which would be published soon thereafter.

Standing in the kitchen trying to process what this meant and if I had missed God, He almost instantly gave me a peace and gently whispered to my heart, "You are still going to go." I love when His voice calms the storm in our souls like that. I so love when our Beloved comes for us like that!

A few weeks later I wrote a letter to Dr. Rutland's ministry pouring my heart out about what I sensed God saying to me. They graciously responded just a few days later with an e-mail informing me of the Florida classes that would fit into the timetable the Lord seemed to be on.

I also sensed I should have my manuscript done and ready to take with me when I went. Now, I was a long way from finished. When you are walking in faith like this you either have to keep walking and wonder if you are a little bit crazy or just sit down and have a freak-out session. That should have caused a freak-out session because I only had a few weeks to pull it all together. However, I am happy to say that I kept on walking. Thanks to my wonderful husband taking on more domestic duties before leaving, some amazing friends and writing mentors, a book that just *happened* to cross my path at just the right time, and copious amounts of grace, the manuscript was done just in time! I laugh because I guarded that thing during our trip like I was carrying the Dead Sea Scrolls!

In Florida, I was not sure how to go about approaching the book subject, because the class was technically not about writing or books; it just happened to be at one of the largest Christian publishers around. The second day I asked Mark Rutland's advice on who to approach and what to do, and he gave me some wonderful advice, which I followed. As a result, I found myself meeting on the last day of classes with the very lady who receives all incoming manuscripts. Amazing!

Was I nervous? Yes and no. I am not so spiritual that I do not get nervous (remember my fear chapter?), but I just knew He had been ordering my steps and that He was with me. That made *all* the difference. I just kept walking.

I boarded the plane home not believing that it was me who just experienced everything I did. At times the changes He has made in me cause me to look at myself and wonder who I am because they have been so radical. The same girl who began this journey in so much fear and shame was now taking some bold steps to share with the world what He has done in me. At times I still have to pinch myself! I arrived home sensing a great relief and release. It was as if God were saying that it was in His hands now. I knew it was all along, but now I *really* knew it.

I was reeling the night I received the e-mail informing me that the publisher wanted to publish my book and would have a proposal to me within the week. I could not believe it, yet it seemed so normal. Within two weeks of turning in my manuscript, Charisma had a proposal for my book; it is very rare to have such a quick response. It is amazing how one e-mail or phone call can change your life forever.

Sometimes we have this crazy notion that when God is moving so quickly in our lives all the pieces just fall into place. It is great when this happens, but it is not always true. Up until now they had for me, but now He has me in some weird waiting period, but I have learned how to hang on to Him for dear life, because I do not always comprehend what He is up to while I am waiting. Remember the wind I was talking about earlier? The wind that rips all the beautiful but dying leaves off the trees with such force? The wind that seems to blow everything away that is not tied down? Yes, that wind. That wind has been blowing with great force and without letting up since

I have been home. This is what has been causing me to lean on my Jesus like never before. He is now requiring me to believe Him for some gigantic things. I am sure glad He had me begin believing Him for some smaller things first.

I cannot blame the tension and pressure I have to wrestle with on the devil. I cannot blame it on anyone or anything other than the season. You see, God has been speaking to my husband and I about enormous changes coming to our life and ministry for some time now, and His wind is preparing us for that. Fun? Not always. I have been more cranky, edgy, and out of sorts. Maybe someone more spiritual would be just floating around all the time on a cloud while life was being changed very drastically right before their eyes. I have those days, but more than anything I feel the wind—the wind that is blowing away everything that is not anchored in Christ Jesus, the wind that is blowing away some more fears and doubts. You see, this wind is drawing me closer to Him. It is blowing me toward His heart and plans for me.

It seems like all I can do is to look up again and see His beautiful eyes of fire that continue to refine me into His image. This is the thing He wants us all to get a life-changing glimpse of. Yes, I went through very difficult times with my physical challenges. Yes, I feel like I gleaned all He wanted me to from that season. And yes, He will never stop changing me; He will never stop transforming us into the image of His beautiful and perfect Son. Hence the wind. It will blow on all of us.

Beloved, we are free to fight for our lives now but not free from the fight. See the difference? I cannot and should not look at the season that I have written about and think that it is all He has for me, that now I can just sit back and rest. Neither should you look at your dark seasons with that finality. Because of what I experienced I now have the tools I need and the knowing of my Father that will get me through anything. Anything. I am confident that there is nothing that He and I cannot face together. That is what this season has given me—my precious and powerful Savior. It has given me the deep assurance of His love.

One of the events that has taken me and our family by surprise is that we are no longer leading Awaken Fellowship, the church that we began about two and a half years ago. After returning from our leadership classes, I naturally expected to go home and put into practice much of what I learned. Instead I had a sense that the grace to do what we were doing was lifting. I had a sense that God was getting ready to open some new doors for ministry. I asked God about this, because in the natural it did not make sense. Because of this and some other circumstances, the only option that gave us peace was to put our meetings on hold, attend somewhere else, and seek God for a season about what is next. It has, in all honesty, been a little rattling, but it is also very freeing to be able to follow Jesus that simply. Sometimes the best thing we can do is to walk away from something. I know I am messing with some of you now! At times we make hearing from God and being free enough to follow Him even when it does not make sense way too hard and weighty. I know I have.

More freedom to just flat out follow Him has come and is coming .We do not know if God will have us start back up or not. Weird. Good weird. One thing I do know: He led us to begin that work, and I gleaned so much from learning at His feet that I am convinced I could not learn anywhere else or any other way. He is so wise. The people that we ministered to are so very precious and dear to our hearts! We continue to be able to love on many of them.

In light of all that, I can stand bravely as the wind hits my face. And hits my mind. And hits my heart. I can stand as the wind of His Spirit and the torch of His love blow on my life. After all, I know that when He is done I will emerge looking and sounding and loving a bit more like Jesus! I never would have grasped this in the smallest sense without Him allowing all He did in my life physically.

Are you game? What wind is blowing in your life today? Oh, I bet He is doing some amazing work in you! Let Him. Let Him in. When you feel like breaking, do it. When you feel the branches of your life bending, bend into His Word and heart for you. Bow your knees to the Holy One of heaven, to the only One worthy of all of you. Let the wind blow you into the plans the Father has had fashioned for you from the foundations of the world.

I still walk around in utter amazement at all He has done in my life. I never, ever imagined that He would desire to do so much with an ordinary girl! Years ago I would never have dreamed that a book would be birthed from this journey that Jesus and I have been on. I would have just been happy to escape alive, whole, and sane. And to think that He has even given me some glimpses of the future and what is in store for my family and I! He seems to be rapidly preparing us—even my children—for those changes. I have a difficult time trying to put it into words or thoughts in my own brain, much less to try and explain it to anyone else, even my hubby.

My heavenly Father has taught me that while He loves being my Daddy who can come and heal His broken daughter, He does not want me to stay broken. As much as He adores me and loves coming running to my aid as Daddy and Healer, He is showing me how much *more* He has for Him and I. He is showing me more of who He is and more of who He has made me and how to live it out.

God has called me to rule and reign with Him (Rom. 8:17). These are not fancy words for spiritually elite people. Instead, they come from the confidence that He has given a bunch of ordinary people His authority and an avenue to extend His kingdom. Yes, He has called me to walk out this wild journey of expanding *His* kingdom. He could swoop down to this earth and do it all on His own, but

He desires so much more than that. He thrives off the intimacy it takes for us to pull this off! He lets me in on the process of redeeming all things back to Himself: people, families, and nations.

But first, healing had to come. First I had to bow. First He had to rule my heart; only then could I rule *with* Him. First I had to see beyond myself and what was going on in my life. All this has happened to a very ordinary girl. Now this ordinary girl gets to see frequent glimpses into His heart and the plans that He desires to accomplish with me alongside of Him. I would not trade away one second of my painful journey with Him because of all I have with Him now as a result of it!

You see, our God has so much for us than we could ever ask, think, or imagine (Eph. 3:20–21). What may seem ordinary to you, our Redeemer can take in His hands and bless the world with. Whether you are a stay-at-home mom, a businessman, pastor, teacher, or grandma—He wants to use us *all!* Our most joy-filled and abundant lives come from letting Him use us right where He has us. Our past sins, mistakes, and stumbles can all be shaped by the Potter's hands to bring us and others to the place of freedom and abundant life.

Who knows what God has for *you!* You can be confident that no matter your place in life, He wants to use you to shape history and even whole nations. You are called to rule and reign with Him. Let Him bring you out of your past and inadequacies into *knowing* you are complete in Him. Let Him bring you to the place of walking confidently side by side with Him to advance His kingdom. Lay all your unanswered questions at His feet, and let Him be your answer. This is how true freedom comes.

Writing this book is one way He is allowing me to come alongside of Him in His plans. While He may not be calling you to write, you are called to something great! Raise those babies to love Jesus. Love your husband. Share Jesus with people wherever you go. This is ruling and reigning with Him. Just do what He says, and don't make it more complicated than that!

Being complete in Him does not mean we have it all together or do not have anything else in our lives that needs to be worked out. Here is what I think God's heart is for us to hear when we read Colossians 2:10: We are dead to ourselves and our old life. We are alive to Him. Everything we could ever need and desire is in Him. If we are in Him and Jesus fills all in all, then we are complete. Being complete in Him means just what you have read about in the story of the pages of this book. It just means we know He is our everything, that He is our identity, and that His Word is the absolute ruler over all in our lives. It means that His Spirit gets to move us where He wishes. This type of closeness will ever be His unceasing desire for all His people.

I am complete in Him. God always saw that I was; I just needed to see it, believe it, and receive it. Now I am walking in it, though not perfectly and not without some stumbles. I allow those mistakes to point me again to the grace of God that empowers me to continue living out the calling He has placed on my life. Friends, there is so much grace available for our imperfections that it's crazy!

How about *you*? Are you feeling rather ordinary today? I bet those fishermen were the day that Jesus walked up to them and said, "Follow Me!" It probably seemed like another ordinary day casting their nets into the sea. The day I prayed and asked God to heal me seemed very ordinary to me too. Who knew throwing myself across my bed while my babies were down for a nap would totally change my life and my story?

It still really rattles me at times that He lets us in on *His* story! The disciples, like myself, had no idea the places Jesus would take them—the journeys, the adventures, and yes, for some of them, on to death, all for His name. But they had to have known He was worth it. Isn't He worth it, beloved? I cannot think of anything or anyone else that I would follow and give my life for, not after Jesus has so captured my heart! Not after the hours in His presence as His love washes over me. Not after having Him believe in me in the middle of my mess. I have truly been honored and humbled that He has entrusted me with some of the secrets and thoughts and the love that so abundantly pours forth from His heart.

Let Him capture your heart. All of it. Throw open the doors of your heart and the secret places, and let Him love on you so fiercely that your heart can do nothing but love Him back. Sit back and dream with your Father about what may come out of your journey, my friends.

I have so enjoyed this journey with you! My heart is experiencing so many emotions just trying to close out this final chapter. God has had to remind me that this will not be my last opportunity to share all He has put on my heart, so I do not have to spill it all out here. But know this: you are precious to Him and to me! With all my heart and with all His heart, we are for you. You *will* make it to your finish line.

Your healing, victory, deliverance, and commission are ready and waiting. God may want to use the very struggles that you are trying to escape to catapult you into your destiny, the one formed for you and written in His book from the beginning of time. Who knows? Maybe we will all be reading the story of *your* journey next! I cannot wait to hear it. Until the perfect day when we see Him face to face, let Him find us following Him so closely that we are walking in His footsteps, going where we never could have gone alone.

ABOUT THE AUTHOR

Gabby Heusser has a passion to see people come to intimately know Jesus Christ. Her heart is for them to experience His love and presence in a very tangible way. She desires all to live in the freedom and wholeness that Jesus died to bring. Gabby graduated from Christ for the Nations Institute in Dallas, Texas. It was there she met her husband, Andy, and she is blessed to serve alongside him in ministry. Together they have two beautiful princesses, Sarah and Emily. Gabby and her family live in Salem, Oregon.